T0092034

Programming ML.Net

Dino Esposito
Francesco Esposito

Programming ML.Net

Published with the authorization of Microsoft Corporation by:

Pearson Education, Inc.

ISBN-13: 978-0-13-738365-8

ISBN-10: 0-13-738365-7

Library of Congress Control Number: 2021952995

1 2022

Trademarks

Microsoft and the trademarks listed at http://www.microsoft.com on the "Trademarks" webpage are trademarks of the Microsoft group of companies. All other marks are property of their respective owners.

Warning and Disclaimer

Every effort has been made to make this book as complete and as accurate as possible, but no warranty or fitness is implied. The information provided is on an "as is" basis. The author, the publisher, and Microsoft Corporation shall have neither liability nor responsibility to any person or entity with respect to any loss or damages arising from the information contained in this book or from the use of the programs accompanying it.

Special Sales

For information about buying this title in bulk quantities, or for special sales opportunities (which may include electronic versions; custom cover designs; and content particular to your business, training goals, marketing focus, or branding interests), please contact our corporate sales department at corpsales@pearsoned.com or (800) 382-3419.

For government sales inquiries, please contact governmentsales@pearsoned.com.

For questions about sales outside the U.S., please contact intlcs@pearson.com.

Editor-in-Chief
Brett Bartow

Executive Editor
Loretta Yates

Sponsoring Editor
Charvi Arora

Development Editor
Rick Kughen

Managing Editor
Sandra Schroeder

Senior Project Editor
Tracey Croom

Copy Editor
Rick Kughen

Indexer
Timothy Wright

Proofreader
Abigail Manheim

Technical Editor
Bri Achtman

Cover Designer
Twist Creative, Seattle

Compositor
codeMantra

To Silvia, Michela and new dreams
— Dino Esposito

To my loved ones, to whom I couldn't help but dedicate a book
— Francesco Esposito

Contents at a Glance

Contents

Chapter 7 Anomaly Detection Tasks 119

Chapter 8 Forecasting Tasks 141

Acknowledgments

FROM DINO:

It's the second time that the two of us, father and son, have written a machine learning book and a lot has changed since our last one, two years ago. In this book, we really joined forces—I put my software experience on the table, and Francesco gave his freshness, energy, and mathematical skills. We learned both how tricky it can be to put machine learning solutions in production and how "easy" it can be to hide those little gems in the folds of "normal" ASP.NET applications.

In the past two years, we achieved other results and, for example, we solidified our grasp of software for professional tennis and expanded to healthcare, agriculture, and customer care. The common denominator is always that one: intelligent software that ends up doing intelligent things. It's not about replacing humans and killing jobs—quite the reverse. It's about replacing tasks with automated procedures, thus freeing humans from boring, automatable tasks and keeping them engaged in more interesting activities.

With Giorgio Garcia-Agreda and Gaetano Guarino, and the entire Crionet crew, we're making our tennis fanatic dreams bigger every day. We are changing the games. With Vito Lanzotti and the KBMS Data Force team, we're making silent history by turning doctors' operating dreams into concrete and applicable artifacts, thus smoothing the way patients receive care. With Salvo Intilisano and Daniel Intilisano of Karma Enterprise, it was really a matter of technical karma. Same mindset, same vision, and same father-and-son business model! Agriculture won't be the same after the project ends, and the bees will be grateful!

The Youbiquitous team is growing, and the business is now spread over multiple pairs of strong shoulders—mainly those of Matteo, Luciano, Martina, Filippo, and Gabriele. Thank you all for taking the time to keep the business running while we were having fun with ML.NET.

Finally, any book is teamwork, and it is our pleasure to call out the names of those who made it ultimately possible. Last but not certainly least! A monumental thank-you goes to Loretta Yates as the acquisition editor, Charvi Arora as the sponsoring editor, Rick Kughen as the development and copy editor, and Bri Achtman as the technical editor.

FROM FRANCESCO:

I'm 23, grown enough to live alone but young enough to feel my heart beating for my grandparents. Sadly enough, the number is smaller than a book ago. A warm thought goes to Grandpa Salvatore and a hug to Grandma Concetta and Grandma Leda: I love you. On an even more personal side, this book is for Gianfranco—friend, business partner, second father, and grandfather. He taught me how to do things right and forgot to teach me how to do it wrong. And this book is also for Michela, who is strong enough to pursue her own way—no matter what—and smart enough to choose a good path!

Introduction

*We need men who can dream of things that never were, and ask,
"why not?"*

—John F. Kennedy, Speech to the Irish Parliament, June 1963

Today, the quest for data scientists is continuous, the data seems to be abundant, and cloud computing power is available. Is it the perfect world for the definitive triumph of machine learning? As we see things, we have all the necessary ingredients to cook up the "applied AI," but we still lack a clear and effective method for combining them.

The purpose of data science is, like the purpose of science, to show that something is possible. Data science, though, doesn't productionize solutions. That's the purpose of another branch of the machine learning universe—data engineering.

Companies are wildly looking for data scientists, but the outcome of a good data science team is typically a runnable model whose software quality is often that of a prototype rather than of a production-ready artifact. Algorithms are tightly bound to data, and data must be complete, clean, and balanced. Who's in charge of this part of the job is often unclear, and as a result, the job is often partially done at best. Yet, a data science team disconnected from the rest of the applied AI pipeline that makes it to production is still a due investment for a large organization whose business produces large quantities of data (such as energy utilities, financial institutions, and manufacturing farms). For smaller companies with significantly more limited budgets, the outcome of some applied data science can be cheaper to buy as a service.

From data science to production, there is usually a long way in between and a lot of work on data. Following are a few points to consider:

- How is data stored? On a daily or hourly basis?

- Should data be temporarily copied in some intermediate format?

- What kind of transformation is required for the model to work? How can you automate that?

- How is the performance of the model once deployed to production?

- How often is the model expected to need retrained to stay adherent to live data?

- If retraining is a frequent operation, how to automate any related tasks?

- What about collecting updated datasets, running the training, and deploying the up-to-date model?

The biggest issue we experience with machine learning models traces back to the data employed. In July 2021, the *MIT Technology Review* published an article about the impact of AI in facing the COVID pandemic. The article's bottom line is that many of the problems uncovered by a large review of aptly developed models are linked to the poor data quality that researchers used to develop their tools. Hence, nearly all tools were of nearly no effective use. This leads to a better understanding of the role of data engineering and data quality. Treating data via CSV sparse files is sufficient for probing an idea, but in order to build a robust infrastructure, you need to switch to some database (relational, NoSQL or graph) and some serious query language, and for this purpose, likely move beyond Python and enter into classic programming. Data science is not enough without serious programming and database skills. On the other hand, isn't searching for business-specific insights in data all that you do?

AI in general, and machine learning in particular, are now played as a tradeoff between commodity and direct solutions for vertical problems. Commoditized cloud services offer security, stability, and acceptable quality. They don't cover every possible scenario, though. But they're expanding, and more will expand in the near future.

All this is creating the environment for building the same old software but with more powerful tools. We're not just talking about the primitives of programming languages and classes from some frameworks. We're also talking about intelligent and predictive tools backed by machine learning algorithms and commoditized cloud (or containerized) services.

In this scenario, ML.NET acts as a perfect bridge between data engineering and commoditized data science, and it is fully integrated with the .NET framework. ML.NET commodities come in different forms: built-in algorithms for shallow learning, facilitated access to Azure cloud services, and integration with pre-trained models, such as Keras or TensorFlow networks.

Who Should Read This Book?

In our vision, if you adopt the .NET stack, then ML.NET is the perfect tool to do machine learning, whatever that ultimately means in terms of the internal gears of your chosen algorithms and models.

Hence, this book is for .NET developers willing (or needing) to approach the world of machine learning. It's ideal if you're a software developer adding data science and machine learning skills to your arsenal. It's ideal if you're a data scientist willing to learn more about software beyond Python. Both categories, though, need to learn more and more about the other.

Who Should Not Read This Book?

This book discusses machine learning through the lenses of ML.NET, which is a platform-specific library. It is tailored more to data engineers and ML engineers than plain data scientists. To clarify, the core responsibilities of an ML engineer are to physically incorporate an externally trained model into client applications and perform the much more delicate task of supervising the building and training of a model based on data science specs. The book discusses the tools for doing this.

If you're not much interested in the actual productionizing of the machine learning solution, this book is probably not the best you can get. It doesn't open your mind to cutting-edge data science techniques, but it teaches you how to start leveraging what the ML.NET team has been doing for years—to integrate simple but effective machine learning solutions in .NET.

Organization of This Book

This book is divided into three sections.

- Chapters 1-3 provide a foundational overview of the library.

- Chapters 4-10 outline the dedicated tasks for data processing, training, and evaluation for common problems, such as regression, classification, ranking, anomaly detection, and more.

- Chapters 11-13 are dedicated to neural networks that might come into play when none of the shallow learning tasks is found to be suitable. Also, we include an overview of neural networks and an example of passport recognition that uses both commoditized Azure cognitive services and a handmade custom Keras network.

Lastly, Appendix A discusses model explainability.

System Requirements

You will need the following hardware and software to complete the practice exercises in this book:

- A computer running Windows 10, Linux, or macOS

- Visual Studio 2019, any edition, or superior; Visual Studio Code

- Internet connection to download software or chapter examples

Code Samples

All the code included in the book, including possible errata and extensions, can be found at MicrosoftPressStore.com/ProgrammingMLNET/downloads.

Errata, updates, & book support

We've made every effort to ensure the accuracy of this book and its companion content. You can access updates to this book—in the form of a list of submitted errata and their related corrections—at:

MicrosoftPressStore.com/ProgrammingMLNET/errata

If you discover an error that is not already listed, please submit it to us at the same page.

For additional book support and information, please visit *http://www.MicrosoftPressStore.com/Support.*

Please note that product support for Microsoft software and hardware is not offered through the previous addresses. For help with Microsoft software or hardware, go to *http://support.microsoft.com.*

Stay in Touch

Let's keep the conversation going! We're on Twitter: *http://twitter.com/MicrosoftPress.*

CHAPTER 1

Artificially Intelligent Software

Let us calculate, without further ado, to see who is right.
—*Gottfried Wilhelm Leibniz, "The Art of Discovery," 1685*

Software is the ultimate result of the embryonal vision that crossed the minds of a handful of great thinkers since the seventeenth century. A few mathematicians, philosophers, and scientists in the most general sense of the word, in various ways and at different levels of abstractions, had the vision of a universal language able to mechanize the acquisition and sharing of knowledge. In particular, Gottfried Leibniz (1646 to 1716) concluded (or was it just a bit less than a dream?) that at least part of the human reasoning could be mechanized. He even devised an abstract engine—the *calculus ratiocinator*—that could act as a universal processor of statements written in some symbolic language and appropriate notation.

Leibniz's visionary notes on the *calculus ratiocinator* remained unpublished for more than two centuries, but the idea of a symbolic language found an immediate application in the notation for the calculus of infinitesimals he introduced in 1684 at nearly the same time that Isaac Newton was developing his mathematical methods to explain the physics of motion and gravitation.

In the late 1800s, Leibniz's work two centuries before stimulated logicians to boldly move beyond Aristotle's logic that was still predominant at the time. In particular, the German scientist Gottlob Frege dedicated his entire life to devising a comprehensive theory that could be used to represent all mathematical statements. There was a sort of a bug in his work, though, that *ante litteram* beta tester Bertrand Russell found just days before the whole work went to printers.

Interestingly, Russell's paradox when going through Frege's theory was not identifying some error or misstatement. Decades later, Godel's theorems of incompleteness showed that nothing was wrong in either Frege's or Russell's reasoning. Godel, in fact, proved unrealistic the expectation set by Frege and denied by Russell with a counterexample.

Then, Alan Turing started an immortal journey in abstract mathematics, culminating in Turing's machine—the first-ever fully defined model for symbolic calculation.

Great! But what about software then?

How We Ended Up with Software

Godel's incomplete theorem draws the line beyond which mathematical logic can't just go. In essence, incompleteness means that there are things that cannot just be proven true or false through any flavor of formal reasoning. Period.

However, the flip side of such an apparently negative outcome is just what opened the floodgates of what today we call software. Incompleteness killed the dream of a sharp seventeenth-century polymath, but, at the same time, it showed that within the boundaries of a consistent formal system, any reasoning can always be expressed as a set of formal transformation rules and then, in some way, mechanized.

This fact represents the theoretical foundation for any computer-based reasoning and marks the birth of what ended up being the software of today.

The Formalization of Computing Machines

Godel's theorems of incompleteness (1931) gave the spark to a few independent research paths that conveyed the same result around the mid-1930s:

- **General recursive function**   Defined by Godel himself, a general recursive function is a computable logical function that takes a finite array of natural numbers and returns a natural number.

- **Lambda calculus**   Formalism devised by Alonzo Church to define some mechanic computation on natural numbers.

- **Turing machine**   Theoretical model of a computing machine capable of performing calculations via symbols written on an infinite tape.

Next, in 1936, the Church-Turing thesis unified the three classes of computable functions. The thesis proved that a function is computable in the lambda calculus if and only if it is computable in the Turing machine and if and only if it is a general recursive function. The ultimate effect of the thesis made imaginable the building of a mechanical device that could reproduce any conceivable process of mathematical deduction through the manipulation of symbols.

The explosion of the Second World War accelerated the development of electrical machines able to crunch numbers and automate tasks. Well-known ancestors of modern computers were the cypher- and code-breaking Enigma; its breaking counterpart, The Bombe (built with a significant contribution from Alan Turing); the German Army's Lorenz machine; and the British giant machine Colossus, which ultimately broke the Lorenz cypher. All these models were built in Europe, whereas the United States completed the building of the ENIAC computer in the final days of the war under the supervision of another big name of modern computer science, John von Neumann.

All these machines were based on the theoretical foundation laid by the Church-Turing thesis.

The Engineering of Computing Machines

In the 1950s, far from the pressure of the war, research resumed, and scientists faced the compelling problem of devising the architecture of a computing machine. Imagine being in the shoes of one of those great people.

Consider this: It's the 1950s, and the world is getting a facelift after the hardships of the war. In the past few years, you and your peers built dedicated machines starting from the sole theoretical evidence that it was possible. The contingency of the war forced you to build machines around the accomplishment of very specific tasks, mostly calculating numbers from numbers, but you know that more is possible. The same theory that resulted in building number-crunching agglomerates of electro-mechanical valves, wires, and rotors can be leveraged to engineer a machine that can compute anything that can be expressed through a consistent grammar of symbols. It's about creation. It's not about getting numbers from other numbers.

In the shoes of any such great person, you would probably feel like a god.

And you would probably foresee a machine that can behave in much the same way as humans do. And then, probably, you would wonder about this crucial question: *Can machines think?*

Faced with engineering a computing machine, it seemed natural to look at the human brain and imagine such machines as a surrogate of the human brain. The initial focus was on the engineering part—how to connect the physical parts in an overall architecture that could afford flexible processing of numbers and representation of more complex information. Nobody ever figured out anything like what we call software today.

The goal was to create an intelligent machine, and the model was the human brain.

The Birth of Artificial Intelligence

The term *artificial intelligence* (AI) was officially coined in 1956 when John McCarthy organized a six-week summer research workshop at Dartmouth College in New Hampshire; this research workshop was open to a number of mathematicians, engineers, neurologists, and psychologists.

The workshop was devised to be a brainstorming session around the idea of thinking machines. At the time, the abstract theme of thinking machines was debated in two distinct and largely opposed research contexts. The Automata theory directly descended from Church and Turing's work and cybernetics, which directly descended from Babbage's theory and was turned into concrete hardware by Von Neumann.

In an attempt to please and attract researchers from both camps, McCarthy chose the new name of *artificial intelligence* because of its neutrality. Also, McCarthy wanted to unify the two souls of the ongoing academic research that he perceived to be the same entity.

Yet, the ultimate purpose of the workshop was to lay the groundwork for a number of shared methods and practices to build the artificial counterpart of a brain.

Many declined the invitation to the workshop, and no concrete outcomes resulted from it. Yet, it is remembered as the birth of artificial intelligence.

Software as a Side Effect

Computing machines were born to emulate the human brain and represent intelligence in a formal and computable way. But, as in many popular Internet memes these days, at some point, something went unexpectedly wrong. The result is just what we currently call software, which was, in a way, the waste product of the quest for artificial forms of intelligence.

What is software?

We belong to successive generations, and it is interesting to note that younger developers might still miss the fact that software derives from the definition of the Von Neumann computer architecture that introduced the key concept that instructions had to be separated from hardware and not hard-coded in the physical parts. The Von Neumann architecture is the same architecture that modern devices use and consists of a processing unit (CPU) that provides basic computation logic, multiple levels of memory, and input/output mechanisms.

Programming languages to arrange instructions for the machine to execute started appearing in the 1950s and rapidly developed until the end of the next decade. At that point, it was clear that software was necessary to use computers and an unavoidable tool to build intelligent automated behavior. In the 1960s, it became evident that writing software to achieve any minimally acceptable behavior required dedication, discipline, and method. Not coincidentally, the term *software engineering* started gaining popularity around 1968.

Software played a crucial role in getting astronauts to the moon, but it was nothing like artificial intelligence; the software required the human brain to dictate action. However, the industry decided that the software was enough, and the dreams of artificial intelligence could wait. Then the early 1970s brought us relational databases and the definitive direction: Software is for business, and artificial intelligence moved to the academic back office.

The Role of Software Today

We're well into the twenty-first century, and every day we experience the pervasiveness of software in every aspect of our lives. It was not the same in the beginning. For a few decades, software was devised to be a relatively thin layer of abstraction around core and raw data. Storing and reading business data was the major goal, and software was just the necessary grease to smooth the gears of business processes. The software was devised to execute tasks correctly and (ideally) quickly.

There was no care for the user. In a way, some using a computer had to feel happy and grateful just to be there. Twenty years ago, the Internet—followed by the iPhone ten years later—changed the landscape in favor of introducing a bunch of new methodologies and, more than everything else, woke up engineers and managers to the relevance of users.

To be nice to users and make information that's available at their fingertips (an old slogan attributed to Bill Gates), software had to be designed in different ways and around different—radically different—user stories. All in all, in modern society, any software has three main goals:

- Save people from having to do repetitive and boring tasks

- Mirror the processes as they happen in the real world

- Assist and empower people

These goals haven't changed significantly since the early days of ENIAC, Fortran, IBM mainframes, and workstations. The era of cloud (and, why not, the possible futuristic era of quantum computing) won't change these basic goals. They form the very essence of software and are, in a way, universal.

What *has* changed over the past decades and what *might* further change is the relevance of these goals for people, companies, organizations, and businesses in general. The software is not expected to have different goals; neither is it expected to change its nature. Instead, it is expected to change to give those goals more and more relevance. Software is expected to be closer and closer to the real world and empower more and more people while saving time for other human-specific gigs or just more fun.

For these goals, the software just needs to be more intelligent.

We don't have artificial intelligence to use as a magic wand; we wish to have it, but it's not here yet. At a minimum, though, we should be writing more intelligent software. One way to do so is to use the tools created by research under the umbrella of artificial intelligence.

Automating Tasks

In the beginning of the software industry, something as simple as storing and retrieving data was seen as a successful form of automation. Over the years, though, the need for automation and the definition of an automatable task have changed. Today, many tasks that would have been happily taken over by a human user 20 years ago are considered boring, repetitive, and, as such, ideal for another smarter software application.

A good example of such tasks for which simple forms of artificial intelligence might be helpful is the analysis of timelines, scanning of documents, and standard processing of documents such as resizing photos or passport reading. In this context, we could compare artificial intelligence to barcode readers. Years ago, barcode readers incredibly smoothed and accelerated data-entry processes. Likewise, relatively standard neural networks—or even implementations of dedicated algorithms—can give a similar boost to analogous business domains today.

Mirroring the Real World

New cars make it simple: As you turn the key, the embedded software welcomes you, and if it's a Saturday, it immediately offers to set up the same route to the mall you seem to take almost every weekend. Wow, that's smart! When you drive and happen to be too close to another car, the same embedded software warns you or brakes for you, depending on the model and circumstances. Wow, that's even smarter!

It's not so much about being smart. It's more about understanding and mimicking things as they happen in the real world. Having been in the software industry for well over three decades, Dino remembers very well the early days in which users had to adapt to software—not the other way around. Doubtless, it still happens—even in the code he writes today, though the frequency has diminished.

Note that it's not only the user experience that's affected, AND it's not simply frontend and interfaces. To be able to offer a valuable user experience, a serious, flexible, and scalable backend is required more often than not.

On the way to making software closer to the human-level interactions that people are used to, you should certainly look at existing cognitive services (chatbots and voice-based input of data). You blissfully fail, though, if you stop at a cloud service shop and just buy subscriptions. The intelligence of cognitive services is a tremendous plus, but it shouldn't be at the cost of skipping user-friendly forms and menus and implementing business processes and ubiquitous languages.

Let's say you are a software engineer who designs a software system that is still under cover of cognitive services. If that software were to fail to recognize crucial business entities because it doesn't name them properly, that would mean you're not properly mirroring the real world and you're not providing a great service to your customer. As emphatic as it may sound, a simple misnomer here or the less-than-optimal design of a storage structure there multiplied by years of everyday use can be measured as noticeable damage.

These days, it's too easy to fall into the trap of putting AI everywhere and to favor the use of a pet technology rather than focusing on what could solve the problem, at least in the short term. We've seen projects stuck because of inadequate design and product choices. And, unfortunately, we're not the only ones.

Empowering People

The more the software is able to mirror the real world, the more it ends up empowering people in their everyday personal, social, and business activities. And it also works the other way around: the more people use software regularly, the more software evolves and improves.

Today, to really empower users, the software has to be intelligent and proactive. A nice user experience seems more and more like a commodity. It is assumed to be a nice one, but it makes a difference less and less often. AI is an effective tool to investigate ways to provide more powerful features to users and more insights about the data they use.

For nearly any user activity, timely suggestions, recommendations, and accurate estimations and forecasts are immensely helpful. Today, AI is no longer an obscure area of research but is fully integrated in a large-use framework such as .NET 6, so there are no more excuses for not using it. The challenge is in how to use it in the context of real-world applications that mirror the real world as closely as possible.

AI Is Just Software

Artificial intelligence is no different from the software that companies are already using. In fact, AI is just another face of software; it's a new type of fuel for the software that can reinforce the benefits for users. In spite of this, the hype around AI is high.

To be really effective and widely used, AI solutions must be easy to code and even easier to integrate into new and existing applications. No AI solution is a stand-alone piece, and the challenge is in making smart features plug seamlessly into regular software. Even the most sophisticated neural network is not very usable by users if it's not nicely hidden behind a friendly interface.

Expert systems have been the first concrete form of artificial intelligence put to work in a number of business domains such as cruise control systems, legal, tax, finance, and healthcare. Those intelligent software systems do the work of a human expert and can give the same insightful answer to a fixed number of questions. Expert systems are expensive to update, but at some point, they face obsolescence. Machine learning is the next step.

Machine learning is a subset of AI and works by creating a model that can answer questions it was never explicitly programmed to answer. An expert system, in fact, for the most part is made of an intricate but fixed network of branches. Any answer an expert system can give comes at the end of a hard-coded learning path. In a machine learning system, this is not true. In action, a machine learning model uses a previously identified mathematical function to calculate the output from a given input. Before it can be used, the model is trained on a large sample dataset, and training is aimed at discovering just that mathematical function that captures the hidden relationships between input and output.

The point is not which flavor of machine learning you should be using or whether Python is preferable to ML.NET. The point is to find the most appropriate technical solution for adding a new smart feature to your applications that turns the existing software into more intelligent software.

AI, in the end, is just software.

In this first chapter, we barely scratched the surface of intelligence in modern software. Given the level of sophistication of the average software of today, the entire challenge is to make it smarter and closer to the user's needs. Machine learning techniques—whether shallow learning algorithms or neural networks—are an effective approach. In the rest of the book, we delve into the features and capabilities of ML.NET—the machine learning framework native in the .NET 6 platform.

CHAPTER 2

An Architectural Perspective of ML.NET

"In mathematics, the art of asking questions is more valuable than solving problems."
—Georg Cantor, Doctoral thesis, 1867

As consumers, we continuously experience the pleasant effects of cognitive AI (for example, Amazon, Google, Apple, Microsoft, and Netflix). As people, we hope to see the same power applied to healthcare. In the general enterprise sector, where companies much smaller and rich than the web giants strive, the adoption of AI is slow and steady. This is precisely the feeling that descends from the point of intelligent software. Very few running businesses need the same level of cognitive AI we find in, say, Alexa or Cortana. All running businesses, though, would benefit from smarter features.

What is intelligent software, then?

Any software is statically designed to be aware of the context, but only intelligent software is designed to run while being dynamically aware of the business context. On the other hand, isn't this just what intelligence is supposed to be—the ability to acquire knowledge and turn it into expertise? In a nutshell, intelligence combines cognitive capabilities, including perception, memory, language, and reasoning and uses a specific learning approach to extract, transform, and store information. Turning all this into code requires ad hoc tools that are different from the basic logical equipment provided in any programming language or core framework.

Marketing departments love to generally identify these tools as artificial intelligence, specifically in the machine learning (ML) section. How do we do ML?

Most ML solutions today are built using tools from the Python ecosystem. It's a matter of convenience, however, rather than a matter of technological merit. In this chapter, we introduce the ML.NET platform—the .NET way to machine learning and the core topic of the book. More than just that, though, we will aim at providing an architectural perspective of a generic ML solution and presenting the reasons that, in our opinion, make ML.NET the right thing at the right time.

Life Beyond Python

In the collective imagination, ML is tightly coupled to using the Python programming language. Even from a surface-level look at job descriptions in tons of recruitment posts, this is clear. There are both historical and convenience reasons for languages like Python and C++ to be at the forefront of ML. However, there's no strict business reason or technical argument that prevents .NET and related languages (C# and F#) from being effectively used to build ML models.

Why Is Python So Popular in Machine Learning?

Python is an interpreted and object-oriented programming language created by Guido Van Rossum in the late 1980s with the declared goals of syntax minimalism and readability. The vision of Python as a programming language is that of a small core language engine with a large standard library and an easily extensible interpreter.

Python, which was born in a scientific environment, has become the de facto standard programming language for scientists to practice, explore, and experiment with numbers. In a way, it took the place that Fortran held in the 1960s and '70s. In the beginning, using Python in a hot new scientific field such as machine learning was a natural choice, and over time—given the natural extensibility of the language—it led to the creation of a vast ecosystem of dedicated libraries and tools. In turn, that reinforced the belief that using Python for building computational models was the best option.

Today, most data scientists find Python comfortable to use for machine learning projects, and that is probably because of a combination of the language's simplicity, the available tools, and plenty of examples. As developers, we also find Python comfortable to use to reshape data quickly to find the most appropriate format, test algorithms quickly, and explore different directions.

Once a clear path is outlined, the ML model must be trained and integrated into a runtime environment, its performance with live data must be monitored, and due changes must be applied and redeployed. It's the ML life cycle that is also known as MLOps. When you move away from experimenting with tools and libraries and look just for what enterprises need—working and maintainable code—Python shows structural limits. At the very minimum, it's yet another stack to integrate into .NET or Java stacks, which is how most business applications are written.

> **NOTE** It's difficult to go from ML experimentation (often done in Python and via Notebooks) to deployment. In fact, according to a 2020 State of Enterprise Machine Learning report, only 22 percent of companies using machine learning have successfully deployed a machine learning model into production. See https://bit.ly/3y8BxOH
>
> That's one of the advantages of ML.NET—.NET makes it super easy to bring projects to production.

Taxonomy of Python Machine Learning Libraries

The ecosystem of tools and libraries available in Python can be divided into five main areas: data manipulation, data visualization, numerical computing, model training, and neural networks. It's probably not an exhaustive list because many other libraries exist that perform other tasks and focus on some specific areas of machine learning, such as natural language processing and image recognition.

When using Python, the steps to build a machine learning pipeline are typically performed within the boundaries of a notebook. A notebook is a document created in a specific web or local interactive environment called Jupyter Notebook. (See *https://jupyter.org*.) Each notebook contains a combination of executable Python code, richly formatted text, data grids, charts, and pictures through which you build and share your development story. In some way, a notebook is comparable to a Visual Studio project solution.

In a notebook, you perform tasks such as data manipulation, plotting, and training, and you can use a number of predefined and battle-tested libraries.

Data Manipulation and Analysis

Pandas (*https://pandas.pydata.org*) is a library centered around the `DataFrame` object through which developers can load and manipulate in-memory tabular data. The object can import content from CSV files, text files, and SQL databases, and it provides core capabilities, such as conditional search, filtering, indexing and sorting, data slicing, grouping, and column operations (such as add, remove, and rename). The `DataFrame` object has built-in capability to flexibly reshape and pivot data and merge multiple frames. It also works well with time-series data.

The Pandas library is ideal for data preparation operations. Its integration with interactive notebooks enables you to perform on-the-fly testing of different configurations and data groupings.

Data Visualization

Matplotlib (*https://matplotlib.org*) is a helper library that isn't directly related to any of the common tasks of a machine learning pipeline, but it comes very handy to visually represent data during the various phases of the data preparation step or metrics obtained after evaluating trained models.

In general terms, it's a mere data visualization library built for Python code. It includes a 2D/3D rendering engine and supports common types of graphs, such as histograms, pie charts, and bar charts. Graphs are fully customizable in terms of line styles, font properties, axes, legends, and the like.

Numeric Computing

Because Python is a language that is largely used in scientific environments, it can't be without a bunch of extensions specifically designed for numerical computation. In this area, NumPy and SciPy are popular libraries, though they have slightly different capabilities.

NumPy (*https://www.numpy.org*) focuses on array operations and provides facilities to create, manipulate, and reshape one-dimensional and multidimensional arrays. Also, the library supplies linear algebra, Fourier transform, and random number operations.

SciPy (*https://scipy.org*) extends NumPy with polynomials, file I/O, image and signal processing, and more advanced features such as integration, interpolation, optimization, and statistics.

In the area of scientific computation, another Python library that is worth mentioning is Theano (*https://github.com/Theano/Theano*). Theano evaluates mathematical expressions based on multidimensional arrays, very efficiently making transparent use of the GPU. It also does symbolic differentiation for functions with one or more inputs.

Model Training

Though it was originally designed for data mining, today, scikit-learn (*https://scikit-learn.org*) is a library mainly focused on model training. It provides implementations of popular algorithms for regression, classification, and clustering. Also, scikit-learn provides methods for data preprocessing, such as dimensionality reduction, feature extraction, and normalization.

In a nutshell, scikit-learn is the Python foundation for shallow learning.

Neural Networks

Shallow learning is an area of machine learning that covers a broad array of fundamental problems such as regression and classification. Outside the realm of shallow learning, there are deep learning and neural networks. For building neural networks in Python, more specialized libraries exist.

TensorFlow (*https://www.tensorflow.org*) is probably the most popular library for training deep neural networks. It is part of a comprehensive framework that can be programmed at various levels. For example, you can use the high-level Keras API to build neural networks or manually build the desired topology and specify via code forward and activation steps, custom layers, and training loops. Overall, TensorFlow is an end-to-end machine learning platform providing facilities also to train and deploy.

Keras (*https://keras.io*) is probably the easiest way to get into the dazzling world of deep learning. It offers a very straightforward programming interface that at least comes in handy for quick prototyping. As mentioned, Keras can be used from within TensorFlow.

Yet another option is PyTorch, available at *https://pytorch.org*. PyTorch is the Python adaptation of an existing C-based library specialized in natural language processing and computer vision. Of the three neural network options, Keras is, by far, the ideal entry point and the tool of choice as long as it can deliver what you're looking for. PyTorch and TensorFlow do the same job of building sophisticated neural networks, but they use different approaches to the task. TensorFlow requires you to define the entire topology of the network before you can train it. In contrast, PyTorch follows a more agile approach and provides a more dynamic method for making changes to the graph. In some ways, their differences can be summarized as "waterfall versus agile." PyTorch is younger and doesn't have TensorFlow's huge community behind it.

End-to-End Solutions on Top of Python Models

With Python, you can easily find a way to build and train a machine learning model. Ultimately, a model is a binary file that must be loaded into a client application and invoked. Usually, a Java or .NET application serves as the client application for an ML model.

There are three main ways to consume a trained model:

- Hosting the trained model in a web service and making it accessible via a REST or gRPC API.

- Importing the trained model as a serialized file in the application and interacting with it through the programming interface provided by the infrastructure it is built upon (for example, Tensor-Flow or *scikit-learn*). This is possible only if the founding infrastructure provides bindings for the language to which the client application.

- The trained model is exposed via the new universal ONNX format, and the client application incorporates a wrapper for consuming ONNX binaries.

While the web service option is the most commonly used, a direct API that is specific for the client language of choice might seem the fastest way to consume a trained model. There are a couple of aspects to review, however:

- Using a direct API can prevent you from taking advantage of hardware acceleration and network distribution. In fact, if the API is hosted locally, any dedicated hardware (such as a GPU) is up to you. For this reason, if you want to invoke a graph at a very high rate in real-time, then you should consider using an ad hoc, hardware-accelerated cloud host.

- A binding for the specific trained model might not exist for the language of your choice. For example, TensorFlow natively supports Python, C , C++, Go, Swift, and Java.

Invoking a Python (or C++) library from within .NET code is not an unsurmountable technical issue. However, invoking a specific library, such as a trained machine learning model, is usually harder than calling a plain Python or C++ class.

In summary, an ML solution doesn't live on its own and must be framed in the context of an end-to-end business solution. Because many business solutions are based on the .NET stack, it was about time that a platform for training ML models natively in .NET came out. Using ML.NET, you can stay in the .NET ecosystem and don't have to deal with integrating Python into .NET applications.

Introducing ML.NET

First released in the spring of 2019, ML.NET is a free cross-platform and open-source .NET framework designed to build and train machine learning models and host them within .NET applications. See *https://dotnet.microsoft.com/apps/machinelearning-ai/ml-dotnet.*

ML.NET aims to provide the same set of capabilities that data scientists and developers can find in the Python ecosystem, as described earlier. Specifically built for .NET developers (for example, the API reflects common patterns of .NET frameworks and related development practices), ML.NET is built around the concept of the classic ML pipeline: collect data, set the algorithm, train, and deploy. In addition, any required programming steps sound familiar to anybody using the .NET framework and C# and F# programming languages.

The most interesting aspect of ML.NET is that it offers a quite pragmatic programming platform arranged around the idea of predefined *learning tasks*. The library comes equipped to make it relatively easy—even for machine learning newbies—to tackle common machine learning scenarios such as sentiment analysis, fraud detection, or price prediction as if they were just plain programming.

Compared to the pillars of the Python ecosystem presented earlier, ML.NET can be seen primarily as the counterpart of the scikit-learn model building library. The framework, however, also includes some basic facilities for data preparation and analysis that you can find in Pandas or NumPy. ML.NET also allows for the consumption of deep-learning models (specifically, TensorFlow and ONNX). Also, developers can train image classification and object detection models via Model Builder. It is remarkable, though, that the whole ML.NET library is built atop the tremendous power of the whole .NET Core framework.

The ML.NET framework is available as a set of NuGet packages. To start building models, you don't need more than that. However, as of version 16.6.1, Visual Studio also ships the Model Builder wizard that analyzes your input data and chooses the best available algorithm. We return to Model Builder in Chapter 3, "The Foundation of ML.NET."

The Learning Pipeline in ML.NET

A typical ML.NET solution is commonly articulated in three distinct projects:

- An application that orchestrates the steps of any machine learning pipeline: data collection, feature engineering, model selection, training, evaluation, and storage of the trained model

- A class library to contain the data types necessary to have the final model make a prediction once hosted in a client application. Note though that the input and output schemas do not strictly require its own project since these classes can be defined in the same project where training or consumption occurs

- A client application (website or a mobile or desktop application)

The orchestrator can be any type of .NET application, but the most natural choice is to have it coded as a console application.

It is worth noting, though, that this particular piece of code is not a one-off application that stops existing once it has given birth to the model. More often than not, the model has to be re-created many times before production and especially after being run in production. For this reason, the trainer application must be devised to be reusable and easy to configure and maintain.

Getting Started

As simple as it sounds, you can start by creating three such projects manually in Visual Studio and make them look like Figure 2-1. The figure presents three embryonal projects with many files and references missing but with sufficient details to deliver the big picture.

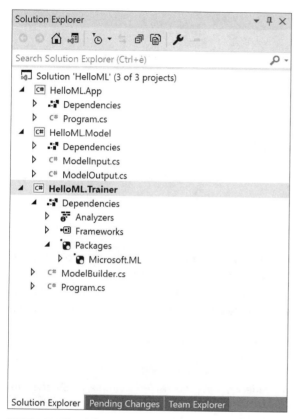

FIGURE 2-1 The skeleton of an ML.NET project in Visual Studio

Aside from the core references to the .NET framework of choice (whether 3.x or 5), the only additional piece you need to bring in is the `Microsoft.ML` NuGet package.

The package is not comprehensive, meaning that depending on what you intend to do, installing more packages might be necessary. However, the package is sufficient to get you started and enables you to experiment with the library. Let's focus on the trainer application and see what it takes to interact with the ML.NET library.

The Pipeline Entry Point

The entry point in the ML.NET pipeline is the `MLContext` object. You use it in much the same way you use the Entity Framework `DBContext` object or the connection object to a database library. You need to have an instance of this class shared across the various objects that participate in the building of the model. A common practice employed in most tutorials—including the sample code generated by the aforementioned Model Builder wizard—is wrapping the model building workflow in a dedicated class, often just named `ModelBuilder`.

```
public static class ModelBuilder
{
    private static MLContext Context = new MLContext();

    // Main method
    public static void CreateModel(string inputDataFileName, string outputModelFileName)
    {
        // Load data

        // Build training pipeline

        // Train Model

        // QUICK evaluation of the model

        // Save the output model

    }
}
```

The instance of the `MLContext` class is global to the class methods, and the name of the files containing train data and the final output file are passed as arguments. The body of the `CreateModel` method (or whatever name you choose for it) develops around a few steps that involve more specific classes of the ML.NET library for activities such as data transformation, feature engineering, model selection, training, evaluation, and persistence.

Data Preparation

The ML.NET framework can read data from a variety of data sources (for example, a CSV-style text file, a binary file, or any `IEnumerable`-based object) and does that through the services of a few specialized loaders built around a specific interface—the `IDataView` interface, a flexible and efficient way of describing tabular data.

An `IDataView`-based loader works as a database cursor and supplies methods to navigate around the data set at any acceptable pace. It also provides an in-memory cache and methods to write the modified content back to disk. Here's a quick example:

```
// Create the context for the pipeline
Context = new MLContext();

// Load data into the pipeline via the DataView object
var dataView = Context.Data.LoadFromTextFile<ModelInput>(INPUT_DATA_FILE);
```

The sample code loads training data from the specified file and manages it as a collection of `ModelInput` types. Needless to say, the `ModelInput` type is a custom class that reflects the rows of data loaded from the text file. The snippet below shows a sample `ModelInput` class. The `LoadColumn` attribute refers to the position of the CSV column to which the property binds.

```
public class ModelInput
{
  [LoadColumn(0)]
  public string Month { get; set; }

  [LoadColumn(1)]
  public float Sales { get; set; }
}
```

In the code, there's an even more relevant point to emphasize. The code makes a key assumption that the loaded data is already in a format that is acceptable for machine learning operations. More often than not, instead, some transformation is necessary to perform on top of available data—the most important of which is that all data must be numeric because algorithms can only read numbers. Here's a realistic scenario:

Your customer has a lot of data coming from a variety of data sources, whether timeline series, sparse Office documents, or database tables populated by online web frontends. In its raw format, the data—no matter the amount—might not be very usable. The appropriate format of the data depends on the desired result and the selected training algorithm. Therefore before mounting the final pipeline, a number of data transformation actions might be necessary, such as rendering data in columns, adding ad hoc feature columns, removing columns, aggregating and normalizing values, and adding density wherever possible. Depending on the context, these steps might be accomplished only once or every time the model is trained.

> **NOTE** At first sight, it might seem that integrating data processing in the pipeline is a waste of time and that there's no value in doing it every time the model is built. More in general, instead, it is a matter of trade-off. We're usually talking about large quantities of data, and processing it to some intermediate format may be expensive. On the other hand, if the gap between raw and cleaned data is not that big, transforming data on each build of the model can deliver tremendous flexibility because you can change the transformation parameters as is convenient. It's a pure speed versus flexibility trade-off.

Trainers and Their Categorization

Training is the crucial phase of a machine learning pipeline. The training consists of picking an algorithm, setting in some way its configuration parameters, and running it repeatedly on a given (training) data set. The output of the training phase is the set of parameters that lead the algorithm to generate the best results. In the ML.NET jargon, the algorithm is called the *trainer*. More precisely, in ML.NET, a trainer is an algorithm plus a task. The same algorithm (say, L-BFGS) can be used for different tasks, such as regression or multiclass classification.

Table 2-1 lists some of the supported trainers grouped in a few tasks. We cover ML.NET tasks in more depth throughout the rest of the book and investigate their programming interface.

TABLE 2-1 ML.NET Tasks Related to Training

Task	Description
AnomalyDetection	Aims at detecting unexpected or unusual events or behaviors compared to the received training
BinaryClassification	Aims at classifying data in one of two categories
Clustering	Aims at splitting data in a number of possibly correlated groups without knowing which aspects could possibly make data items related
Forecasting	Addresses forecasting problems
MulticlassClassification	Aims at classifying data in three or more categories
Ranking	Addresses ranking problems
Regression	Aims at predicting the value of a data item

Figure 2-2 presents the list of ML.NET task objects as they show up through IntelliSense from the `MLContext` pipeline entry point.

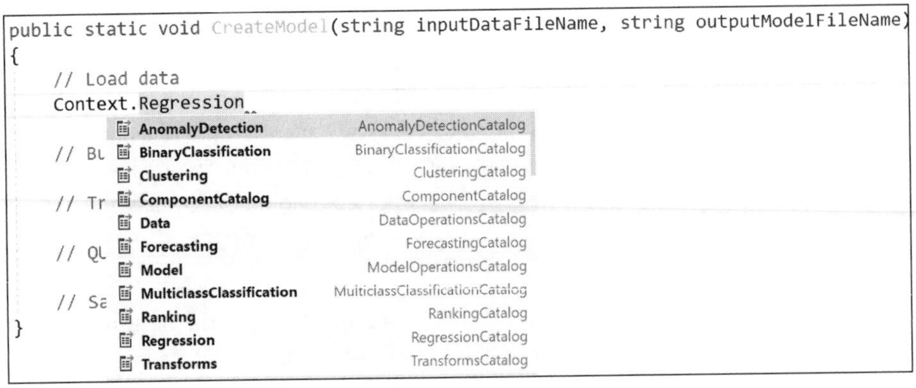

FIGURE 2-2 The list of ML.NET task objects

Each of the task objects listed in Table 2-1 has a `Trainers` property that lists the predefined algorithms supported by the framework. For example, for a prediction task, a good algorithm is the Online Gradient Descent algorithm.

```
var dataProcessPipeline = mlContext.Transforms.Text.FeaturizeText(...);
var trainer = mlContext.Regression.Trainers.OnlineGradientDescent(...);
var trainingPipeline = dataProcessPipeline.Append(trainer);
```

The code snippet selects an instance of the algorithm and then appends it to the data processing pipeline at the end of which the compiled model will come out. This short code contains the essence of the whole ML.NET programming model. This is the way in which the whole pipeline is built step by step and then run.

It is also worth noting that ML.NET supports several specific algorithms for each predefined task. In particular, for the regression task the ML.NET framework also supports the "Poisson Regression" and the "Stochastic Dual Coordinate Ascent" algorithms, and many more can be added to the project at any time through new NuGet packages.

Once the pipeline is built and fully configured, it is ready to run on the provided data. In this regard, the pipeline is a sort of abstract workflow that processes data in a way comparable to how in .NET LINQ queryable objects work on collections and data sets.

Once trained, a model is nothing more than the serialization of a computation graph that represents some sort of mathematical expression or, in some cases, a decision tree. The exact details of the expression depend on the algorithm and to some extent, the nature of the problem's category.

Model Training Executive Summary

Explaining the mechanics of model training is well beyond the scope of this book, which remains strictly focused on the ML.NET framework. However, at least a brief recap of what it means and how it works is in order. For an in-depth analysis, you can easily find online resources as well as books. In particular, you can take a look at our book *Introducing Machine Learning* (Microsoft Press, 2020), in which we mainly focus on the mathematics behind most problems and the algorithmic solutions discovered so far for each class.

Purpose of the Training Phase

Abstractly speaking, an algorithm is the sequence of steps that lead to the solution of a problem. In artificial intelligence, there are two main classes of problems: classification of entities and predictions. In each of these classes, we find several subclasses, such as ranking, forecasting, regression, anomaly detection, image and text analysis, and so forth.

In fact, the output of a machine learning pipeline is a software artifact made of an algorithm (or a chain of algorithms) whose parametric parts (settings and configurable elements) have been adjusted based on the provided training data. In other words, the output of a machine learning pipeline is the instance of an algorithm that, much like the instance of an object-oriented language class, has been initialized to hold a given configuration. The configuration to use for the instance of the algorithm is discovered during the training phase. The schema is outlined in Figure 2-3.

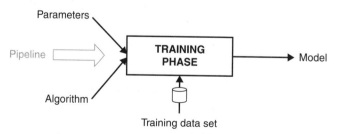

FIGURE 2-3 Overall schema of the training phase in a machine learning process

The Computation Graph

As mentioned, the model is a mathematical black-box—a computation graph—that takes input and computes an output. Input and output are lists of numbers, and in an object-oriented context—as in .NET—they are modeled using classes.

Figure 2-4 presents an abstract and concrete view of how a client application ultimately uses a trained model. Input data flows in, and the gears of the graph crunch numbers and produce a response for the application to deal with.

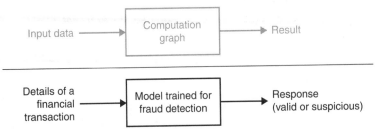

FIGURE 2-4 Overall schema of a trained model being used in production

For example, if you have a model trained to detect possible fraudulent transactions in a financial application, the graph in the model will be called to process a numeric representation of the transaction and produce some values that could be interpreted as to whether the transaction should be approved, denied, or just flagged for further investigation.

Performance of the Model

The term *machine learning* sounds fascinating, but it is not always fully representative of what really happens in a low-level ML framework such as ML.NET or Python's scikit-learn. At this level, the training phase just iteratively processes records in the training data set to minimize an error function.

- The function that produces values–the computation graph—is defined by the selected algorithm.

- The error function is yet another element added to the processing pipeline and also depends, to some extent, on the selected algorithm.

- The error function measures the distance between values produced by the graph on testing data and expected data embedded in the training data set.

- The graph enters the training phase with a default configuration that is updated if the measured error is too large for the desired goal.

- When a good compromise between speed and accuracy is reached, the training ends, and the current configuration of the graph is frozen and serialized for production.

The whole process develops iteratively in the training phase within the ML.NET framework. The steps are summarized in Figure 2-5.

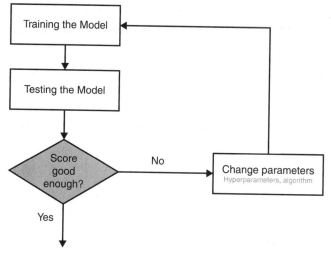

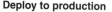

FIGURE 2-5 The generation of an ML model

It should be noted that the evaluation phase depicted here happens within the ML.NET framework and, more in general, within the boundaries of the ML framework of choice. The actual performance evaluated is obtainable on training data with a given set of algorithm parameters (referred to as hyperparameters) and internally computed coefficients.

This is not the same as measuring the performance of the model in production. At this stage, you only measure how good the model is at work on sample data. However, sample data is only expected to be a realistic snapshot of data the model will face once deployed to production. A more crucial evaluation phase will take place later and might even take to rebuilding the model based on different hyperparameters and—why not?—a different algorithm.

In ML.NET, the quality of the model during the training phase is measured using special components called *evaluators*.

A Look at Evaluators

An evaluator is a component that implements a given metric. Evaluation metrics are specific to the class of the algorithm and, in ML.NET, to the ongoing ML task. A good introduction on which evaluator is deemed appropriate for each ML.NET task can be found at

https://docs.microsoft.com/en-us/dotnet/machine-learning/resources/metrics.

A more in-depth discussion about the mathematical reasons that make each metric qualified for a given task can be found in the aforementioned book *Introducing Machine Learning*.

For example, for a prediction problem such as estimating the cost of a taxi ride (and in general for regression and ranking/recommendation problems), a key metric to consider is Squared Loss, also known as Mean Squared Error (MSE). This metric works by measuring how close a regression line is to test expected values. For each input test value, the evaluator takes the distance between the computed and the expected response, squares it, and then calculates the mean. The squaring is applied to increase the relevance of larger differences.

Interestingly, Model Builder, which is embedded in Visual Studio, does some of the work for you. It first lets you choose the class of the problem (the ML task) and indicate the training data set. Based on that, it automatically selects a few matching algorithms, trains them, and measures the performance according to automatically selected metrics. Then it makes a final call and recommends how you should start coding your machine learning solution.

In general, there are a few things that could possibly go bad in a machine learning project:

- The selected algorithm (or algorithm hyperparameters) might not be the most appropriate to explore the given data set.

- The original data set needs more (or less) column transformation.

- The original data set is too small for the intended purpose.

As an example, Table 2-2 summarizes the scores of various algorithms selected by Model Builder for a prediction (regression) task.

TABLE 2-2 Multiple algorithms (and scores) for a sample regression task

Algorithm	Squared Loss	Absolute Loss	RSquared	RMS Loss
LightGbmRegression	4.49	0.38	0.9513	2.12
FastTreeTweedieRegression	4.70	0.44	0.9491	2.17
FastTreeRegression	4.83	0.41	0.9486	2.19
SdcaRegression	10.52	0.87	0.8845	3.27

After a test run of Model Builder, it shows that all featured algorithms ended up with good marks, but Model Builder ranked them in the order shown, thus suggesting we use the LightGbmRegression algorithm based on the evidence provided by metrics. Look in particular at the Squared Loss column. The score is acceptably good for the first three ranked algorithms and significantly worse for SdcaRegression. On the other hand, SdcaRegression is much faster to train. The golden rule of machine learning is that everything is a trade-off.

> **NOTE** Another aspect to consider is that once the model goes to production—even with the best metrics—there might still be chances that things go wrong and the predictions are not in line with business expectations. When this happens, the odds are that an inadequate set of data rows was used for training. Inadequate, at least, in comparison to the real data the model was called to manage in production.

Consuming a Trained Model

At the end of the training phase, you have a model that contains instructions on which algorithm to run and which configuration to use. The model file is a zipped file in some serialization format. Note that a universal, interoperable format exists and is the ONNX format. ML.NET supports it.

As is, however, the model is a dead thing. To bring it to life, you need to load it in a runtime environment so that an API can be exposed to invoke the computation from the outside.

Making the Model Callable from the Outside

Once saved to a file—typically a ZIP file—the model is simply the flat description of a computation to be done on some input data. The first step is wrapping it into a framework engine that knows how to deserialize the graph and execute it on some input data.

ML.NET has a tailor-made set of methods ready to use. Here's the skeleton of the code you need to invoke a previously trained model in ML.NET.

```
public ModelOutput RunModel(string modelFileName, ModelInput input)
{
    var ml = new MLContext();
    var model = ml.Model.Load(modelFileName, out var schema);
    var engine = ml.Model.CreatePredictionEngine<ModelInput, ModelOutput>(model);
    return engine.Predict(input);
}
```

The sample function takes the path to the serialized model file and the input data to which a prediction is made. If the model estimates the cost of a taxi ride, then the class ModelInput describes the ride for which a quote is required. Typically, you will find that the model uses details such as distance, time of day, type of service requested, traffic conditions, area of the city involved, and whatever else is established. The ModelOutput class describes the output of the algorithm used for training. Usually, it's a simple C# class with just a few numeric properties. Here's an example:

```
public class ModelOutput
{
  public double Prediction { get; set; }
}
```

The ML.NET shell code creates an instance of a prediction engine that will carry the task of deserializing and executing the graph and return the calculated value. From the software developer's perspective, invoking an ML model is in no way different from calling a class library method.

Other Deployment Scenarios

Direct embedding of a trained model in the client application is one—and by far the simplest—deployment scenario. There are a couple of potentially sore points to emphasize.

One is the cost of deserializing the model and turning it into an executable computation graph for the runtime environment of choice—in this case, the .NET framework. The other is the (related) cost of setting up a prediction engine. Both operations can be quite expensive to perform if the client application is, say, a web application subject to thousands of calls per second. This is where an artifact like `PredictionEnginePool` comes in handly.

Therefore, the code snippet shown earlier is great for understanding the process but not necessarily good for production. More realistically, a company trains a model to expose a business-critical process as a service to various running software applications. This means that the model should be incorporated in a kind of web service, and proper layers of caching and balancing should be used to ensure proper performance.

In a nutshell, a trained model can be seen as a business black box to be used as a local class library, as a web service, or even as a microservice with its own storage and micro frontend. No option is favorable over the others, but all are feasible options for the architect to choose.

From Data Science to Programming

If you look at the trained model as an autonomous, black-boxed artifact integrated in a given type of software application, you should be able to see also the frontier between data science and programming. Data science contributes the model; programming makes it usable. Both aspects are strictly needed and unavoidable.

A trained model is nothing if not surrounded by a decent programming interface, whether in the form of a class library or a web service. To build an effective model, specific skills are required. First, you need domain expertise. Second, statistics and mathematics and the ability to discern between algorithms and metrics and interpret numbers are required. In extreme cases, the ability to develop new algorithms (including neural networks) or customize existing ones are also required. These skills very rarely belong to developers.

In much the same way, exposing a functional model requires due attention to the overall performance and scalability of the host application and care of the user experience. A taxi ride predictor model ultimately needs numbers to represent any sort of information. But you can hardly expect that people using the app on the go enter their destination through numbers. This is programming work.

In this scenario, ML.NET takes an interesting challenge: enabling developers to code their own machine learning tasks autonomously at least for relatively simple instances of problems and where a sharp precision is not the goal. This is just the ultimate purpose of ML tasks and AutoML—the engine that lies behind Model Builder. In this book, we deeply cover ML tasks but also dedicate a few final chapters to give problems a more real-world perspective. High precision, if necessary, comes at a cost!

Summary

ML.NET is now slated to become the reference platform for machine learning in the .NET space. It is mainly limited to shallow learning and doesn't offer direct support for building neural networks and deep learning (the support is only for consuming existing networks). On the other hand, also in the Python space there are libraries for shallow learning (scikit-learn) and libraries for building neural networks.

It is, instead, much more interesting and promising is the overall approach aimed at making machine learning easy to consume and relatively easy to design for developers. No developers will turn into expert data scientists overnight—not even after digesting the content of this book—but any savvy developer passionate about newer technologies and artificial intelligence would be incredibly comfortable with getting into the dazzling world of machine learning through ML.NET.

We've already mentioned something, but it helps to reinforce the concept: Although Python is quite popular among data scientists, there's no strict reason why machine learning models can't be developed and tested in .NET (or other languages, including Java and Go). It's all about the ecosystem and ease of use. ML.NET relies on the .NET Core infrastructure and Visual Studio.

Let's now go with a simple but not-so-trivial and complete example: taxi fare prediction. The next chapter includes a bit of feature engineering, feature selection, and, more importantly, a client web application.

CHAPTER 3

The Foundation of ML.NET

"My brain is open."

—Paul Erdos, Mathematician, 1913—1996

A common distinction of roles we observe in applied machine learning is between data scientists and programmers. The former are perceived as the wizards who know the (mathematical) tricks to create gold from data, whereas the latter are no more than helpful and willing assistants.

Without beating around the bush, we think data science and programming are dichotomous roles that can only hold at a very high level of abstraction. From a 10,000-foot view, you realize that just modeling the data is not enough. The ability to engineer data into workable structures and pipelines is crucial for putting AI-based systems into production.

In Chapter 2, "An Architectural Perspective of ML.NET," we discussed Python and introduced ML.NET to point out that convenience has been the key driver for using Python. Python is great for data science practices, though it stops being a great tool when moving from prototyping to production. ML.NET, which is well integrated with the .NET framework, sits at the beginning of the data engineering field—beyond mere data science on the way to plain intelligent software.

In this chapter, we analyze the foundation of ML.NET, focusing on data processing, training, and "productionizing" a machine learning–based software solution.

On the Way to Data Engineering

To start off, let's outline the principal professional roles we could realistically encounter in machine learning projects. We identify three crucial roles:

- Data scientist
- Data engineer
- ML developer

In this context, a role is just a named collection of skills, and the same individual can cover multiple roles in the same project or company. In fact, the actual skills necessary for the various roles tend to overlap to some extent, as represented in Figure 3-1.

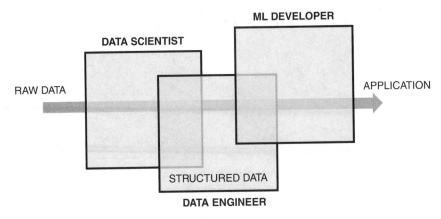

FIGURE 3-1 Roles necessary to an ML project

The Role of a Data Scientist

As the name emphasizes, a data scientist is required to use science to turn the raw material of data into a commodity for the company. In doing so, the data scientist borrows techniques from mathematics and statistics to sift through the raw data available and make reasonable guesses about what that data can be turned into.

As we see things, the primary responsibility of a data scientist is determining what a company can learn from its data and ideally point at which artifacts or, more specifically, which products can be planned and for which business purpose. Some good knowledge of the domain is a critical plus for any data scientist. Abstract mathematics is a powerful tool, but a clear business focus is necessary to provide substance.

The data scientist looks at the data, reshapes it in many different ways, analyzes quality parameters, attempts to fix what can be fixed, and identifies additional or alternative sources. The data scientist also likely builds runnable models to probe ideas and verify assumptions. Python is the perfect tool for these activities because it's easy to pick up for nondevelopers and trivial to manage for everyday tasks.

The outcome of the data scientist's work is typically a runnable model whose software quality is often that of a prototype rather than that of a production-ready product.

In our opinion, a team of data scientists is a due investment for a large organization producing very large quantities of data (such as an energy utility, a financial institution, or a manufacturing farm). For smaller companies with significantly more limited budgets, the outcome of some applied data science can be cheaper to buy as a service. A smaller organization willing to set up an ML solution will probably want to prioritize the acquisition of resources that can start from a prototype or detailed specs and build up some robust and scalable data processing pipeline that can be turned into a production-ready deliverable.

The Role of a Data Engineer

Chapter 1 takes you through an historical journey of how artificial intelligence developed. In short, it was an abstract idea (close to a dream) in the seventeenth century that a handful of mathematicians turned into a new branch of mathematical logic in the nineteenth century and became the theory of computation with Alan Turing in the 1930s. However, the Turing machine was an abstract model—not even a concrete prototype—but it proved what we could do with it.

In life, scientists discover and produce the abstract model of new things, but then it is engineers who do their part to produce actual goods. It is exactly the same with data.

The role of the data engineer is between a data scientist and a software engineer who knows some basics of machine learning. A company that has figured out what can be learned from its data is only halfway done. Here are a few points that need to be addressed:

- How is data collected and stored on a daily or hourly basis?

- Should data be temporarily copied in some intermediate format?

- What kind of transformation is required for the model to work? How can that be automated?

- How is the performance of the model live?

- How often is the model expected to need retraining to stay adherent to live data?

- If retraining is a frequent operation, how can any related tasks—such as collecting updated datasets, running the training, and deploying the up-to-date model—be automated?

All these tasks require the manipulation of data in persistent data stores that are more structured and faster than plain text files. Treating data as sparse files might be sufficient, but to build a robust infrastructure, you might want to switch to some flavor of database (whether relational, NoSQL, or graph) and a related query language.

In general, a dedicated Extract-Transform-Load (ETL) pipeline must be in place and fully automated to copy, sort, map, and munge raw data into a more usable format and shape that is easy to maintain and evolve. The term "data wrangling "is often used to describe this kind of data engineering work. Bear in mind that data science focuses on a static sample of data that is representative of the business domain. Companies want applications that drive dynamic, live data through a model that is scalable enough to support real workloads.

An ETL pipeline is just software.

The Role of an ML Engineer

Data in an easy-to-process format enables further steps of machine learning, such as building a training infrastructure, following the guidelines of the data science team, and more generally productionizing the model for client applications to consume the solution.

An ML engineer is primarily a software developer with some specific skills in machine learning. An ML engineer has some degree of familiarity with machine learning frameworks (including Python-based frameworks) and the activities of the overall ML pipeline. The engineer can also write good code by applying best practices such as object orientation, dependency injection, and unit testing and is comfortable with API endpoints, web services, REST, and gRPC.

The core responsibility of an ML engineer is that of physically incorporating an externally trained model into client applications or the much more delicate task of supervising the building and training of a model based on data science specs.

Expecting business and learning guidance from an ML engineer is probably unrealistic, as much as it is unrealistic to hire a data scientist and believe you're done. It is unlikely—but far from impossible—that a single individual would be able to serve in the three aforementioned roles. However, any professional in any of the roles should be ready to acquire some knowledge in side sectors. Machine learning is the combination of many things. A Y-shaped approach to learning sounds like a much more rewarding alternative than, say, a T-shaped model.

> **NOTE** *T-shaped* refers to extremely deep professional skills in one area but relatively flat skill levels in all surrounding areas. In other words, a Y-shaped set of skills is as deep as a T-shaped set in one area, but the Y-shaped skills also bring deeper expertise in other sectors that are closer to the main expertise. Thus, outside the specialty, a Y-shaped skilled professional is more well-rounded.

If you're still wondering where ML.NET can help and how it is related to Python, we believe ML.NET is the perfect tool to support data engineering efforts in the .NET technology stack.

The Data to Start From

Let's go through an end-to-end journey in ML.NET to see what it means to spot available data, build a business idea, proceed to the model's definition, the training, and finally, the client application consuming it.

Let's say your company processes thousands of consumer transactions every day in a specific geographical area. Your customers are ready to pay for the service, but the nature of the business is such that the fee for this service is not fully determined until the service is completed. Yet, you have the full log of all transactions, day after day.

Is there anything you can learn from your data?

Making Sense of the Available Data

The ultimate goal of data science is to look at the available data from many different angles and perspectives to spot any hidden value. A data scientist in front of data is comparable to a sculptor in front of a block of marble. Legend says that Michelangelo was inspired to shape his sculpture of David by looking at a marble block from a cave in the Apuan Alps, North Tuscany. Reportedly, Michelangelo said the marble was talking to him and guiding his hands to create a masterpiece.

With data and data science, it is much easier. And, above all, there's no need to create masterpieces all the time. The definition of a masterpiece is much looser when we're talking about data and data science than with sculpture and marble.

The Way Data Science Looks at Data

Suppose the data owner is a taxi company, and the data consists of the log of a few million paid transactions for many taxi rides in a certain geographical area. What stories could the data tell? One possible story is the density of transactions that may reveal which subarea is in highest demand at a certain time of day. The money is another story—where and when did the company get most of the money? In other words, when and where were the rides the most rewarding?

These two sample stories belong to a well-known class—statistical market analysis. They're definitely useful, but there's nothing new in any of them. A new story that a data scientist can spot in the data is guessing the dynamic elements that make the final price. This information—a prediction descending from data analysis—can be used to forecast earnings but also to tell customers how much they might be asked to pay.

The story told by a dataset depends on the nature and shape of the data itself. Clearly, not every dataset will tell you the same story, but every dataset can have the potential to tell you business-attractive stories. Which stories and how attractive they are depends on the quality of data science analysis and is also a matter of causality and creativity.

Exploring a Sample Dataset

As an example, our data science team is given a CSV file made of seven columns and a couple of million rows. Each row represents a paid transaction, specifically a taxi ride. The direction of the analysis is driven by the actual features of the data and the source. In this case, it is realistic to assume that data comes from the company's back-end system that tracks rides, cars, and payments.

Each data row contains the time of day, the number of passengers, the time it took to complete the ride, the distance traveled, the type of payment (cash or card), and the fare paid. There's enough to attempt price prediction, but at the same time, it's unrealistic to expect high accuracy from this data. At the very minimum, the dataset lacks information about the pick-up and drop-off addresses and an indication of the traffic conditions and weather at the time of the ride.

The task of data science is measuring the accuracy of the prediction that results from the available data and, at the same time, exploring ways to get hold of missing data to integrate with the original dataset.

So much for plain data science and analysis. What about data engineering?

Raw data must be organized in manageable and tidy data structures. With ML.NET, each row of the dataset can become a C# class to make it easier to build and consume the final model. The following class is a realistic representation:

```csharp
public class TaxiTrip
{
    [LoadColumn(0)]
    public string VendorId;

    [LoadColumn(1)]
    public string RateCode;

    [LoadColumn(2)]
    public float PassengerCount;

    [LoadColumn(3)]
    public float TripTime;

    [LoadColumn(4)]
    public float TripDistance;

    [LoadColumn(5)]
    public string PaymentType;

    [LoadColumn(6)]
    public float FareAmount;
}
```

The LoadColumn attribute establishes a static binding between the specific property and corresponding column in the original dataset. The position is indicated by name or position if the source is a CSV (comma-separated value) or TSV (tab-separated value) text file.

This class is important because it represents the smallest data item in the project, and the entire dataset is described as a collection of TaxiTrip objects. The TaxiTrip class is also very close to the input passed to the model to get a response. In programming terms, this class will be placed in a separate assembly to be referenced by any .NET client applications entitled to use the final trained model.

Building a Data Processing Pipeline

As mentioned, data engineering is about doing the things envisioned (and prototyped) by data science. Any machine learning algorithm requires numbers to work nicely. In this context, therefore, the first aspect to consider is the rendering of the data.

In most datasets, several columns of data are made of text. In our example, we have textual features such as the vendor ID, the code for the paid rate, and the payment type. Therefore, the values in those columns must be turned into numbers in some way that doesn't alter the distribution and relevance of individual values.

Common Data Transformations

The ML.NET library provides helper classes to do these kinds of transformations. Here's an example. Note that the mlContext object is the root object that identifies the ML.NET context:

```
var dataTransformationPipeline = mlContext
            .Transforms
            .Categorical
            .OneHotEncoding("VendorIdEncoded", "VendorId")
      .Append(mlContext
            .Transforms
            .Categorical
            .OneHotEncoding("RateCodeEncoded","RateCode"))
      .Append(mlContext
            .Transforms
            .Categorical
            .OneHotEncoding("PaymentTypeEncoded", "PaymentType"));
```

The OneHotEncoding object applies a common data transformation to categorical values. The algorithm consists of adding one binary (0/1) column for each distinct categorical value found in the specified column. The first parameter of the method is the prefix to name new columns.

Another transformation that might make sense to apply is the normalization of mean variance on numeric columns:

```
pipeline.Append(mlContext.Transforms.NormalizeMeanVariance("PassengerCount"));
```

The purpose of normalization is to minimize the impact of outliers in columns so that the model isn't skewed outside the normal range of values. In addition, you might also want to remove outliers from the dataset. An outlier is a value too far away from the mean. This step may not be necessary all the time, but if you have reasons to believe that outliers affect results, by all means, do so. You remove outliers by simply filtering the loaded dataset. In the example dataset, we're removing all rows in which the FareAmount column value is lower than 1 and higher than 150.

```
mlContext.Data.FilterRowsByColumn(rawData, "FareAmount", 1, 150);
```

Finally, there are a couple of further transformations required because of the internal mechanics of the ML.NET library. You need to have a column named Label that represents the target of the prediction. Also, you need a column named Features containing all row values serialized in an array.

```
mlContext.Transforms.CopyColumns("Label", "FareAmount");
mlContext.Transforms.Concatenate("Features", ...);
```

In this way, we will tell the training algorithm to target the values of the original FareAmount column (now duplicated in the Label column) and process the input values in the Features column made by the concatenation of all other values in the row.

Loading Data for Processing

ML.NET takes a sort of functional approach to training a model. First, you define a pipeline of actions (loading, transformation, training, and evaluation). Next, you fire it up and pass the link to the actual data to process for training. We've already touched on the common transformations applicable to the dataset used for training a model. Now we should focus on loading the data, which is a foregone point with no fancy comments to make. Yet, it's one of the most compelling reasons to consider abandoning Python even when a full Python solution is acceptable.

Training a dataset is a matter of crunching large quantities of data, and this large quantity has to be read in memory to become available. Just loading all the data in memory is often expensive in terms of resources. ML.NET addresses this aspect—a frequently insurmountable issue in Python solutions—in a custom way by means of a dedicated object—the data view—that acts as a classic database cursor and moves back and forth one item at a time.

The data view works like a plain enumerable object works in the .NET framework and provides methods to count and visit all reachable elements in the collection. The interface behind the data view—the IDataView interface—represents the fundamental type for input and output in all data query operations. It wraps an enumerable collection (including schema information) and provides a cursor-based navigation system that proceeds row by row. The data view object works hand in hand with the data loader object, characterized by the IDataLoader interface. The data loader is respon-sible for the actual loading of the data from some external data source and for returning a valid IDataView object.

In ML.NET, navigation of data is cursor-based and centered on the GetRowCursor method of the data view. This method just returns the cursor for the client application to use to move over the view in a forward-only mode. The method also allows access to a subset of the columns available.

Interestingly, the optional method GetRowCursorSet on the data view interface returns an array of cursors that can be run in parallel to cover a larger section of the data view through multiple threads. If implemented in the specific data view object, the method GetRowCursorSet enables you to set a limit on the number of cursors to be created and returned.

Although from a functional perspective, ML.NET offers the same capabilities as machine learning frameworks available in other languages when it comes to technical details, it looks like a very carefully crafted framework that was specifically designed to overcome reported issues with other frameworks and languages. This alone makes ML.NET a powerful tool to use for data engineers, along with data-base tools and cloud software facilities.

Further Considerations on the Dataset

Before we focus on the training step of the ML.NET pipeline, a few sparse considerations on the nature of the training dataset are in order. Considering that any machine learning model is a transformer that works on whatever you pass to produce whatever it can figure out, it stands that any time the input data is inadequate, insufficient, or unbalanced, then you will get inadequate or insufficient or unbal-anced answers. Therefore, the training dataset must contain information about all possible factors that could influence the result.

We started this chapter by presenting the three major roles in machine learning. First, we discussed how data science is at the beginning of the chain, and data engineering follows. Although this is definitely a quite common scenario, sometimes things might go differently, and data engineering might precede any data science analysis. This is true when it's not obvious which data can be detached and processed to train some model in a business context.

Sometimes data engineers can be called to arrange some ETL infrastructure to flow live data into a manageable container where data scientists can play their tricks and figure out what can be learned and how. In doing so, some preliminary data transformations (which require specific skills of database tooling) may be necessary, such as hot encoding of categorical values, computed and/or aggregated columns, or normalization of values.

The skills of transforming data for training purposes can be part of data engineering and data science, and the neutral term feature engineering is used to indicate it. While feature engineering refers to data transformation, the tools employed to perform it may be different if the actor is a data scientist or a data engineer. It will likely be some Numpy or Pandas function in the hands of a data scientist; it might be the SQL-related (or ML.NET-related) tool in the hands of a data engineer.

As a final example, what could be missing from the sample taxi rides that can't be extracted easily? The traffic condition at the time of each ride is one piece of data that's crucial to have for accurate predictions. This information can be brought from the outside, or the team can decide to hard-code it based on information, such as calculating the categorical value that looks at the time of day the ride took place. This represents an appropriate example of data transformation that would help the data scientist do a better job but could be tricky to perform without some solid knowledge of ETL.

The Training Step

With all data in place and an infrastructure ready to pump it all the way down the pipeline, it's time to focus on the trainer—namely, the algorithm that will try to make sense of the input to output a classification or a prediction. Let's focus on a very common use of machine learning—prediction of the price of a service. In this case, the cost of a taxi ride in a known geographical area.

When it comes to predicting a numeric value like the price of a service, the class of algorithms that works most of the time is regression. (We tackle the internals of the most common classes of machine learning algorithms in Part II of the book.) Under the umbrella of regression, there are a number of different algorithms, and choosing the one to try first is a matter of experience, knowledge of the domain, and sometimes even gut feeling.

Whatever algorithm you choose for the first run of training needs to survive the metrics of the post-training test. If numbers don't support the choice, you might consider trying a different algorithm or shape the training set differently.

Machine learning is almost always a matter of trial and error.

Picking an Algorithm

All in all, price prediction is a relatively easy problem to solve. If you can have dense and detailed data, then prediction essentially boils down to choosing the fastest regression algorithm. In ML.NET, the trainers available for the regression task are grouped under the Regression property of the context object. Here's how to add a regression trainer to the pipeline:

```
// Identify the training algorithm
var trainer = mlContext
        .Regression
        .Trainers
        .OnlineGradientDescent("Label", "Features", new SquaredLoss());

// Add it to the current data processing pipeline
var trainingPipeline = dataPipeline.Append(trainer);

// Start training of the model
var trainedModel = trainingPipeline.Fit(dataView);
```

The selected algorithm—the online gradient descent algorithm—is an average good choice, but faster and more precise algorithms exist, such as the LightGbmRegression algorithm. You can use any of those more sophisticated algorithms by referencing additional NuGet packages. With the default configuration of ML.NET, the online gradient descent algorithm is commonly a good option.

The algorithm takes two string parameters to denote the names of the input and output columns (or features) in the dataset. The output column is the column to predict. The third parameter indicates the error function that will be used to measure the distance between the predicted and expected values during the testing phase. The SquaredLoss object refers to the R-squared metric—a fairly common metric for regression problems.

When all is ready, you just call the Fit method to start the training of the model.

> **NOTE** Calling the Fit method on a training pipeline is easy, and we agree that most of the effort up to this point descends from the expertise of data science specialists. However, training the model is not just one method call. The training procedure is hardly a one-off action and, more often than not, has to be repeated regularly. In other words, it's code, and as such, it must be tested and maintained.

Measuring the Actual Value of an Algorithm

The value of a machine learning algorithm results from the combination of multiple factors. One is the time it takes to converge to an acceptable outcome. The speed of a trainer is measured through the formula of computational complexity, namely the number of steps and resources required for running it.

Another aspect is how the specific algorithm—given its internal steps—reacts to the actual data it is presented. The same algorithm, in fact, can produce more (or less) accurate results working on different shapes of the same raw data. This is not surprising at all if you know at least a bit of the theory of computational complexity.

Computational Complexity

Because the complexity of an algorithm may significantly vary for different shapes of the same input, the complexity is expressed for the best-, average-, and worst-case scenarios. The complexity calculated for the worst-case scenario indicates the longest it may take, regardless of the input. The complexity is usually expressed as a function of the size of the input. Only the asymptotic behavior of the function is taken into account when the input size grows indefinitely.

To see how the shape of the data may affect the performance of algorithms, let's consider the Quicksort algorithm. Written in the early 1960s by Tony Hoare, Quicksort remains one of the fastest sorting algorithms and one of the most commonly used in libraries and frameworks.

On average, the Quicksort algorithm has a complexity of $n*log(n)$ where n is the size of the input, that is the array of data to sort. A complexity of $n*log(n)$ is also known to be the fastest asymptotic complexity for any sorting algorithm. In the early implementations of Quicksort, researchers observed an interesting relationship between the algorithm and the input data. In particular, if the data was presorted (ascending or descending), or if all elements in the input dataset were the same, the algorithm had its complexity grow up to an unacceptable n^2.

In more recent real-life implementations of the algorithm, those edge cases have been ruled out. Today, the Quicksort algorithm can run a few times faster than any other sorting algorithm while showing the same (optimal) asymptotic behavior.

The weird behavior of the originally proposed flavor of the Quicksort algorithm reminds us that a given representation of the training dataset can make an otherwise super fast algorithm perform worse than another. Hence, we need to be careful with testing the model and aim at the best possible metrics we're able to achieve. The performance may depend on the organization of data, but the organization of data depends on the raw data available or how they have been initially extracted and composed for data science.

Planning the Testing Phase

In any machine learning project, we have a unique heap of data to work with. Most of this data should be used to train the model; the remaining part should be used to test the trained model and grab some quick metrics to evaluate the model's behavior.

The point is leaving enough data for the trainer to understand and enough for the evaluator to test. Generally, an 80/20 split is good if data is evenly distributed so that the "inner nature" of the data items in the training set matches the "inner nature" o++f the data in the testing set.

Note that a plain 80/20 split refers to a technique called a *holdout*. A holdout is quick and easy to code, but it only works effectively if the data is balanced. And the split keeps both subsets balanced as well. However, it's worth recalling that you're testing the model on only 20 percent of the data.

Cross-validation is another testing technique, longer to run but far more accurate. All these techniques find hard-coded tools in the ML.NET framework. In particular, cross-validation is a resampling technique borrowed from statistics that consists of splitting the original set of data into a few groups (say, five groups) and iteratively using any group as the testing dataset and the remaining (say, four) groups as the training dataset. This technique is recommended in the case of data shortage because it maximizes the use of the available data using all data items for both training and testing.

A Look at the Metrics

Once we have a trained model, ML.NET provides a number of predefined services to evaluate the resulting model's quality. Here's how we can run a testing step and grab metrics:

```
// Run the trained model on the testing dataset
IDataView predictions = trainedModel.Transform(testDataView);
var metrics = mlContext.Regression.Evaluate(predictions, "Label", "FareAmount");
```

The *Evaluate* method on the Regression object gets the testing dataset and goes through all the contained items looking at the input values in the Label column and the expected values as in the *FareAmount* column. In ML.NET, the Evaluate method returns a RegressionMetrics object, as described in Table 3-1.

TABLE 3-1 Properties of the *RegressionMetrics* Type in ML.NET

Name of metrics	Description
LossFunction	Double value. It indicates the average of values returned by the loss function passed to the trainer. In the example, it was a *SquaredLoss* object.
MeanAbsoluteError	Double value. It indicates the average of the absolute errors found between the predicted and the expected values.
MeanSquaredError	Double value. It indicates the average of the squares of the errors found between the predicted and the expected values.
RootMeanSquaredError	Double value. It refers to the square root of the average of squared errors found between the predicted and the expected values.
Rsquared	Double value. RSquared (or R^2) indicates the coefficient of determination of the model. It is given by the ratio of mean squared error of the model and the variance of the predicted feature.

Of all these metrics, the most relevant for a regression algorithm is RSquared because it tells how good the algorithm is to capture the feature's variance to predict. The optimal value of the RSquared metric is as close as possible to 1.

> **NOTE** How do you know about the relevance of the various metrics for the various algorithms? It's expertise, and it's primarily data science expertise. However, this knowledge easily flows from the data science team down the chain to developers and facilitates the transfer of knowledge that ultimately makes it possible to blur the boundaries of the machine learning professional roles, as summarized in Figure 3-1.

Consuming the Model from a Client Application

So, what is a trained model? It's a binary file that is not made of any executable code.

A trained model is a file that stores the description of a computational graph. The information is serialized according to a rigorous, common schema so that it can be read and processed in multiple host environments. In ML.NET, the trained model is a serialized ZIP file. It needs to be deployed as a project file and loaded into a new instance of MLContext to become usable from any client .NET code.

Let's see what it takes to create a sample ASP.NET Core application to consume a taxi fare prediction model we assume to have created. (The full source code of the sample application is available in the Source Code section of the book as well as from the /downloads folder on our *https://youbiquitous.net* website.)

Getting the Model File

The typical ML.NET project you create in Visual Studio consists of a console application that leads the training phase. It contains code to load data from some local or remote source, apply transformations, pick a trainer, train, evaluate, and persist the model. The output is a ZIP file with the serialized trained model and a class library containing the C# classes used to map the training dataset. The following line is an excerpt that shows the serialization of the model:

```
mlContext.Model.Save(trainedModel, trainingDataView.Schema, "model.zip");
```

The schema parameter describes the schema of the data used to train the model. This information is necessary to any newly created MLContext instances that will load the model later.

The Overall Project

As mentioned, a machine learning project is not made of the sole infrastructure needed to produce a single executable. A typical project may include a module for training, one shared library, and the client application. Figure 3-2 shows the solution open in Visual Studio.

Under the Training folder, you find the console application that knows how to train the dataset using a given algorithm. The Output subfolder ends up containing the zipped model files. The Model folder is the class library—specifically, a .NET Standard library project—that shares common-use types necessary to train and invoke the model.

The shared library may not need to reference the ML.NET package. Under the ASP.NET project, you find the core Microsoft.ML package and copies of the trained model files in a child directory.

From the perspective of an ASP.NET web application, the trained model is a static data file and gets processed through the services of a wrapper engine. In an end-to-end scenario, you should see any trained machine learning model as a domain service—part of the business layer of your solution.

The sample application sets up an HTML view to collect some input data and then invoke a controller endpoint. In turn, the controller endpoint calls the wrapper ML.NET engine to have the response.

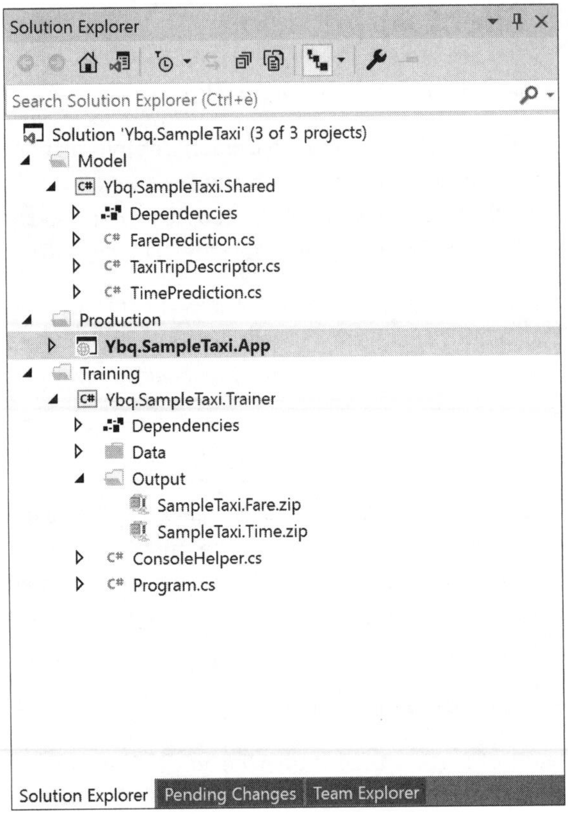

FIGURE 3-2 The sample project in Visual Studio 2019

Making a Taxi Fare Prediction

Even though the example is written for ASP.NET Core, you can use the ML.NET library with .NET framework applications as well, including classic ASP.NET MVC applications. The following is the controller class that, in the sample application, deals with the prediction service. In turn, the prediction service encapsulates the machine learning model:

```
public class FareController : Controller
{
    private readonly FarePredictionService _service;
    public FareController(IWebHostEnvironment environment)
    {
        _service = new FarePredictionService(environment.ContentRootPath);
    }

    public IActionResult Suggest(TaxiTripEstimation input)
    {
        var response = _service.Predict(input);
        return Json(response);
    }
}
```

The `FarePredictionService` class receives the content root path that it will use to locate the ZIP file with the trained model to load. Here's the code necessary to invoke the model:

```
public TaxiTripEstimation Predict(TaxiTripEstimation input)
{
    // Map the input received from the UI to the input required  by the model
    var trip = FillTaxiTripFromInput(input);

    // Predict the amount of the fare given the input parameters
    var ml = new MLContext();
    var fare = MakePrediction(trip, ml, _mlFareModelPath);

    // Copy prediction to the input object
    input.EstimatedFare = fare;
    input.EstimatedFareForDisplay = TaxiTripEstimation.FareForDisplay(fare);
    return input;
}
```

More than the actual prediction, the key thing that's going on here is the mapping between the input data coming from the user interface and the data required by the model—the `TaxiTrip` class imported from the referenced model library. Note that `TaxiTripEstimation` belongs to the client application, and it is a helper class that the `ASP.NET` MVC layer populates from the HTTP context using `ASP.NET` MVC model binding. We've hidden the details—a mere copy of fields—in the `FillTaxiTripFromInput` method.

The actual prediction takes place in the `MakePrediction` method:

```
float MakePrediction(TaxiTrip trip, MLContext mlContext, string modelPath)
{
    // Load the trained model
    var trainedModel = mlContext.Model.Load(modelPath, out var modelInputSchema);

    // Create prediction engine related to the loaded trained model
    var predEngine = mlContext
        .Model
        .CreatePredictionEngine<TaxiTrip, TaxiTripFarePrediction>(trainedModel);

    // Predict
    var prediction = predEngine.Predict(trip);
    return prediction.FareAmount;
}
```

It should be noted that the preceding code is good for understanding the mechanics of the interaction between ASP.NET and the ML.NET library, but it leaves room for a few concerns if the planned use is in a production environment.

In a real-life scenario, in fact, you might want to load the model and build the ML.NET prediction engine once and reuse it across multiple calls.

Scalability Concerns

Specifically, the preceding code has two main issues. One is that the model is being loaded on every HTTP request that causes it to execute. It's just a matter of poor performance that becomes evident when the model is significantly large. At the very minimum, the trained model should be coded as a singleton and shared across the application. Technically, a model in ML.NET is an instance of the ITransformer type, which is known to be thread-safe, and then sharing it as a singleton is acceptable. In ASP.NET Core, the easiest method is to load the model at startup and share via dependency injection. A global variable would also work fine.

The other problem is more serious and relates to the PredictionEngine type. As mentioned, the type wraps up the trained model and invokes it. Getting an instance of the type is time-consuming, so it is not recommended to create a fresh instance every time a specific request comes in. Unfortunately, though, this type is also not thread-safe, meaning that the singleton workaround discussed for the model can't be applied, and a more sophisticated solution is recommended, such as using object pooling. The good news is that you don't have to work out an object pool yourself.

The Microsoft.Extensions.ML package provides a pool object that plugs into the startup service collection easily:

```
public void ConfigureServices(IServiceCollection services)
{
    // Other services here
    // ...
    services.AddPredictionEnginePool<TaxiTripDescriptor, FarePrediction>();

    // More services here
}
```

In this way, you can create a scalable pool of prediction engines that take one specific type in input and one specific type in output.

Devising an Adequate User Interface

In spite of its overall simplicity, the example still raises a number of practical questions about the trained model, the client application, and the whole feedback cycle for the project.

One issue is that the model needs to know the distance of the ride to make a price prediction. (See the definition of the TaxiTrip class, derived from the considered dataset.) It's reasonable, but how would you devise the user interface around it? Should you ask customers to type the distance they want to travel?

More realistically, the user interface on top of this sample taxi service will let users enter two addresses and will calculate the distance using some third-party geographical information system. In addition, how would you render the response to the user? Should you go with a plain float number, or is calculated range preferable? (See Figure 3-3.)

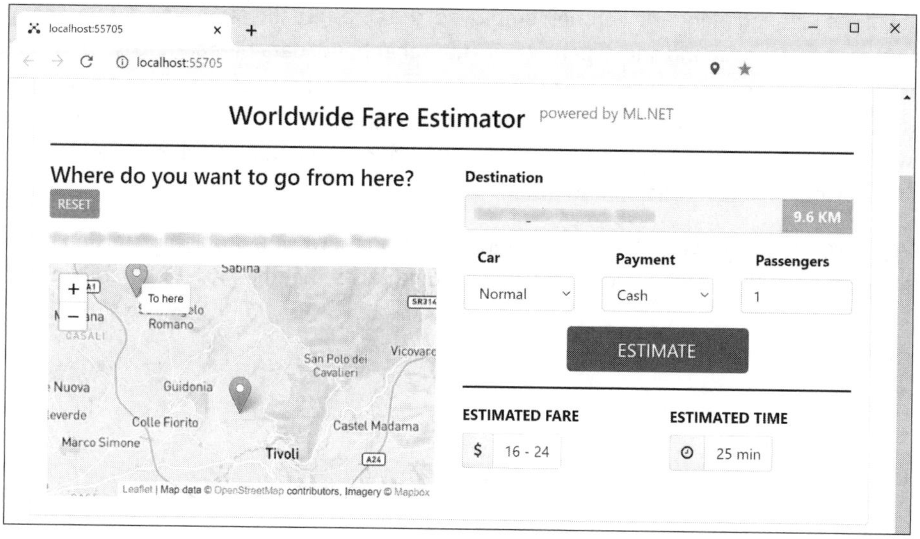

FIGURE 3-3 The user interface of the sample application.

As you can see in the figure, the type of car, payment, and the number of passengers are collected from the user interface and passed to the controller via HTTP. Those values are mapped to corresponding properties of the model-specific TaxiTrip class. The addresses, instead, must be programmatically converted into a distance. (The JavaScript API of the GIS service does it in this example.) The Estimate button posts the form back to the ASP.NET Core application and receives the text to display as the estimated range for fare and time.

> **NOTE** It is interesting to remark that although the model was trained using public data from the city of New York, in a number of cases, the predictions were not much further away from what it would really take in Rome for similar distances! This should remind us that machine learning is only about guessing, and despite metrics and evaluators, it's the business scenario that determines when a guess is acceptable.

Summary

This chapter covered the canonical steps of machine learning projects as the ML.NET library implemented them and provided an end-to-end, full .NET example of a sample model in action. In this demo, we started from the model. In the real world, instead, you should start from the problem and review all aspects of it before you commit to building a machine learning model.

In spite of the language (and the libraries) employed, the steps are the same, and data preparation is by far the most time-consuming and expensive. On the other hand, data preparation is often neglected in demos as most demos start from ready-made data. Just data preparation, however, suggests that sticking to one language and platform may not always be a great idea. In Python, for example, you tend to work with CSV files, whereas sometimes, a plain relational database (and some Java or C# code to populate it) would make it cheaper and faster.

Anyway, beyond data preparation, this chapter focused on regression problems. Starting with the next chapter, we'll review the whole set of machine learning tasks that the ML.NET library supports.

CHAPTER 4

Prediction Tasks

"I know that two and two make four, though I must say that if by any sort of process I could convert 2 and 2 into five, well, that would give me much greater pleasure."
—Lord George Gordon Byron, letter to future Lady Byron, 1812

Machine learning—and everything else that falls under the umbrella of artificial intelligence—addresses applications of two main scenarios: prediction and classification.

Prediction is about guessing numbers. More precisely, it is about identifying a mathematical function whose curve well approximates the (present and future) distribution of data faced in a specific business context.

Classification is about identifying the category an object belongs to. An object is intended as a data item and is fully represented by an array of values (referred to as *features*). Each value refers to a measurable property that makes sense to consider in the scenario under analysis. Whereas prediction returns numbers in a continuous and potentially unbounded range, classification returns values in a discrete, categorical set.

All machine learning techniques—from shallow learning algorithms to sophisticated neural networks (and any combination thereof)—are good at addressing these two general classes of problems. How good they are depends on the constraints and nonfunctional requirements of the specific business problem to solve.

Whenever you are faced with a software task—and more than everything else, a machine learning task—bear in mind that any technology is a mean and never the ultimate goal. Figure 4-1 is inspired by a cartoon in which two characters face the problem of passing through a door with a huge skewer larger than the width.

In the cartoon, the two characters go for a brute-force, kind of blind approach and break the wall around the door enough to make the skewer pass horizontally laid out. Perhaps a more thought-out approach would have conducted them to a simpler solution, such as slightly rotating the skewer to make it pass diagonally laid out.

Turning to machine learning, a 100-layer neural network might not be preferable and objectively more precise than a far simpler and quick regression algorithm for the same (prediction or classification) problem!

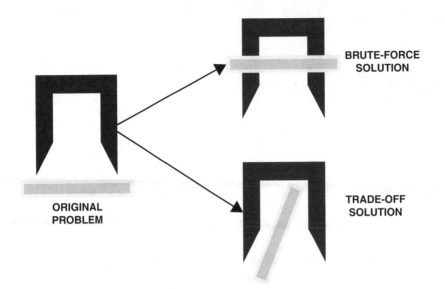

BRUTE-FORCE
SOLUTION

ORIGINAL
PROBLEM

TRADE-OFF
SOLUTION

FIGURE 4-1 Brute-force approach vs. trade-off approach

In this chapter, we go through the prediction scenario through the shallow learning algorithms provided by ML.NET. In successive chapters, we face classification tasks and more specific aspects of both prediction and classification, such as categorization, anomaly detection, recommendation systems, and image classification.

The Pipeline and the Chain of Estimators

The ML.NET training infrastructure is centered on three pillars: data views, transformers, and estimators. A dedicated interface describes the core capabilities of each component: `IDataView`, `ITransformer`, and `IEstimator`.

Data Views

A data view component guarantees access to data, both input and output, transformers, and estimators. A data view component provides rather advanced features as far as data streaming and memory management are concerned.

Devised as a lazy object, a data view should not be seen as an in-memory container of data but rather as a tool to view (and, at some point, access) data. In plain database terms, it is much closer to a view than to a table. Data views work side by side with data loaders that are ultimately responsible for defining access paths to physical stores of data (for example, text files, relational tables, and JSON endpoints).

It is remarkable to note that data view objects are immutable. As mentioned, a data view doesn't contain values but limits at transforming values as read from the source. Immutability of data views is a key factor in ML.NET because it enables concurrency and guarantees thread safety—no shared data. In addition, data views as virtual views over physical data minimizes I/O operations and memory consumption. Read and write operations still occur, but they're only on demand and consequently with a highly reduced frequency.

Transformers

A transformer is a (chainable) object that transforms source input data into new data that has a different output schema or modified content. The role of transformers is crucial for feature engineering and data preparation and their ultimate purpose is turning a source dataset into a transformed dataset that is appropriate for training. In particular, the ITransformer interface features (but is not limited to) the following native members:

```
DataViewSchema GetOutputSchema(DataViewSchema inputSchema);
IDataView Transform(IDataView data);
```

The GetOutputSchema method returns the schema of the data once the transformations have been completed. The input parameter refers to the initial schema of data. For example, if the transformation consists of adding one column, the input schema will list, say, three columns, and the output schema will have four.

The Transform method takes the data in, applies transformations, and outputs a modified data view to access the data. It should be noted that the method doesn't actually perform changes on the data. All it does is return a virtual view of the data that must be finalized to provide access to real data. The pattern here is nearly the same as what you have in LINQ with IQueryable objects and finalizer methods such as ToList and First. Therefore, the method doesn't physically edit data; instead, it checks to see that requested transformations are compatible with input and output schemas.

In addition, a transformer object features a couple of interesting extension methods:

```
DataDebuggerPreview Preview(IDataView data, int maxRows);
TransformerChain<ITransformer> Append<ITransformer>(ITransformer additionalTransformer);
```

Devised only for debugging scenarios, the Preview method provides a preview of the transformations being made on the given data view. The effect on performance is attenuated by the maxRows parameter, which limits the view to the specified number of data rows.

The Append method creates and returns a new chain of transformers, just appending a new one to the current transformer (or chain thereof).

Estimators

The estimator is also a chainable object, as shown here:

```
interface IEstimator<out TTransformer> where TTransformer : ITransformer
```

The generic type TTransformer, which is prefixed by the out keyword in the preceding definition, is covariant, meaning that you can use either ITransformer (as required by the *where* clause) or any other type that is more derived.

The term *estimator* comes from statistics, in which it refers to the rule for calculating an estimate looking at some available data. A more machine learning–oriented definition for estimators came from Apache Spark—a very popular analytics engine. An estimator is an algorithm that can be fit on a dataset and produces a transformer. In turn, a transformer is an algorithm that transforms a dataset into another dataset. These same definitions are used by ML.NET.

In ML.NET, an estimator features the following two methods:

```
TTransformer Fit(IDataView);
SchemaShape GetOutputSchema(SchemaShape inputSchema);
```

The GetOutputSchema method works in much the same way as the method of the same name on transformers. The only difference is in the type that defines the schema. Estimators use the SchemaShape type instead of DataViewSchema. SchemaShape is only a promise of the output schema—merely a collection of columns without a strictly defined type. Both types refer to a data schema, but SchemaShape supplies a more relaxed definition.

The beating heart of an estimator is the method Fit, which is where the estimator learns from provided data and builds a chain of transformers that ultimately form the model. The interesting thing is that the final trained model is still a transformer and, as such, it can turn other data (for example, test data) into predictions. This is typically done at the end of the training phase to evaluate the quality and accuracy of the results against known metrics that work for the specific training applied.

Pipelines

A composition of transformers and estimators forms a pipeline. The pipeline, or a chain of estimators, begins with a single transformer or estimator, and others are appended using the method *Append*.

The pipeline is an immutable object. This means that whenever you append a new estimator, it doesn't append it to the current pipeline instance. Instead, it creates and returns a new pipeline object. As a developer, you always need to catch and store this object in a specific variable for further use.

The Regression ML Task

In a shallow learning scenario (as opposed to a deep learning scenario where neural networks reign), prediction tasks, such as predicting the price of goods or services, are tackled through regression algorithms.

Note that regression is not a single, well-defined algorithm; instead, it is the moniker to a class of different algorithms. ML.NET provides a native implementation for a number of them, which are grouped under the concept of a machine learning task (ML task).

General Aspects of ML Tasks

Behind the implementation of an ML task lies the idea of grouping common machine learning use cases under a common (and familiar) programming pattern.

Whether you're a data scientist, data engineer, or ML software developer, if you're going to build a trained model for a business problem using the native shallow learning algorithms of ML.NET, you first have to choose which of the available tasks works for your scenario. Second, you cherry-pick the best available algorithm to train the model. Note that the notion of what is "best" is a moving target and can hardly be determined by reasoning on paper without evidence of numbers and errors both in training and production.

We already presented the following table in Chapter 2, but it is useful to take a second look at it. Table 4-1 lists the supported ML tasks you can find in ML.NET. In light of this, your first step is mapping the business problem (that is, predicting the cost of some goods or services) to one of the following tasks.

TABLE 4-1 ML.NET Tasks

Task	Description
AnomalyDetection	Aims to detect unexpected or unusual events or behaviors compared to the received training.
BinaryClassification	Aims to classify data in one of two categories.
Clustering	Aims to split data in a number of possibly correlated groups without knowing which aspects could possibly make data items related.
Forecasting	Addresses forecasting problems in which the input being passed to the model is a time-series (sequence of values).
MulticlassClassification	Aims to classify data in three or more categories.
Ranking	Addresses ranking problems in which the ultimate goal is computing the relevance of data. To some extent, it can be approximated with multiclass classification.
Regression	Aims to predict the value of a data item. To some extent, it can be seen as a superclass of forecasting problems.

For the purposes of this chapter, we are entering the realm of the Regression task.

Supported Regression Algorithms

The Regression task is a catalog with three main endpoints: a list of training algorithms (property *Trainers*), an evaluator to score results of training against the configured error function (method Evaluate), and a cross-validator tool (method CrossValidate).

Available Trainers

The regression task provides a few algorithms in the core implementation of the ML.NET library and a lot more via additional NuGet packages. Overall, you can train a regression model using at least the algorithms shown in Table 4-2.

TABLE 4-2 Regression Algorithms in ML.NET

Algorithm	Method	Additional Package
FastForestRegressionTrainer	Based on the random forest method	Microsoft.ML.FastTree
FastTreeRegressionTrainer	Based on MART gradient boosting (an ensemble method)	Microsoft.ML.FastTree
FastTreeTweedieTrainer	Based on the Tweedie compound Poisson model	Microsoft.ML.FastTree
GamRegressionTrainer	Generalized Additive Model using shallow gradient-boosted trees	Microsoft.ML.FastTree
LbfgsPoissonRegressionTrainer	Based on the Poisson regression method	
LightGbmRegressionTrainer	Based on LightGBM, an open-source implementation of the gradient-boosting decision tree	Microsoft.ML.LightGbm
OlsTrainer	Based on the Ordinary Least Squares regression method	Microsoft.ML.Mkl.Components
OnlineGradientDescentTrainer	Based on the standard, non-batch, stochastic gradient descent	
SdcaRegressionTrainer	Based on the Stochastic Dual Coordinate Ascent method	

In a nutshell, a business problem that can be formulated as a regression problem can be solved through a number of different methods. From Table 4-2, we can list methods like gradient descent, Poisson regression, dual coordinate ascent and decision trees, random forests, and ensemble methods. To some extent, each method can be further considered as a base class of concrete algorithms that are often based on academic papers and advanced research. From an ML developer's perspective, all these methods call from the Regression ML task catalog. Admittedly, choosing the most appropriate method for the specific problem and available data is often a task well beyond a software person's reach. This is where data science skills kick in.

Configuration of a Trainer

If you decided on the Online Gradient Descent, here's the code you would need to have in your ML.NET training application:

```
var trainer = mlContext
    .Regression
    .Trainers
    .OnlineGradientDescent("Label", "Features", lossFunction: new SquaredLoss());
```

In ML.NET, training algorithms take two types of parameters:

- Options to control the internal behavior

- More foundational parameters, such as the label column name, the feature column name, and the error function to use to determine when a sufficiently good result has been obtained, and training can be stopped

Optional values are specified to pass the trainer object an ad hoc container class such as `OnlineGradientDescentOptions`. Specifically, the online gradient descent training algorithm would accept additional tuning parameters such as the following:

- Whether to accord more relevance to more recent updates.

- The number of passes through the training dataset.

- Whether to shuffle data for each training iteration (the learning rate). Namely, this is the step size to apply at each iteration while moving toward the minimum of the error function.

The label column refers to the column's name in the training dataset that contains the known answer the algorithm has to approximate. In ML.NET, it is common to duplicate the actual dataset column with answers to a new column named `Label` or any other arbitrarily chosen name. For each row in the training dataset, the error function (`SquaredLoss` in the preceding code snippet) takes the calculated value and compares it to the value found in the `Label` column of the row. The errors on each data row are then combined according to the characteristics of the selected error function (for example, the mean value, the max, the min, and the sum).

Finally, the feature column name refers to a specific trait of the ML.NET library. All the algorithms designed for ML.NET expect to find all values to process (commonly referred to as *features*) available as a numeric vector. This requires an extra column where all feature values are concatenated. The name of this additional column defaults to `Features`. This column is not done manually but is a service requested by ML.NET.

Preparing the Training Dataset

Some preliminary work is required on the dataset to ensure that the algorithm can find a label and feature column. In ML.NET, this is done by configuring a data processing pipeline. The following code shows how to duplicate and rename an existing column and how to generate a new computed column that combines the value of multiple individual columns in the dataset:

```
var pipeline = mlContext.Transforms
    .CopyColumns("Label", nameof(TaxiTripDescriptor.FareAmount))
    .Append(mlContext.Transforms.Concatenate("Features",
                "RateCodeEncoded",
                "PaymentTypeEncoded",
                "PassengerCount",
                "TripTime",
                "TripDistance");
```

The `Transforms` object on the ML context provides ad hoc methods to copy and concatenate columns. In the code snippet, strings like `RateCodeEncoded` and `TripDistance` refer to columns in the dataset available for training.

Note that, in general terms, there would be no need to concatenate multiple columns into one for machine learning processing purposes. This is a design choice of the ML.NET internal training engine.

Supported Validation Techniques

The quality of a machine learning model depends on how good it can be at predicting (or classifying) data it has never seen before. The challenge here is that you can train the model on one sample dataset and sometimes not even a particularly large, well-balanced, and highly representative one.

A number of techniques have been developed to make better and more proficient use of the training dataset and, subsequently, to capture a good grasp of the precision the model can develop once it's in production.

Cross-validation is the primary technique used to estimate the performance of a machine learning trained model.

Holdout Cross-Validation

Cross-validation comes in two flavors: *holdout* and *k-fold*. The *holdout* technique is fairly trivial to arrange. It basically consists of splitting the source dataset in two segments: approximately two-thirds of it is used for training, and the remaining part (approximately one-third) is for test purposes.

When not used in combination with other techniques, the holdout presents two key drawbacks. One is that only a subset of the available data is used to train and test the model and, worse yet, that dataset that might not even be sufficiently large. A better approach consists of applying the holdout technique multiple times.

This is the essence of the k-fold cross-validation technique.

K-Fold Cross-Validation

In the k-fold technique, the training dataset is partitioned into k subsets, and on each partition, the holdout validation is applied. In the end, k-fold consists of repeating holdout cross-validation k times—each time using one of the k subsets as the test dataset and the remaining k-1 subsets as the training data.

The k-fold technique has a number of benefits. In the first place, it is not subject to the risk of underfitting as long as the algorithm is a good fit for the problem. In general, fitting (or *goodness of fit*) refers to the skills actually learned by the algorithm and indicates how good it is at doing its job. Underfitting, therefore, describes a condition in which the algorithm is not particularly good at predicting.

With the k-fold technique, the risk of underfitting is low because the model is ultimately trained on all the available data. By the same token, the variance of the model is minimized because the entire dataset is used to test the model.

In machine learning, the variance refers to the deviation of the model from the mean. Because the model is trained and tested on the whole dataset, the variance can only be as low as the adherence of the selected algorithm to the problem allows.

Furthermore, the k-fold technique is a win even when the dataset is packed with a relevant percentage of outliers—data rows with values patently different from the mean of others. For the nature of this technique, outliers are evenly split across all folds and evenly distribute the noise over the training and testing data.

There are no strict rules for setting the value of k, but 5 and 10 are commonly used values. Figure 4-2 offers a visual representation of the k-fold technique where *k* equals 5.

Iteration 1	Fold 1 **TEST**	Fold 2	Fold 3	Fold 4	Fold 5
Iteration 2	Fold 1	Fold 2 **TEST**	Fold 3	Fold 4	Fold 5
Iteration 3	Fold 1	Fold 2	Fold 3 **TEST**	Fold 4	Fold 5
Iteration 4	Fold 1	Fold 2	Fold 3	Fold 4 **TEST**	Fold 5
Iteration 5	Fold 1	Fold 2	Fold 3	Fold 4	Fold 5 **TEST**

Training data	Testing data

FIGURE 4-2 K-fold cross-validation explained

Regularization

Quite obviously, the trained model should not be underfitting the sample dataset. At the same time, though, we don't want it to be overfitting the sample model. Overfitting, in particular, refers to the situation in which the model is too close (overfits) to the training data. Consequently, it is not necessarily able to process data accurately that it has never seen before.

Regularization is another excellent technique to detect overfitting—when the trained model gives excellent performance on the sample data leaving the (concrete) doubt that it won't be as precise on other similar-looking data.

Regularization intervenes in the training phase when results are not convincing, and the team is tempted to add more features to the model in the hope of achieving better results. In this case, the risk of a model too close to the source dataset is concrete.

Regularization works by simply placing a penalty on each new feature (column) added to the dataset. Of course, adding a penalty increases the error, so it's a matter of adding just the features that bring an inherent value and reduce the error.

Regularization is a guard against making the model uselessly complex.

Permutation Feature Importance

Another aspect to consider when it comes to evaluating the skills of a trained model is which features have the biggest effect on the final results, whether a prediction or a classification. This concept is referred to as *feature importance*.

Technically, the permutation feature importance is defined as the decrease of the score of a model when a single feature value is randomly shuffled. The concept is fairly intuitive: if you scramble the values of a column and still get a similar score, then it means that the acted feature is not particularly important in the internal economy of the model. From this standpoint, a low-importance feature can be removed without worries. Should you do it, however?

Note that importance here refers to the role played by that feature in that model. As you switch to another algorithm, all numbers of importance are canceled and lose all of their relevance. In other words, permutation importance does not reflect the intrinsic predictive value of a feature. Instead, it only reflects the importance of that feature for a particular model.

Using the Regression Task

Quite naïvely, many tend to associate artificial intelligence with the possibility of magical predictions about future events. Unfortunately, artificial intelligence is not magic, although it can still make reliable predictions. However, the ability to predict doesn't come from superpowers. More simply, it is the result of a few statistical techniques, the most relevant of which is regression analysis.

At its core, regression measures the strength of the numerical relationship set between one output variable and a series of input variables. A regression algorithm attempts to discover such a relationship by processing sample data and the expected results. The net effect of a regression algorithm is computing one (or more) output values based on some input data. Regression is a supervised machine learning technique (meaning it needs to be provided with exact answers during training) and can predict a continuous value (as opposed to discrete categorical values typical of classification algorithms).

Let's see how to use the regression ML task to tackle a specific prediction problem. The problem we'll consider here is the same we touched on in Chapter 3, "The Foundation of ML.NET": predicting how much a taxi ride in a given city could cost. In the coming pages, we explore the training pipeline in much more detail.

A Look at the Available Training Data

To try to predict the cost of a taxi ride, you need to look at a relevant number of past rides in the area of interest. A taxi ride can be realistically described at least by the following features:

- Amount paid

- Distance

- Pick-up and drop-off addresses

- Company

- Time of day

- Day of the week

- Overall traffic conditions

- Payment type

- Passenger count

- Number of bags

A reasonable dataset would then be made by a list of records, including the aforementioned columns. How many records? The more, the better, we would say. An acceptable order of magnitude is a few million records. However, be aware that more data doesn't always mean you are in a better situation.

Data You Have and Data You Would Like to Have

The preceding list of features has been determined via pure reasoning and business analysis and is nothing more than a wish list. The actual list of features for arranging some regression comes from the company's back-end system that tracks (or aggregates) rides, cars, and payments.

We have seven features in the sample dataset we borrowed from the ML.NET website (and also shared through the source code that comes with this book). The sample dataset is available as a CSV text file, and a glimpse of it is shown in Figure 4-3.

```
taxi-fare-train.csv    ⊕ ✕
    vendor_id,rate_code,passenger_count,trip_time_in_secs,trip_distance,payment_type,fare_amount
    CMT,1,1,1271,3.8,CRD,17.5
    CMT,1,1,474,1.5,CRD,8
    CMT,1,1,637,1.4,CRD,8.5
    CMT,1,1,181,0.6,CSH,4.5
    CMT,1,1,661,1.1,CRD,8.5
    CMT,1,1,935,9.6,CSH,27.5
    CMT,1,1,869,2.3,CRD,11.5
    CMT,1,1,454,1.4,CRD,7.5
    CMT,1,1,366,1.5,CSH,7.5
    CMT,1,1,252,0.6,CSH,5
    CMT,1,1,314,1.2,CRD,6
    CMT,1,1,480,0.7,CRD,7
    CMT,1,1,386,1.3,CRD,7
    CMT,1,2,351,0.8,CSH,5.5
    CMT,1,1,407,1.1,CSH,7
    CMT,1,2,970,5.6,CSH,19
    CMT,1,3,371,0.6,CRD,6
```

FIGURE 4-3 The CSV file with training data opened in Visual Studio 2019

While such a dataset can be used to make some predictions, not much can be said about the precision and accuracy. Comparing the columns in Figure 4-3 and the bullet list discussed earlier, we find some relevant pieces of information missing: pick-up and drop-off addresses, time and day of the ride, traffic conditions, and the number of bags. This makes a case for some data engineering work on the original data that natively comes from the back-end systems.

Augmenting the Dataset

Information such as the number of bags and the time of the ride might reasonably be available somewhere in the back-end system. Getting a larger dataset is then an option. If not, the time of the ride might be figured out from the log of payments, assuming that the payment took place at about the time the ride ended. Knowing the duration of the trip and the time when the ride started can be easily obtained.

If not natively tracked by the system, pick-up and drop-off information is hard to obtain. However, traffic conditions can be read from some free or paid services and incorporated into the training dataset.

Data scientists and/or data engineers are responsible for an Extract/Transform/Load (ETL) pipeline that consists of the following:

- Exporting data from the original back-end system

- Adding computed columns

- Integrating with external data (that is, traffic conditions)

Loading the Dataset in ML.NET

The first step in the training application is loading training and testing datasets into a new ML context. In its simplest yet effective form, a training ML.NET application is a console program. The first instructions look like the following:

```
// Main container for ML operations
var mlContext = new MLContext();

// Load data to be used for training
IDataView dataForTraining = mlContext.Data
    .LoadFromTextFile<TaxiTripDescriptor>(_trainDataPath, hasHeader: true, separatorChar: ',');

// Load data to be used for testing the model
IDataView dataForTesting = mlContext.Data
    .LoadFromTextFile<TaxiTripDescriptor>(_testDataPath, hasHeader: true, separatorChar: ',');
```

The TaxiTripDescriptor class describes in C# the structure of the training record: the columns in the CSV file:

```
public class TaxiTripDescriptor
{
    public string VendorId;
    public string RateCode;
    public float PassengerCount;
    public float TripTime;
    public float TripDistance;
    public string PaymentType;
    public float FareAmount;
}
```

To simplify the binding between C# properties and the columns in the source CSV file, you can use the aptly provided LoadColumn attribute. Any property decorated with the attribute will receive as a value the content of the CSV column at the specified ordinal position.

```
[LoadColumn(4)]
public float TripDistance;
```

Loading data from a single static file describes a basic, common scenario. More likely, you have multiple files to deal with or an entire folder dynamically populated by some background task and integrated into some MLOps context.

ML.NET provides a bunch of ad hoc data loaders to deal with multiple files, folders, and databases.

Supported Data Sources

In general, ML.NET is designed to allow data access from a variety of data sources, such as multiple text files, databases, JSON, XML, and even in-memory collections. Regardless of the data source, data in ML.NET is always presented through an IDataView object—an ad hoc frontend specifically designed to deal with potentially large sets of tabular data.

Each dataset is associated with a schema. As long as the schema is the same, in ML.NET, you can load rows of data from multiple files in the same folder or even scattered through multiple folders. The following line shows how to load all text files from the Dataset folder:

```
IDataView data = mlContext.Data
    .LoadFromTextFile<TaxiTripDescriptor>("dataset/*", hasHeader: true, separatorChar: ',');
```

It takes a bit more code to enable the loading of text files from multiple disk folders. In this case, you first create a text loader component and then have it load content from a variety of places:

```
TextLoader = mlContext.Data
    .CreateTextLoader<TaxiTripDescriptor>(hasHeader: true, separatorChar: ',');
IDataView data = textLoader
    .Load("dataset/week01/data.csv", "dataset/week02/data.csv", "dataset/week03/data.csv");
```

Similarly, you can access data stored in a number of relational databases. ML.NET supports all databases from which the .NET System.Data namespace provides a driver. The list grows over time and, at a minimum, includes SQL Server, Azure SQL Database, Oracle, SQLite, PostgreSQL, Progress, and IBM DB2.

From a programming standpoint, you first create a database loader object, as shown here:

```
DatabaseLoader loader = mlContext.Data.CreateDatabaseLoader<TaxiTripDescriptor>();
```

Next, you set up a database source and load data:

```
var source = new DatabaseSource(SqlClientFactory.Instance, connectionString, sqlCommand);
IDataView data = loader.Load(source);
```

In addition to the connection string and the command to query data, you pass a reference to the factory to be used to create the necessary DbConnection object. For a SQL Server database, it is the SqlClientFactory object.

As far as loading data from other common sources such as JSON and XML files is concerned, you have to go through in-memory collections:

```
var list = LoadJsonOrXml(...);
IDataView data = mlContext.Data.LoadFromEnumerable<TaxiTripDescriptor>(list);
```

The idea is that you write a loader for JSON or XML files or endpoints and turn the content into a list of instances of the specified type.

Feature Engineering

Machine learning algorithms can work only on numbers, whereas training data often contains some text fields. For example, in the sample dataset, a couple of columns are made of text: the vendor ID and payment type. Those values must be turned into numbers.

Suppose a reference to a street address is added to enrich the dataset. In that case, the reference has to be converted into numbers, whether a numerical code that identifies the ZIP Code or latitude and longitude. If you find a way to collect traffic information, you should also think of how to render it as a normalized value, typically in the 0 to 1 interval.

In general, the values in all text columns must be turned into numbers before proceeding with training. However, any applied transformation mustn't alter the distribution and relevance of individual values.

The whole set of transformations performed on the selected dataset goes under the name of feature engineering.

Preliminary Physical Operations

Before you get into data transformation, sometimes you might want to do some preliminary work on the dataset. The most common operation is identifying and removing (or normalizing) outliers.

Envisioning a data row with N features as a point in an N-dimensional space, an outlier is a point located too far away from the rest of the points. Put another way: An outlier data row refers to a tracked record that deviates significantly from the other rows.

Any quantitative measures involved in the preceding definition are to be agreed on: What is intended by "the other rows"? What is the distance? What is the maximum tolerable distance? Removing (or normalizing) outliers is a common technique to reduce variance in the final model. (See Figure 4-4.)

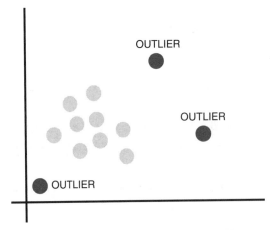

FIGURE 4-4 Graphical representation of outlier data rows

In ML.NET, removing outliers should not be considered the same as a data transformation step because removing outliers is a direct change to the loaded dataset. In contrast, the application of a data transformation step occurs on the whole set of rows you actually intend to process. Here's some code that removes all transactions higher than $150 and lower than $1 from the taxi ride dataset:

```
// Removing outliers for fares higher than $150 and lower than $1
private static IDataView RemoveOutliers(MLContext context, IDataView data)
{
    var modifiedDataView = context.Data.FilterRowsByColumn(data, "FareAmount", 1, 150);
    return modifiedDataView;
}
```

Conceptually, removal (or, in general, addition) of rows is an optional operation that precedes the execution of any transformation pipeline.

Building the Transformation Pipeline

In ML.NET, the output of feature engineering is the data transformation pipeline. The pipeline is the description of the sequence of actions that will happen when the pipeline is actually run—a promise of transformations on data to take place later.

If you are familiar with .NET and LINQ, then you should recognize here a conceptual similarity between an IQueryable tree and related executor methods such as ToList and First and the ML.NET pipeline. Building a pipeline is like building an IQueryable tree.

Which operations concur to feature engineering?

Normalization and Featurization

There are quite a few different types of operations, the majority of which are usable across the entire set of ML tasks. Feature engineering methods are exposed out of the Transforms catalog object in the ML context:

- **Adding and removing columns** The CopyColumns method of Transforms duplicates an existing column to a new column with a given name. The DropColumns method, instead, removes the listed columns from the dataset.

- **Normalization** Refers to adding a column of normalized numeric column values. Normalization uses various techniques to fit all values in the column to a common interval, typically the 0 to 1 interval. The original distribution of values is maintained. The goal of normalization is improving the accuracy of the training algorithm of choice. MinMax normalization operates by finding minimum and maximum values in each column and setting the minimum to 0 and the maximum to 1; all other values are scaled in between. Another type of normalization is MeanVariance, which first subtracts the mean of the column values and then divides by the variance. Yet another variation is LogMeanVariance, which operates on the logarithm of the column values.

- **Binning** Refers to partitioning actual values of a column of data into a number of reference values (bins). It works by normalizing all values in a given range to a fixed, common value. The canonical example is age, such as 0 to 18 turns to 1; 19 to 25 turns to 2, and the like.

- **Missing values** Any input dataset may have a missing value here and there. This feature engineering step aims at filling the gaps in some algorithmic way. In ML.NET, the native missing values estimator works only with numerical columns and offers to replace missing values either with the default value of the type (0 for numbers) or with the mean of values in the column. Other options are possible but require ad hoc estimators or some preliminary batch procedure run on the dataset.

The normalizers mentioned so far act on numeric data. However, categorical data are also fairly common in datasets. In machine learning, categorical data refers to an enumeration of fixed values, much like enum types in C# and other high-level programming languages. When it comes to columns made of categorical values, other normalization techniques apply:

- **Key-value mapping** Used to map string values in a column to a unique integer value for training purposes, such as CRD to 1 and CASH to 2.

- **One hot encoding** This technique maps each distinct value of the column of possible values to a number whose binary representation has just a single 1 value in a unique position. It is the same as when in C# you define an enum type with values that are powers of 2. For example, 1, 2, and 4 in binary format are 001, 010, and 100. One hot encoding is typically the ideal choice if there is no implicit ordering of values.

- **Hashing** The hashing technique condenses a categorical value (including strings) to a number of a fixed size. ML.NET has a normalizer that can deal with strings, numbers, and dates.

A whole different space is reserved for text transforms. We delve deeper into this family of normalizers in later chapters when we cover sentiment analysis—a specific branch of classification problems founded on text.

Accessing the Content of Datasets

In ML.NET, actual data access is performed through the services of classes that implement the IDataView interface, designed from the ground up with the declared goal of handling as efficiently as possible large datasets both in width and depth. All ML.NET training algorithms consume data through the methods of the interface. IDataView objects can contain numbers, text, Booleans, vectors, and more.

> **IMPORTANT** The IDataView interface is designed with cursoring and laziness in mind but does not directly address more sophisticated aspects, such as dealing with distributed data and distributed computation. At the same time, it is suitable for single-node processing of data partitions belonging to larger, distributed datasets. Put another way, if the dataset is already partitioned and distributed, then each agglomeration of data can be treated via IDataView, but the interface doesn't automatically split and distribute your data in autonomy.

Working with Data Views

The `IDataView` subsystem comprehends different flavors of software components to compose data processing pipelines. The most relevant are the aforementioned loaders and transformers (for example, normalizer and featurizer components).

Even though the `IDataView` subsystem is crucial for the internal working of the ML.NET machinery, as a developer, your contact with it is very limited. First, you define necessary data loaders and get a data view reference:

```
var dataViewTraining = mlContext.Data.LoadFromTextFile<TaxiTripDescriptor>(_trainDataPath);
```

Second, you optionally pass the data view reference to any method that might physically remove or add rows. You obtain back a modified data view. Note that the data view reference doesn't carry actual data around. Compared to a classic database table, a data view is a virtual data container much like a database view. Whereas tables physically contain the values in the rows, a (data) view computes values on demand and doesn't own any.

The net effect of the next line is modifying the logical tree of actions behind the view so that when asked to materialize data, the data view filters out any data rows that looks like an outlier:

```
// Modify the view adding the command that will filter out outliers when actually reading data
dataViewTraining = RemoveOutliers(mlContext, dataViewTraining);
```

Third, you further modify the data view processing pipeline by adding data transformations. Here's a good example for a taxi ride prediction scenario:

```
var pipeline = mlContext.Transforms.CopyColumns("Label", "TripTime")
        .Append(context.Transforms.Categorical.OneHotEncoding("IdEncoded", "VendorId"))
        .Append(context.Transforms.Categorical.OneHotEncoding("RateEncoded", "RateCode"))
        .Append(context.Transforms.Categorical.OneHotEncoding("PaymentEncoded", "PaymentType"))
        .Append(context.Transforms.NormalizeMeanVariance("PassengerCount"))
        .Append(context.Transforms.NormalizeMeanVariance("TripDistance"))
        .Append(context.Transforms.Concatenate("Features",
                    "IdEncoded",
                    "RateEncoded",
                    "PaymentEncoded",
                    "PassengerCount",
                    "TripDistance"));
```

At the end of transformations, the data available to the training algorithm consists of the original columns plus a few new columns: one named `Label` and one named `Features`. Also, a new column (with the name suffixed by `Encoded`) has been added for each of the listed normalizers. The `Features` column contains a numeric vector composed from the values of the listed columns.

The pipeline object now fully defines the set of operations that the original data will undergo to serve data to the training algorithm we'll select in a moment.

Dealing with Very Large Datasets

One of the major issues you might encounter while doing shallow machine learning is that Python might run short of memory when the dataset to process is particularly large—in the order of gigabytes.

The ML.NET team was aware of this pure memory shortage, so it designed the data view subsystem to efficiently handle high-dimensional data and large datasets containing many columns and many rows.

A data view can be used in two different ways. You can load and enumerate data as a classic in-memory collection object would do, but you can also stream data from the original data source via a cursoring mechanism conceptually similar to database cursors and ADO.NET data readers. Streaming data is what most algorithms do during training.

This native feature allows ML.NET training applications to easily handle huge datasets that go well beyond the gigabyte order of magnitude and get into terabytes.

Composing the Training Pipeline

The data processing pipeline is the logical container that brings data to the training algorithm. Yet picking the algorithm is the most delicate choice. If you lack direct machine learning experience and theoretical knowledge of statistical learning, picking a training algorithm for a business problem is like taking a shot in the dark, even when you have correctly identified the problem's class.

Identifying the Training Algorithm

The ML task components in ML.NET do a good preliminary job of selecting a few algorithms that might be appropriate for regression, binary classification, ranking, or image detection problems. It's not a definitive analysis, though. You might decide to try a neural network or a Support Vector Machine (SVM) algorithm—the most sophisticated class of shallow learning algorithms. ML.NET comes with an integrated Visual Studio tool—Model Builder—that helps choose from the available algorithm options in the ML.NET framework. (See Figure 4-5.)

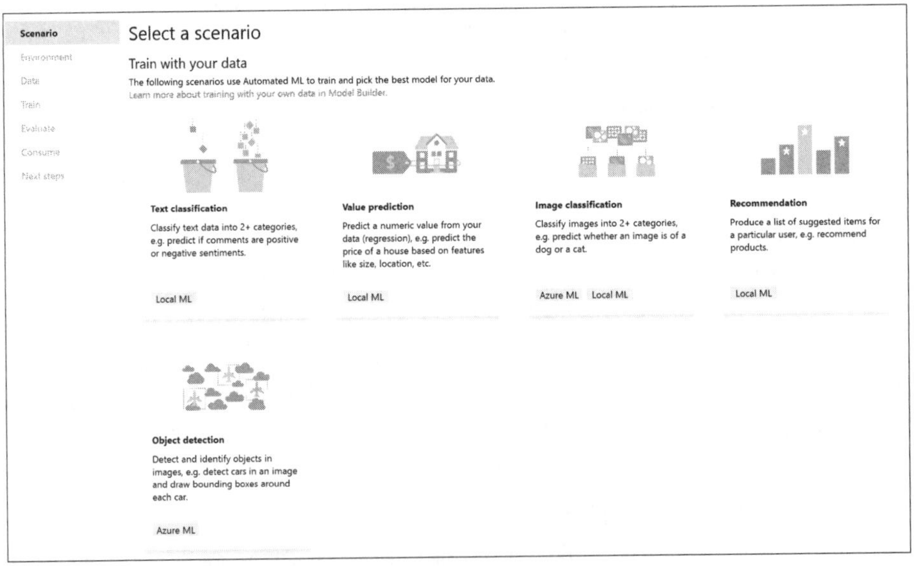

FIGURE 4-5 The home page of the Visual Studio Model Builder

Model Builder is a valuable attempt to guide developers with limited data science skills to select a valid algorithm to try for a given scenario, whether value prediction, text or image classification, or recommendation.

In a nutshell, picking the algorithm is a decision in between implementation and architecture. It can even be seen as an implementation detail once the class of the problem has been correctly identified. At the same time, the selection of the algorithm is comparable to an architectural, hard-to-change decision because if scores prove poor in production, a relevant subsystem of the deployed solution must be amended.

Fitting the Model

Let's suppose we have identified, in some way, the training algorithm to start with and assume we want to use the SDCA trainer for the taxi ride cost prediction problem. Here's how we code it:

```
// Get the trainer reference
var trainer = mlContext
                .Regression
                .Trainers
                .Sdca("Label", "Features", lossFunction: new SquaredLoss());

// Attach the trainer to the data processing pipeline and get a modified pipeline
var trainingPipeline = pipeline.Append(trainer);

// Train the model fitting to the training dataset
var model = trainingPipeline.Fit(trainingDataView);
```

First, we obtain a reference to a configured instance of the algorithm. This is the `trainer` variable. The trainer is then appended to the data processing pipeline and produces a modified pipeline that knows how to prepare data and run the algorithm on it. Finally, the `Fit` method gets the data view pointing to the sample dataset and runs it through the trainer. The output of the `Fit` method is the trained model, which has to be serialized to be made available to client applications.

The Loss Function of the Model

Let's return to the configuration of the trainer. As shown earlier, the `Sdca` method receives the scoring column (`Label`) and the input column (`Features`). The scoring column is the name of the column that contains the expected output to compare with the computed values. In other words, the `Label` column contains the actual fares paid given the input values, namely passenger count, taxi company, rate, and the like.

The score of the model—how good it is at predicting values—is measured through an error function. This is the loss function—the third parameter passed to the `Sdca` method. The error function measures the distance between the actual value computed by the algorithm on the provided features and the expected value as set in the `Label` column.

Each algorithm (and more generally, each class of machine learning problems) has its own preferred set of loss functions. Choosing the most appropriate is, again, a matter of data science skills. In particular, the SquaredLoss function passed to Sdca measures the distance between computed and expected values using the square of the numerical difference.

The error (or loss) function acts as a controller and determines when the algorithm has reached an acceptable accuracy in the processing of a given set of input features.

Validation of the Model

The code shown earlier for the prediction problem at hand uses a basic holdout approach in which training and testing datasets are provided as distinct entities. The same application that runs the code discussed so far that produces a trained model has the responsibility of running some automated tests on the model to score its inherent quality. In brief, we want to verify that a model trained on a sample dataset behaves well enough on different test data. Here's the code that runs the trained model on a test data view and evaluates the results:

```
IDataView predictions = trainedModel.Transform(testDataView);
```

The Transform method validates the schema of the provided data view to be used for testing the model. It ensures the compatibility between the model schema and the data schema. The method is lazy and performs no actual operation other than checking the schema of data. The returned data view must be passed to the Evaluate method of the ML regression task to get some task-specific metrics:

```
var metrics = mlContext.Regression
        .Evaluate(predictions, labelColumnName: "Label", scoreColumnName: "Score");
```

In addition to the test data, the Evaluate method also receives instructions about the column to use as the source of true values and the column to populate with scores.

The method returns a RegressionMetrics object. The object contains five metrics, as shown in Table 4-3.

TABLE 4-3 Regression Metrics Properties

Metrics	Property	Description
Loss function	LossFunction	Gets the result of user-defined loss function. In our example, this is an instance of the SquaredLoss class.
R2 score	Rsquared	Gets the R-squared value of the model. In statistics, the R-squared value is also known as the coefficient of determination and is the ratio between the values calculated by the model and the mean of the target values. In our scenario, this value is the actual fares paid. The value of this indicator is ideally close to 1. However, having it close to 1 is not sufficient to guarantee high quality, but having it close to 0 is a clear indicator that something doesn't work.
Absolute loss	MeanAbsoluteError	Gets the absolute loss of the model. The absolute loss is defined as the mean of the sum of absolute errors (difference between calculated and target values).
Squared loss	MeanSquaredError	Gets the squared loss of the model defined as the mean of the sum of the squares of the errors (difference between calculated and target values).
RMS loss	RootMeanSquaredError	Gets the root mean square loss, namely the square root of MeanSquaredError.

No metrics are universally valid by themselves, but all indicators provide insights to an expert eye. Some clear ranges of acceptability exist for all metrics, but it is not realistic to expect all numbers to be close to their ideal thresholds. For example, the RSquared value is expected to be close to 1, but determining whether any value near 1 is really good is often beyond the reach of an ML.NET developer.

(Not much different from having blood tests and trying to make sense of the overall health. While you can easily check whether all values are within an acceptable range, you might want to see a doctor to have an expert evaluation of your health.)

Cross-Validation of the Model

As mentioned earlier, the holdout approach to select, train, and test data might not always be realistic. In some cases, you just have a relatively small dataset to be used for training and testing. In this case, cross-validation is a valid technique. In ML.NET, using cross-validation to select training and testing data requires some slightly different lines of code.

Let's say we have reasons to try out a different algorithm—the online gradient descent. Here's the code that sets up the trainer reference:

```
var trainer = mlContext
        .Regression
        .Trainers
        .OnlineGradientDescent("Label", "Features", lossFunction: new SquaredLoss());
```

In the previous example, we considered a single pipeline for both data preparation and model training. We took the data processing pipeline, added the selected trainer, and then ran the *Fit* method to get a trained model. A single pipeline is just a possibility and probably the simplest to use for prediction scenarios.

However, for completeness, let's just show what it takes to use separate data processing and model training pipelines. One of the benefits of separate pipelines is that it's easier to inspect the learned model parameters. The following code deals with the data preparation:

```
// Obtain a transformer that fits on provided data (ie, normalized columns in the dataset)
ITransformer dataPrepTransformer = dataProcessPipeline.Fit(trainingDataView);

// Transforms data ready for training
IDataView transformedData = dataPrepTransformer.Transform(data);
```

The first step is preparing the transformer to operate on a given data schema; the second step relates to getting a modified data view ready to be processed by the training algorithm. This modified data view is the visible effect of separate preparation and training pipelines.

To split the data view into training and validation datasets and use all the data for both training and testing (the cross-validation approach to training), you don't use the Fit method but the CrossValidate method.

```
// The trainer here is the OnlineGradientDescent class referenced above
var results = mlContext
        .Regression
        .CrossValidate(transformedData, trainer, numberOfFolds: 5);
```

The provided data is split into five folds, and the folds are used interchangeably for training and testing. As a result, the entire set of data is used to train and test over five iterations. The method's return value is an object that contains five trained models and related regression metrics—one for each iteration.

The `results` variable is a collection, so it can be processed using LINQ for whatever purposes you may have. For example, to pick up the best model (and related metrics) according to the RSquared metrics, you proceed as follows:

```
var listOfModels = results
            .OrderByDescending(fold => fold.Metrics.RSquared)
            .Select(fold => fold.Model)
            .ToArray();
var listOfMetrics = results
            .OrderByDescending(fold => fold.Metrics.RSquared)
            .Select(fold => fold.Metrics)
            .ToArray();

// Get the best model and related metrics
ITransformer trainedModel = listOfModels[0];
RegressionMetrics metrics = listOfMetrics[0];
```

Needless to say, you can arrange any sort of automatic analysis of models and metrics or just print it out and let some data science experts come to their conclusion.

> **NOTE** A pipeline is always a chain of estimators, even when it is only made up of data transformers, as was the case of the `dataPrepTransformer` in the earlier code snippet. Because a pipeline is always a chain of estimators, you can fit it on the dataset to obtain trained transformers. When do you need it? For example, when you have transformers that are not simply value converters or column managers but need to look at the entire dataset, such as one-hot encoders or normalizers.

Packaging the Trained Model

That crazy little thing called the trained model is ultimately the expression of a computation graph. In simplest scenarios, such as linear regression, it can be as simple as a polynomial or a decision tree. In contrast, it can be a much more sophisticated mathematical model if neural networks are used. Training a model is about discovering the most appropriate coefficients to complete a computation graph whose composition depends on the specific algorithm used with a sufficiently high level of accuracy.

Once returned by the `Fit` or `CrossValidate` method, a model in ML.NET is an in-memory object. It needs to be saved to disk to be made available to client applications. Here's the code you use to save a model to disk:

```
mlContext.Model.Save(trainedModel, trainingDataView.Schema, modelPath);
```

The saved model is a ZIP file (see Figure 4-5) and contains serialized data in a proprietary way, the list of necessary transformers, and the data schema. The saved model will be deployed to reach a client application (that is, a web application). As long as the client application is a .NET application, the model can be loaded in process, which results in much faster predictions. Otherwise, it can be embedded in a .NET web service or gRPC shell and be consumable from clients regardless of their hosting platform.

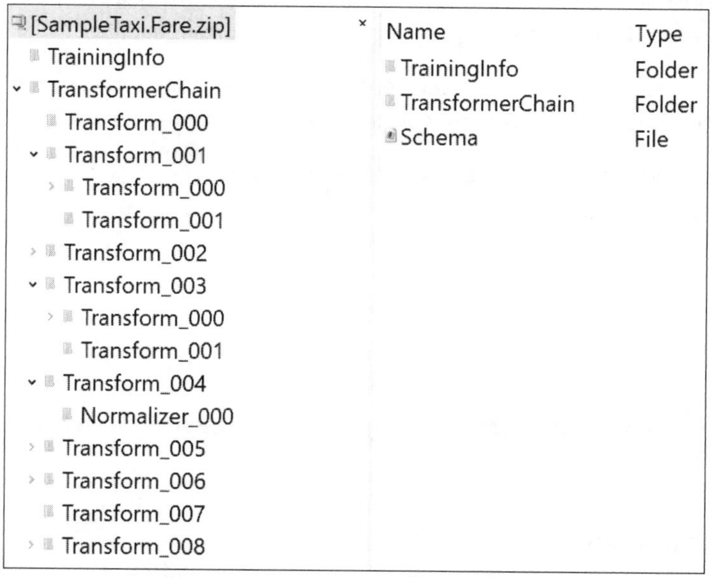

FIGURE 4-6 Internals of a saved ML.NET model produced by the Regression ML task

Setting Up a Client Application

There are two main scenarios for using an ML.NET trained model and, in both cases, you need to take the same programming steps. One scenario is when you host the model in a web service. The other is when you host the model in a native .NET executable. In both cases, the model host needs to take the following actions:

- Instantiating a prediction engine

- Invoking the prediction engine using input data and receiving output data, as dictated by the model's schema

The way you instantiate the prediction engine depends on whether the client is a desktop application or runs in a server environment, such as a web application or an Azure function.

In a nonserver environment, or whenever you don't have scalability concerns, you go with the following rather intuitive code:

```
ITransformer trainedModel = mlContext.Model.Load(modelPath, out var modelInputSchema);

// Create prediction engine related to the loaded trained model
var predEngine = mlContext
        .Model
        .CreatePredictionEngine<TaxiTripDescriptor, FarePrediction>(trainedModel);
```

```
// Predict
var prediction = predEngine.Predict(trip);
```

First, you load the model (previously saved as a ZIP file) and pass it to the CreatePrediction-Engine method in the Model catalog of the ML.NET context object. Once you've got a prediction engine, you simply call the method Predict to have a prediction out of some input data.

What you pass and what you receive from Predict depends on the schema supported by the model and the classes defined in the training phase to represent feature and score columns.

In our example, the TaxiTripDescriptor is the class that describes the training data. The FarePrediction data is as shown here:

```
public class FarePrediction
{
    [ColumnName("Score")]
    public float FareAmount;
}
```

Both TaxiTripDescriptor and FarePrediction may go in the same assembly shared by the training application and the client.

A Better Way to Invoke a Model

In a server, multithreaded environment such as an ASP.NET application, a web API, or Azure functions, for performance and scalability reasons, you need to minimize the impact of creating a new instance of the prediction engine for every HTTP request. Real-life models can be significantly large, and loading one on each request could negatively impact the total time the request takes to complete.

The trained model object in the example (the trainedModel variable) should be made a single-ton and shared across the whole application. Its type, in fact, is ITransformer, which is thread-safe and can be safely declared as a singleton or a global variable. If you make it a singleton, however, you can easily plug it into the dependency injection framework of ASP.NET Core. In a desktop application, instead, you can just treat it as a global reference.

An even bigger issue is the creation of the prediction engine. The method CreatePrediction Engine is relatively time-consuming, and calling it on every request might affect the overall perfor-mance. Worse yet, the returned type, the PredictionEngine type, is not thread-safe, so the singleton shortcut is not an option here. Again, this is probably not a big deal for a desktop application, but it's a relevant drawback for a web application. For multithreaded applications, like web applications, a more advanced approach is recommended, such as using object pooling.

The good news, though, is that the ML.NET team has created an ASP.NET Core integration pack-age that provides a prediction engine pool out of the box that is well-integrated with the dependency injection layer in ASP.NET Core. As a result, here's the recommended way to call the prediction engine from within an ASP.NET Core application.

In Startup.cs, you add a pool of prediction engines for each scenario: in this case, one engine for predicting the time (length) of ride and one for predicting the cost of the ride.

```
public void ConfigureServices(IServiceCollection services)
{
    // Other startup code here
    // ...

    services.AddPredictionEnginePool<TaxiTrip, TaxiTripTimePrediction>()
            .FromFile(modelName: "TimeModel",
                      filePath:"ml/TaxiFair.Model.Time.zip",
                      watchForChanges: true);
    services.AddPredictionEnginePool<TaxiTrip, TaxiTripFarePrediction>()
            .FromFile(modelName: "FareModel",
                      filePath:"ml/TaxiFair.Model.Fare.zip",
                      watchForChanges: true);
}
```

The controller takes the following form:

```
public class FareController : Controller
{
    private readonly FarePredictionService _service;

    public FareController(
        PredictionEnginePool<TaxiTrip, TaxiTripTimePrediction> timeEngine,
        PredictionEnginePool<TaxiTrip, TaxiTripFarePrediction> fareEngine)
    {
        _service = new FarePredictionService(timeEngine, fareEngine);
    }

    public IActionResult Suggest(TaxiTripEstimation input)
    {
        var response = _service.DoWork(input);
        return Json(response);
    }
}
```

The two prediction engine pools are injected into the controller, and the controller injects in a worker service class that ultimately does the job:

```
public TaxiTripEstimation DoWork(TaxiTripEstimation input)
{
    var trip = new TaxiTrip()
    {
        VendorId = "VTS",
        RateCode = input.CarType.ToString(),
        PassengerCount = input.NumberOfPassengers,
        PaymentType = input.PaymentType,
        TripDistance = input.Distance,

        // To predict
        FareAmount = 0,
        TripTime = 0
    };

    // Predict time
    trip.TripTime = _timeEngine.GetPredictionEngine(modelName:"TimeModel")
                                .Predict(trip).Time;
```

```
// Predict amount
trip.FareAmount = _fareEngine.GetPredictionEngine(modelName:"FareModel")
                            .Predict(trip).FareAmount;

// Prepare for UI
input.EstimatedFare = trip.FareAmount;
input.EstimatedTime = trip.TripTime;
input.EstimatedFareForDisplay = TaxiTripEstimation.FareForDisplay(trip.FareAmount);
input.EstimatedTimeForDisplay = TaxiTripEstimation.TimeForDisplay(trip.TripTime);
return input;
}
```

Now, imagine you use this prediction model in a taxi app on the go. As a user, are you really interested in the exact fare amount, or do you want a human-readable price range, such as $5 to $10? Likely, you want the latter. As a developer, you also would probably be more comfortable if you returned a range rather than a precise value such as $7.36. Here's how to make the actual numerical prediction more user-friendly:

```
input.EstimatedFare = trip.FareAmount;
input.EstimatedFareForDisplay = TaxiTripEstimation.FareForDisplay(trip.FareAmount);
return input;
```

The preceding code goes right at the bottom of the implementation of the Predict method that was shown earlier. The user will receive the exact prediction and a human-readable string for display.

As a final note, from the client application's perspective, there's only one more dedicated class to call, and there's no real perception of artificial intelligence. It's just (slightly more intelligent) code!

The ML Devil's Advocate

Regression, as well as classification, is a huge area that encompasses myriad practical problems. In this chapter, we showed how to implement the apparent magic of predicting the cost of a taxi fare in a specific city of the world. But the fundamental question remains: Is this sufficient to say that you're making use of AI in your application? The answer is both yes and no.

Yes, this is AI because you're using models trained with machine learning. No, because with a single shallow learning algorithm—by construction—you can do only small things and subsequently address only relatively simple problems.

Simple and Linear Regression

Regression is the task of predicting a continuous value, whether a quantity, a price, or a temperature. Here are some examples:

- Price prediction (houses, stocks, taxi fares, energy)

- Production prediction (food, goods, energy, availability of water)

- Income prediction

- Time series forecasting

Time series regression is interesting because it can help understand and, better yet, predict the behavior of sophisticated dynamic systems that periodically report their status. This is fairly common in industrial plants, where thanks to IoT devices, there's plenty of observational data. Time series regression is also commonly used in the forecasts of financial, industrial, and medical systems. Time series regression is so interesting that ML.NET provides a dedicated task that we cover in Chapter 8, "Forecasting Tasks."

To help put in perspective the different scopes of simple and not-so-simple prediction scenarios, let's consider (again) the problem of price prediction.

Linear regression is great for quick-and-dirty predictions, such as estimating the time and cost of a taxi ride, though it would have a very limited effect on the people and the business. Predicting the price of houses (or, worse yet, stocks) is a different story. It's quite another to make long-term predictions about the variation of the prices in a given geographical area.

Nonlinear Regression

Linear regression is not applicable to all real-world scenarios because of its structural rigidity and the inherent linearity of the involved mathematical models. Hence, it's often used as a baseline model to address basic scenarios and tasks or to demonstrate the need for a different approach. Instead, regression implemented via neural networks has the advantage of nonlinearity, and data modeling flows closer to reality.

How are real-world prices predicted on various length timelines?

For example, forecasting the price of energy is a problem that requires a cascading approach. Energy is a multifaceted commodity contributed by conventional and renewable sources; predicting the price the customer will pay requires knowing the dynamics of prices for all the possible sources— hence, the cascading approach. In addition, the price of some energy sources depends on the price of other sources and raw materials. This requires sufficient data from a number of different areas of the business world, cleaned and synchronized.

In machine learning, to reduce the error and return an acceptable and usable prediction, you must be able to model real-world processes and data flows. The world is continuous, not discrete. Although sometimes discreteness is a good enough approximation.

Summary

This is the first chapter of the second part of the book fully dedicated to ML.NET tasks. An ML.NET task is a catalog object that exposes all that a developer may need to build and train a machine learning model for a specific class of problems. In this chapter, we went through the canonical steps of machine learning projects as proposed by the ML.NET library and focused on regression (prediction) tasks.

We showed how to massage sample data coming from thousands of taxi ride transactions into a dataset that could make acceptable predictions about the cost of a ride in a restricted given geographical area.

As this is the first of multiple, similarly structured chapters, we presented more general ML.NET information even beyond the strict needs of the Regression tasks. We covered data loaders (files, databases, collections), validation methods (k-fold, holdout), the foundation of feature engineering (normalizers, one-hot encoding), and the composition of data processing pipelines.

Then we moved to consider the algorithms available for a regression task and showed the details of how to build, run, and evaluate a training pipeline. We discussed saving a model and loading it into a client application, specifically an ASP.NET Core application. In doing so, we touched on the topic of smoothly integrating machine learning predictions into the user interface of the client application and what it takes to effectively host ML.NET prediction engines in a server-side, multithreaded application.

Finally, we introduced the "Machine Learning Devil's Advocate" sections, which appear in all the chapters in the second part of this book. These sections aim to provide a deeper and broader vision of the class of problems addressed in the chapter and put them into a real-world perspective. There's a huge difference (in business and performance) between guessing how much a taxi ride could cost to a traveler and predicting how much electricity would cost in the coming days for, say, an energy utility to plan maintenance and shut down of power plants.

In Chapter 5, "Classification Tasks," we'll take the same approach for classification problems.

Classification Tasks

*"A man provided with paper, pencil, and rubber, and subject to strict discipline, is in
effect a universal machine."*

—Alan Turing, "Intelligent Machinery: A Report by A. M. Turing," 1948

For humans, classification is the act of systematically arranging objects in homogeneous groups according to a number of established criteria. For software applications, it is nearly the same. Machine learning would be no different, except that the number of expected groups gives the problem different connotations, leads to different approaches to the solution, and leads to different algorithms.

In particular, if the number of expected groups in which analyzed objects will be partitioned is exactly two, then the problem goes under the name of binary classification. Otherwise, when the number of output groups is larger than two, the problem becomes multiclass classification.

In ML.NET, there are two distinct ML tasks: one for binary and one for multiclass classification.

Let's focus on binary classification first.

The Binary Classification ML Task

Binary classification is a very common task in everyday life that people often accomplish without even realizing they're doing it. Any time you are posed with a yes/no question, you are using binary classification. A real-world example is whether a given email should be classified as spam or a financial transaction should be flagged as suspicious.

However, in this chapter, we focus on sentiment analysis, which tries to train the model to classify the feedback received about a given item as positive or negative.

In ML.NET, the `BinaryClassification` task is exposed as a catalog property from the ML context object.

Supported Algorithms

As with any ML task, the `BinaryClassification` task is a catalog with three main endpoints: a list of training algorithms (property `Trainers`), an evaluator to score results of training against the configured error function (method `Evaluate`), and a cross-validator tool (method `CrossValidate`).

In addition, the `BinaryClassification` task supports two variations of `Evaluate` and `CrossValidate` methods: normal and noncalibrated. Therefore, a new concept appears with the task—the calibrator.

Available Trainers

The binary classification task provides a few algorithms, all of which appear in the standard library of trainers without requiring additional NuGet packages. Overall, you can train a binary classification model using at least the following algorithms. (See Table 5-1.)

TABLE 5-1 Binary Classification Algorithms in ML.NET

Algorithm	Method
AveragedPerceptron	Based on the Perceptron classification algorithm
FieldAwareFactorizationMachine	Based on the factorization machine strategy for supervised learning
LbfgsLogisticRegression	Based on the linear logistic regression strategy
LdSvm	Based on the Local Deep (LD) Support Vector Machine (SVM) approach; specializes in non-linear SVM
LinearSvm	Based on a Support Vector Machine (SVM) approach complemented by a particular descent strategy that alternates stochastic gradient and projection steps
Prior	Based on the concept of prior probability, namely the likelihood that a label is 0/1 regardless of actual features
SdcaLogisticRegression	Based on the calibrated Stochastic Dual Coordinate Ascent (SDCA) method
SdcaNonCalibrated	Based on a noncalibrated Stochastic Dual Coordinate Ascent (SDCA) method
SgdCalibrated	Based on the Stochastic Gradient Descent (SGD) method
SgdNoncalibrated	Based on noncalibrated Stochastic Gradient Descent (SGD) method

Sometimes, a binary classification problem can be reduced to a simplified version of a linear regression problem in which all values below or over a given threshold are mapped to one of the binary classes. Consequently, the algorithms presented in the previous chapter might also work as binary classifiers and should ideally be added to Table 5-1.

However, the final call on this kind of decision belongs to the data science team.

Available Calibrators

In classification, calibration means turning classifier scores into values that indicate the likelihood of some class membership. In ML.NET, for binary classifiers, a number of predefined calibrator objects can calculate probabilities from scores and return the likelihood that a data row belongs to one particular class. Table 5-2 shows the list of calibrators exposed by the `BinaryClassification` task.

TABLE 5-2 Calibrators for binary classification in ML.NET

Calibrator	Method
Isotonic	Based on monotonic calibration
Naïve	Based on binning calibration
Platt	Based on the popular Platt's scaling method that applies logistic regression model to scores

In classification, getting a direct (binary) answer to whether an object belongs to a certain class might not be ideal. Sometimes it is more convenient to calculate the probability that the object belongs to any available class. Models with this characteristic are referred to as *calibrated*.

Calibration can be obtained through a number of methods. Isotonic calibration is the standard method and uses a monotonic logic in which objects with higher predicted scores are more likely to be positive. Naïve calibration, instead, follows the binning logic discussed in Chapter 4, "Prediction Tasks," for feature engineering. Feature binning turns continuous values into categorical values by essentially grouping all values in a range into a dedicated bin. For binary classification, there are only two possible bins.

Supported Validation Techniques

The `BinaryClassification` task supports two flavors of k-fold cross-validation: calibrated and noncalibrated. From the `task` object, two self-describing methods let you choose which strategy you want to use.

The `CrossValidate` method runs cross-validation over the specified number of folds and returns a tailor-made evaluation object, including probabilistic metrics.

The `CrossValidateNonCalibrated` method does the same job except that its returned evaluation object doesn't include any probabilistic metrics.

Binary Classification for Sentiment Analysis

A great example of binary classification is sentiment analysis, which is the process that analyzes text by trying to extract the sentiment hidden in words. Sentiment analysis can be conducted on any sort of text, including sentences synthesized from a voice conversation.

The intended output of the analysis is generally aimed at finding whether the mood is positive or negative, which is what makes it a perfect fit for binary classification.

A Look at the Available Training Data

In the sample application, the dataset consists of a few thousand sentences extracted from the feedback module of a restaurant website. The input file being processed is a text file with a very simple schema: a sentence and a 0/1 value separated by a tab character.

A 0 flags the comments considered negative, whereas a 1 marks those considered positive. The goal of the binary classifier is to evaluate a string of text and return 0 or 1, qualifying the text as positive or negative.

It is important to note that the sample dataset we'll be working on only contains sentences that rate a restaurant. In general, any sentence can be associated with a number of like/dislike scenarios. A blind, context-insensitive interpretation can easily lead to a wrong result. In other words, the same sentence might be labeled as driving positive sentiment when referring to a restaurant, but it might not be labeled positive when referring to another subject. For example, consider the following sentence:

This vacuum cleaner sucks a lot of dirt.

This would be a positive evaluation for any machine learning model targeting some types of household appliances, specifically vacuum cleaners. However, the presence of the words "sucks" and "dirt" might easily lead to some negative sentiment if applied brutally and blindly to any text or to a different context than cleaning appliances.

Schema of the Data

The sample code uses the following familiar lines to load the text file:

```
var filePath = ...;
var mlContext = new MLContext();
var dataView = mlContext.Data.LoadFromTextFile<SentimentData>(filePath);
```

Remember, loading training data from a file is the easiest way to get started and the fastest (and most comfortable) way to proof a concept. However, beyond the boundaries of data science is the territory of data engineering, where loading and processing data can only be a highly automated process. Here, ML.NET can help immensely by bringing the power of database loaders and the flexibility of in-memory collections.

Any machine learning model is characterized by a schema that defines the data flowing in and out of the model once it is trained and deployed. The preceding code—loading data from a text file—is a generic method of working on the SentimentData class. The layout of this class shapes the data being read from the data source.

As mentioned, we're talking about a tab-separated line of text resulting in two columns of data. Here's the implementation of the SentimentData class we'll use to build up the data view:

```
public class SentimentData
{
    [LoadColumn(0)]
    public string SentimentText;

    [LoadColumn(1), ColumnName("Label")]
    public bool Sentiment;
}
```

The LoadColumn attribute (not necessary if data is loaded from a database) maps the column's ordinal position to a class property. The first column of data goes into the SentimentText property, and the second one (feasible values 0/1) sets the Sentiment property.

Note that we're also using the ColumnName attribute to declaratively rename the Sentiment property as Label for the machine learning pipeline. Note that in the previous example, we used a data transformation and the CopyColumns method.

Partitioning the Dataset

For the regression example discussed in the previous chapter, we assumed that we had two distinct datasets: one for training and a smaller one for testing. This configures a holdout scenario. In the regression example, we had these distinct datasets coming in as independent files from the start.

We then also discussed how to train using a cross-validation approach where initially, you hold just one dataset, and then you must split it into training and testing datasets. The cross-validation approach—specifically the k-fold method—partitions the dataset into a fixed (K) number of groups and uses all but one for training; the remaining one is used for testing. Furthermore, the cross-validation method rotates the groups so that all data sections have been used for both training and testing.

Here are some general—and to some extent, abstract—definitions for machine learning datasets:

- **Training dataset**   A training dataset is the data from which the machine learning algorithm learns and discovers any hidden relationships between the features and the target value.

- **Validation dataset**   A validation dataset is the data used to validate the model during the training phase. Sometimes, the validation dataset is a subset of the training set, although it can be a different one that's as large as the training dataset. The validation dataset is mainly used to fine-tune the model hyperparameters. In software development jargon, a validation dataset finds a close analogy with unit tests.

- **Test dataset**   A test dataset is the data used for an unbiased evaluation of the trained model. It provides the measure of how the model will work in the real world. Values and distribution of the test dataset must be comparable to training. In software development jargon, this is analogous to acceptance tests. In literature, this concept is sometimes referred to as a *holdout dataset*. Test (holdout) datasets should never be used to make decisions about which algorithms to use or for tuning the selected algorithm. It's just a plain test of how good the model would be in production. It just gets you a binary answer. Of course, if the answer is negative enough, you might want to reconsider the model (and the algorithm and/or its parameters), the test (holdout) dataset, or both.

NOTE The model testing we're referring to here is comparable to unit tests in programming languages like Java and C#. The ultimate purpose of unit tests is not to ensure the application satisfies all the customers' requirements. More simply, its purpose is to keep the team confident about what they're doing and have a formidable tool to catch regression errors later if there is some deep refactoring. It's nearly the same here—the testing dataset only provides a necessary measure of quality, but there is no guarantee the model will perform that well when facing production data.

Validation Set and Testing Set

The terms *validation dataset* and *testing dataset* are often used interchangeably in literature, as we have done here.

We used (and will use) the term *testing dataset* to refer to, more abstractly, a validation set—namely, a dataset used to validate the model within the training application. A testing dataset refers to yet another level of tests that is triggered when the model is determined to be valid (passed all validation tests) just before putting it into production.

We won't be referring to this scenario in the book. In this book, a testing dataset actually maps to the definition of a validation dataset shown above.

Programmatic Holdout

In this binary classification example, we assume to have a single dataset file coming from some existing data warehouse and split it into training and testing datasets programmatically using the methods in the ML.NET framework. A common way to split data is by taking 80 percent of the dataset for training and leaving the remaining 20 percent of the dataset for testing.

The split can be done manually before getting into the training phase and would generate two distinct files, as described in Chapter 4. A manual split is a flexible solution because it gives you full control over the data rows that go into each file, though it also raises some serious concerns.

The sore point is that the split must return two truly randomly distributed datasets.

If you do the split manually, you take this responsibility on your own. On the other hand, machine learning libraries usually provide ad hoc tools, and ML.NET is no exception. The Data catalog exposes the `TrainTestSplit` method, which takes an `IDataView` and a percentage and returns a `TrainTestData` object.

```
TrainTestData split = mlContext.Data.TrainTestSplit(dataView, 0.2);
```

The percentage you provide (0.2 in the preceding line) indicates the share of the testing dataset. The net effect of the code is that the dataset undergoes an 80/20 split where 80 percent of the data is retained for training and the remaining 20 percent is used for testing. The *TrainTestData* class is a mere container object made of two `IDataView` objects: `TrainSet` and `TestSet`.

Feature Engineering

Machine learning algorithms work on numbers. So, how can they deal with plain text? The (fairly) obvious answer is, they can't.

Text Featurization

To enable (binary) classification algorithms, another preliminary step is required—text featurization. The ML.NET library provides the `FeaturizeText` method from the Text catalog, as shown here:

```
var pipeline = mlContext
    .Transforms
    .Text
    .FeaturizeText("Features", "SentimentText");
```

The method takes the `SentimentText` column of the dataset and transforms it into a new column called `Features` made of an array of float values. The `Features` column—required as the input values carried by all ML.NET trainers—is then added to the transformation pipeline.

Every value in the array saved to the `Features` column represents the normalized count of a discovered *n-gram*. An *n*-gram is a contiguous sequence of *n* words that appear in the text.

To convert text into numeric values, `FeaturizeText` uses an instance of `TextFeaturizingEstimator` set to its default parameters. (See Table 5-3.)

TABLE 5-3 Text Featurizing Options

Setting	Description	Default value
CaseMode	How to change the case of the text (lower, upper, as-is)	Lower case
CharFeatureExtractor	Produces a numerical vector in which each number refers to a distinct sequence of *n* consecutive characters (*n*-gram)	*n*=3
KeepDiacritics	Whether to keep or remove diacritics in text	False
KeepNumbers	Whether to keep or remove numbers from text	True
KeepPunctuations	Whether to keep or remove punctuation	False
StopWordsRemover	Indicates how to deal with stop words (words commonly filtered out before processing natural language text): ignore, default, or custom vocabulary	None
WordFeatureExtractor	Produces a numerical vector in which each number refers to a distinct sequence of *n* consecutive words (*n*-gram)	*n*=1

As far as feature extractors are concerned, note that vector numbers identify the *n*-gram by the index it has been given in a dictionary the extractor creates internally.

Let's do some debugging on the following code to help you get a clear idea of what this means:

```
var preview = mlContext
    .Transforms
    .Text
    .FeaturizeText("Features", "SentimentText")
    .Preview(splitDataView.TrainSet);
```

With a breakpoint placed right after the preceding line of code, you can inspect the effect of text featurization on the rows of the training dataset. To make inspection even easier, you can add a call to the method Preview. Specifically designed for debugging scenarios, this method applies the transformations to the provided data view and saves the snapshot to a local variable. (The method Preview is not for production and should only be used during debugging sessions.)

Snooping into Featurized Text

Figure 5-1 shows a screenshot of the data view as it is being transformed.

FIGURE 5-1 The effect of text featurization on a sample dataset

After the featurization, the items in the data view are made of four columns: SentimentText, Label (originally, Sentiment), SamplingKeyColumn (which has been added for internal purposes during the training/testing split), and Features (which contains vectors of numbers). Figure 5-1 shows the content of the Features column for the sample row whose original text is the following:

```
My tortillas were falling apart from the grease and from the large quantity of the meat, cheese,
and cabbage.
```

If you expand the content, you find more than one hundred float values, each one representing the occurrence of *n*-grams in the content of the SentimentText column. Note also that values have been normalized in the 0 to 1 range.

Composing the Training Pipeline

The next step is appending a trainer to the machine learning pipeline, training the model, and evaluating the results. We face the usual hard-to-answer question: which algorithm?

Selecting the Algorithm

The logistic regression algorithm is one of the trainers you can use from the BinaryClassification catalog, and it is considered one of the best-fit algorithms for the problem at hand, or at least the first option to try. Logistic regression works by modeling the probability of the default class in the dataset. In our example, the default class is the label value we consider default (or just more common) between positive or negative.

Here's the code you need if you go with the logistic regression algorithm.

```
// Appending the trainer to the pipeline (logistic regression algorithm)
var pipeline = mlContext
    .Transforms
    .Text
    .FeaturizeText("Features", "SentimentText");
    .Append(mlContext.BinaryClassification
            .Trainers
            .SdcaLogisticRegression("Sentiment", "Features"));

// Fitting the model on the training dataset
var model = pipeline.Fit(splitDataView.TrainSet);
```

The logistic regression trainer takes two column names: the name of the column with correct answers to learn from (Sentiment) and the name of the column with input values (Features).

Support Vector Machine (SVM) is another binary classification algorithm you should try. SVM is offered by ML.NET through the method LinearSvm in the BinaryClassification catalog.

SVM Versus Logistic Regression

Support Vector Machine is quite an intimidating name for what is more or less the mathematics behind the algorithm. SVM is a supervised algorithm with a proven success record on both classification and regression problems. It shines, however, at text classification, spam detection, and where sentiment analysis is involved. It also performs well when used on images to recognize regular patterns, such as handwritten notes or digits. SVM usually delivers accurate responses, even when trained on relatively small datasets, as long as the data has limited overlapping.

SVM and logistic regression provide nearly the same performance and the same accuracy on similar datasets. Neither are affected by outliers in the dataset. Furthermore, both algorithms are linear, so they can be trained well, even on fairly large datasets.

The interesting thing is that the two algorithms come to their solutions using radically different approaches. Logistic regression uses a probabilistic approach and returns the likelihood that a data item falls in the default class. Instead, SVM tries to find the widest possible separating margin between data items that fall in each class.

> **NOTE** For more details about the internals of classes of machine learning algorithms—including their mathematical foundations—you might want to have a look at *Introducing Machine Learning* from Microsoft Press (2020).

Evaluating the Model

In binary classification, the method `Evaluate` (as well as its twin method `EvaluateNonCalibrated`) can be used to get some metrics to evaluate the quality and accuracy of the algorithm. The following code shows how to use the trained model to generate predictions based on the test dataset and how to evaluate. It's worth recalling the difference between `Evaluate` and `EvaluateNonCalibrated`. The latter returns a metrics object that doesn't include any probabilities.

```
// Generate predictions based on the test dataset
IDataView predictions = model.Transform(splitDataView.TestSet);

// Evaluating the model on testing data
var metrics = mlContext.BinaryClassification.Evaluate(predictions, "Sentiment");
```

The method `Evaluate` returns a `CalibratedBinaryClassificationMetrics` object, which groups a number of relevant metrics for the problem.

In particular, the metrics object tells us the proportion of correct predictions in the test set (regardless of the value, positive or negative). It also tells us about positive and negative recalls, namely the proportion of positives (and negatives) detected as positives (and negatives). The harmonic mean of precision and recall is summarized in the F1-score (or F-score) metrics.

On the sample test dataset, the logistic regression algorithm returns an accuracy of more than 85 percent. However, the sample test set returns a low F-score—about 0.3—whereas the ideal value of the F-score is 1. What's the most appropriate reading of these numbers? What should we do? Change the algorithm? Add or remove transformations? Use a larger dataset? Again, this is where data science fits in nicely!

If you don't have the support of an expert team, you can use ML.NET to take advantage of AutoML, either through the Visual Studio Model Builder plug-in or via the ML.NET command-line interface (CLI). Provided that you run it for enough time (not just seconds), AutoML suggests the ideal algorithm and the set of hyperparameters to use for a given dataset.

Binary Classification Metrics

Table 5-4 briefly defines the measures you might be interested in when using binary classification.

TABLE 5-4 Common Measures for Binary Classification

Measure	Description
Accuracy	Indicates the percentage of items classified correctly in relationship to the entire test set. The ideal value is close to 100 percent.
Precision	Indicates the percentage of positives/negatives classified correctly in relationship to the number of predicted positives/negatives. In other words, it indicates how many of the positives/negatives detected were effectively so. The ideal value is close to 100 percent.
Recall	Indicates the percentage of items classified correctly in relation to the items in the predicted class. In other words, it indicates the percentage of positives/negatives in the dataset correctly detected as positives/negatives. The ideal value is close to 100 percent.
F1-score	Indicates the harmonic mean of precision and recall. It can be calculated on each of the options. The ideal value is close to 100 percent.

The simplest measure to make sense of is accuracy, which just indicates how often the model makes good predictions, whether positive or negative. However, a result of, say, 85 percent, can be considered quite good, but it's certainly not an enthusiastically good one. At the same time, achieving an accuracy near 100 percent, especially in a large test dataset, is less than ideal and probably a sign of overfitting. So, ideally, you want to get close to 100 percent, but not too close.

The metric of accuracy is more than acceptable if the labels are balanced. However, for imbalanced datasets—those with many "false" and only a few "true" values or vice versa—you could have a high accuracy but still have a model that is not well-trained to detect anomalies in the data. In fact, an imbalanced dataset is typical of anomaly detection scenarios such as credit card fraud.

When a Combined Metric Helps

The F1-score is a combined metric, meaning it doesn't represent a direct measure. Therefore, if accuracy (or precision or recalls) is crucial, it can be blissfully ignored. F1-score, however, gains importance and comes into play when the problem at hand doesn't give strict guidance on the ideal training approach and when you want to compare multiple algorithms.

For example, the role of the F1-score is crucial when the dataset is unbalanced, and one of the two scenarios occurs much more frequently than the other. In the case of unbalanced datasets, it's all about the importance of each option for the problem at hand. A good example is fraud detection, where effectively labeling fraudulent transactions is much more important than dealing in any way with nonfraudulent transactions. In this case, you should look at the F1-score only for the more important option and pick the algorithm that maximizes the value.

However, when the dataset is balanced, F1 can be ignored because, in the presence of good accuracy, the risk of erroneous classifications is really low. When both scenarios should be taken into careful account, then the F1-score should be sufficiently high on both options to be safe about the quality of the model.

Setting Up a Client Application

Figure 5-2 presents a sample ASP.NET application that consumes the binary classification model we have just built. An HTML form captures the text to submit as feedback and invokes a controller action method. The controller is injected with a prediction engine, as discussed in Chapter 4:

```
// From the ConfigureServices method of Startup.cs
services.AddPredictionEnginePool<SentimentData, SentimentPrediction>()
    .FromFile(modelName: "SampleClassify.Sentiment", filePath: mlSentimentModelPath);
```

The class `SentimentPrediction` is defined in the next code snippet. The schema of the class depends on the selected algorithm, which outputs specific columns. In particular, the (calibrated) logistic regression algorithm sets two columns—`PredictedLabel`, holding the Boolean answer, and `Probability`, indicating the confidence of the predicted value. Those columns must be mapped to properties in the `SentimentPrediction` class returned by the trained ML.NET model. The trainer also returns a `Score` column, which contains a float value that is the raw, unbounded score calculated by the model from which sentiment and probability are derived.

```
public class SentimentPrediction
{
    [ColumnName("PredictedLabel")]
    public bool ActualSentiment;

    [ColumnName("Score")]
    public float ActualScore;

    [ColumnName("Probability")]
    public float ActualProbability;
}
```

The web page in Figure 5-2 receives a JSON-serialized version of the preceding class and sets up a user interface.

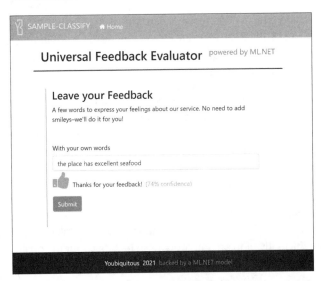

FIGURE 5-2 A sample ASP.NET application using the binary classifier

The Multiclass Classification ML Task

Abstractly speaking, binary classification can be seen as a special case of multiclass classification where there are only two classes to choose from. Nonetheless, dealing with more than two target classes makes a huge implementation difference and leads to a distinct family of algorithms.

The same sentiment analysis problem we just approached as a binary classification instance can be reformulated as a multiclass classification problem by growing the range of choices—positive, negative, neutral, and any other level of sentiment that could make sense. The response of a multiclass classification model is the name of one target class chosen from a collection of more than two feasible classes.

As weird as it may sound, increasing the number of feasible classes to choose from dramatically impacts the various steps of the machine learning pipeline.

Supported Algorithms

Multiclass classification applies to any real-world scenarios in which a data item must be assigned to an existing category. To train an algorithm, you provide a sufficiently large set of classified elements and let the algorithm figure out where the new data item fits better. Unlike clustering (which we discuss next), multiclass classification is a form of supervised learning, meaning that the classes to choose from are known in advance.

Multiclass Versus Multilabel

In spite of similar-looking names, multiclass classification is different from multilabel classification. In particular, multilabel classification is when a single data item can be assigned to one or more categories. Assigning multiple genres to a song or product categorization when a product can fit into multiple marketing categories is a good example of multilabel classification.

Multilabel is usually approached through binary classification on tailormade learning pipelines and aptly transformed data. Most commonly, the solution comes from building a binary classification model for each of the possible categories and running them in a composed pipeline.

Available Trainers

At least, you can train a multiclass classification model using the algorithms shown in Table 5-5. All of them belong to the standard library and do not require additional NuGet packages.

TABLE 5-5 Multiclass Classification Algorithms in ML.NET

Algorithm	Method
LbfgsMaximumEntropy	Based on the maximum entropy model
NaiveBayes	Based on the Naïve Bayes probabilistic classifier method
OneVersusAll	Based on the One-Versus-All method
PairwiseCoupling	Based on the One-Versus-One method
SdcaMaximumEntropy	Based on a linear model that returns probabilities features belong to a class
SdcaNonCalibrated	Based on a linear model noncalibrated to return probabilities

If you compare the names of algorithms in this list and in Table 5-1, you might spot some similarities. In particular, a few algorithms (LbfgsXxx and SdcaXxx) have different monikers in the two tables: maximum entropy for multiclass classification and logistic regression for binary classification.

The maximum entropy method is a generalization of the linear logistic regression and its adaptation to the multiple classes scenario. Let's take a slightly deeper look at other families of multiclass algorithms.

The Naïve Bayes Method

At some point, long before machine learning became as popular as it is now, the scientific community felt the need to add a probabilistic dimension to classification problems. This brought the definition of Bayes classifiers, often also referred to as *naïve classifiers*. Bayesian statistics is the foundation of this method of classification.

In a nutshell, a Bayesian classifier calculates the probability that a given set of features belongs to each of a specified set of outcome classes. Not only does it tell which of the predefined classes a given data item belongs to, but it also tells the related probability. As expected, all probabilities sum to 1.

Why is it considered a naïve technique?

This is because such classifiers assume that all the features are independent from one another. From a purely statistical standpoint, this is a strong assumption that prevents an effective modeling of the real world. Yet, naïve Bayesian classifiers work quite well in machine learning, especially for classification problems and performing the first scan on large volumes of data.

The One-Versus-All Method

This method reduces multiclass classification to multiple instances of binary classification. As a result, a binary classifier is trained to give a yes/no prediction for each target class. Next, for each feature, the binary classifier runs to predict the likelihood for any given class. Finally, the class with the highest probability is chosen and returned as the outcome for the multiclass problem.

In ML.NET, the One-Versus-All method can be used with any of the available binary classifiers listed in Table 5-1. Interestingly, the Microsoft.ML.LightGbm NuGet package includes additional binary classifiers such as LightGbmBinaryTrainer and the multiclass variation based on the one-versus-all method—the `LightGbmMulticlassTrainer` classifier. Both algorithms (binary and multiclass) are based on LightGBM—an open-source implementation of the gradient-boosting decision tree method.

The One-Versus-One Method

Also referred to as *pairwise coupling*, this strategy works by splitting a multiclass classification problem into a number of binary classification problems—one per (unique) pair of target classes.

For example, given four classes such as `Red`, `Orange`, `Yellow`, and `Green`, the method would run a binary classifier for the following pairs:

- `Red` versus `Orange`
- `Red` versus `Yellow`
- `Red` versus `Green`
- `Orange` versus `Yellow`
- `Orange` versus `Green`
- `Yellow` versus `Green`

One-Versus-One (OVO) predicts the class that wins the most comparisons. Suppose two (or more) classes get the same number of wins. In that case, OVO picks up the class with the highest aggregate confidence obtained, summing over the confidence levels computed by the underlying binary classifiers.

The OVO method requires more work than One-Versus-All. In fact, it requires running $n * (n - 2) / 2$ binary classifiers (where n is the number of output classes) for an overall $O(n^2)$ computational complexity. Instead, the One-Versus-All method runs the n binary classifiers exactly.

There's another aspect to consider, though.

OVO triggers more binary classifiers than the One-Versus-All method, but each classifier is set to work on a smaller dataset that only comprises the rows having any of the two classes as their target value. Instead, the One-Versus-All method requires all its binary classifiers to always work on the entire dataset. The trade-off is given by the actual trainer used by the binary classifiers. A binary classifier such as SVM doesn't scale well with the number of rows. Therefore, if SVM is selected as the binary classifier, the OVO method is preferable over One-Versus-All regardless of the higher computational complexity.

Using the Multiclass Classification Task

Classification is about assigning the entity under observation to one of multiple (more than two) feasible target classes. For an effective result, the set of feasible labels must be well-defined beforehand, and data must be organized for supervised learning. In other words, the available dataset must contain a column with the known answer to let the model learn.

Typical instances of multiclass classification regard large chunks of textual information such as emails, feedback notes, or product descriptions to be cataloged into one of a few known categories that make sense for the business scenario. Likewise, images, voice, and videos can be processed for multiclass classification. The specific nature of the source, though, opened up a whole new algorithmic space—object detection and image classification—which we touch on later in the book.

A Look at the Available Data

The sample application we discuss here covers a common scenario—cataloging the feedback that a company may have received through a number of possible channels: websites, bots, social networks, and even tickets entered into some system by some operator following up on customers' phone calls.

As you can guess, for a classification model to be well integrated in a company's business processes, a fully automated collection system must be in place to convey all the feedback received from a variety of channels into a single data warehouse. Data that flows in from users and customers must be cleaned up, structured, anonymized, and then stored. Next, once run through the classification system, the text of the feedback is analyzed and classified as appropriate.

The data we work on in the example is a large text file made of a few tab-separated columns, including description and type of feedback. The dataset comes from the repository of ML.NET samples and contains a collection of over 13,000 GitHub issues.

Schema of the Data

The C# class that describes the features we're considering for multiclass classification is shown in the following code. The property we want the model to predict is Area. We also ignore the ID column in the dataset:

```
public class TicketData
{
    [LoadColumn(1)]
    public string Area { get; set; }

    [LoadColumn(2)]
    public string Title { get; set; }

    [LoadColumn(3)]
    public string Description { get; set; }
}
```

Figure 5-3 shows a glimpse of the source dataset in Microsoft Excel. It's a 15 MB tab-separated TSV file; distinct values in the *Area* column form the list of target classes. There are 22 options.

The columns Title and Description describe—with different levels of detail—an issue in a specific technical area. We expect the final mode to take the title and description and suggest the most appropriate area.

	A	B	
1	ID	Area	Title
2	17	area-System.Xml	Some XPath.XDocument tests are failing
3	20	area-System.Xml	2 XPath.XDocument tests fail because of lacking feature
4	22	area-System.Numerics	Two Numerics Tests are failing only on our CI server
5	36	area-System.Numerics	SIMD test failures on non-ENU configurations.
6	41	area-System.Numerics	Quaternion operator overloads should be using the respective methods
7	49	area-Infrastructure	Add Linux/Mac build script
8	50	area-System.Numerics	Made Quarternion's operator overloads use their respective methods
9	52	area-Meta	ReferenceSource repo license incorrect for individual files
10	54	area-System.Xml	Remove always true "if" and unreachable code in System.Xml.Linq.XObject.SkipNotify method.
11	55	area-System.Xml	[Issue 54] Removed always-true if and unreachable code in XObject.cs
12	58	area-System.Xml	System.Xml.sln fails to build on Mono, error CS0433
13	69	area-Infrastructure	build.cmd does not build solution on HP laptop (when Platform=MCD is pre-set)
14	70	area-Meta	Hello, World! sample
15	71	area-System.Numerics	Behaviour of `Quaternion.CreateFromAxisAngle` when axis is not a unit vector
16	72	area-System.Numerics	`Equals` with NaN values (IEEE vs. reflexivity)
17	77	area-System.Xml	Some Xml encoding tests lost their encoding
18	81	area-System.Xml	Add test coverage for XPath and XDocument
19	94	area-Meta	Necessary bits for Mono.Posix
20	110	area-System.Xml	Add async document/element loading for XLinq.
21	116	area-System.Numerics	Quaternion and public fields
22	118	area-System.Numerics	Matrix4x4 - more useful public properties
23	119	area-System.Numerics	Vector3 - more public static properties

FIGURE 5-3 Content of the dataset viewed in Microsoft Excel

Featurizing Text Columns

Loading the data into a new ML.NET data context is in no way different from what we have seen in previous examples. You can use file or database loaders depending on the actual storage location of the data:

```
var filePath = ...;
var mlContext = new MLContext();
var dataView = mlContext.Data.LoadFromTextFile<TicketData>(filePath);
```

Text properties such as `Title` and `Description` need to be featurized—a necessary step to enable the training algorithm to learn the relevance of words:

```
var pipeline = mlContext
    .Transforms
    .Text
    .FeaturizeText("TitleFeaturized", "Title")
.Append(mlContext
    .Transforms
    .Text
    .FeaturizeText("DescriptionFeaturized", "Description"));
```

The `FeaturizeText` method adds instructions to the pipeline to create two new columns from the values in `Title` and `Description`.

Mapping Target Classes to Numerical Values

Most of the time, target classes are just text, as is the case with the Area column. Therefore, one more step is required: mapping the nonnumerical column to unique numbers for the ease of prediction. We face a similar problem in Chapter 4 while converting the text describing the payment mode of the taxi ride. In that case, we use the one-hot encoding technique.

One-hot encoding works beautifully for categorical data (sort of C# enumerated types) because it creates additional 0/1 columns for each possible categorical value. One-hot encoding is acceptable as long as the options are limited to just a few. Multiclass classification (and the Area column) is a different story because a multiclass column can take hundreds of distinct values—or even thousands for large datasets. For the 15 MB we're considering here, there are just 22 distinct values. One-hot encoding is highly problematic for handling a large number of features. Therefore, we have to opt for adding a new column to map each distinct value in the Area column to a distinct numeric value, typically a progressive index:

```
// Map input column "Area" to output column "IndexOfArea"
pipeline.Append(mlContext.Transforms.Conversion.MapValueToKey("Area", "IndexOfArea"));
```

The IndexOfArea column ends up holding values like 1, 2, and 3 for each distinct value found in the Area column.

Composing the Training Pipeline

It's that time again! We need to choose a trainer and append it to the ML.NET learning pipeline to train the model and evaluate its results. Which algorithm should we start with?

> **NOTE** Model training is made of several logical levels, and the meaning of business terms being used is sometimes slightly different when not blurred in different contexts. For example, an *algorithm* refers to the sequence of steps that, following some mathematical technique, produces an executable computation graph—the model. Different algorithms produce different models. In ML.NET, the same algorithm can be applied to different scenarios, referred to as *tasks*. For example, methods based on the Stochastic Dual Coordinate Ascent algorithm are available to work for binary classification, multiclass classification, and regression. In each scenario, however, the output of the algorithm is interpreted differently. The layer of code that ties a specific algorithm with the appropriate interpretation for a given task in ML.NET takes the name of a *trainer*.

Selecting the Algorithm

Multiclass classification is a special scenario. Most of the trainers available require multiple passes on the training dataset. To avoid reloading the same data over and over from the file on disk, ML.NET provides the tools to force the algorithm to work on cached data within a given pipeline. The primary tool is the method AppendCacheCheckpoint. Bear in mind that the cache checkpoint must be added to the pipeline before the trainer is appended.

To add a cache, you build the chain of estimators in the data processing pipeline as shown here:

```
var dataPipeline = _mlContext.Transforms.Conversion.MapValueToKey("IndexOfArea", "Area")
    .Append(_mlContext.Transforms.Text.FeaturizeText("Title", "TitleFeaturized"))
    .Append(_mlContext.Transforms.Text.FeaturizeText("Description", "DescriptionFeaturized"))
    .Append(_mlContext.Transforms.Concatenate("Features",
                  "TitleFeaturized", "DescriptionFeaturized"))
    .AppendCacheCheckpoint(_mlContext);
```

> **NOTE** All in all, a cache can be used for small or medium datasets. When you are dealing with large datasets, you must not use cache. Here, *a large dataset means it is intended to be larger than the machine's memory*, which is pretty common with real-life datasets. In this case, most trainers will be streaming data from the source (file or database) as needed while training.

Which algorithm should we use?

As in Table 5-3, the Trainers collection on the MulticlassClassification catalog provides several options. However, most of the algorithms work by training one binary classifier for each class or combination of classes. This is the approach taken by the OneVersusAll and PairwiseCoupling trainers. Repeated use of a binary classifier, however, could be less than ideal performance-wise if the client application only needs a default/suggested value to categorize a new data item.

Another option is the NaiveBayes algorithm.

Based on probabilistic theory, this trainer is a valid option for small datasets and also for some quick categorization that might be necessary for a larger and more sophisticated learning pipeline. For example, think of an anomaly detection model aimed at flagging fraudulent transactions. Given the large volumes of transactions flowing in, the majority of which are fine, a Bayesian filter at the gate may widely simplify any further learning, whether it happens via other shallow learning algorithms or neural networks.

For multiclass scenarios, a common way to start is using a linear algorithm such as the Stochastic Dual Coordinate Ascent (SDCA) trainer.

Linearity Is King

A linear algorithm generates a linear combination of the input data and a set of weights. The training effort is then aimed at finding the ideal weights to complete the linear formula. For a linear algorithm to work effectively, all features should be normalized to avoid one having more influence over the result than others. In general, linear algorithms are cheap to train and fast to predict. Given their inherent linearity, they also scale well with the number of features and the size of the training dataset. It is also worth noting that linear algorithms perform multiple passes over the dataset. Hence, if the size of the dataset allows it, you might want to cache it in memory for a better training performance.

Let's opt for the SdcaMaximumEntropy trainer. The algorithm receives the name of the (numerical) column with the known answers and the name of the column (aptly created) with all the input values.

```
var trainer = mlContext
    .MulticlassClassification
    .Trainers
    .SdcaMaximumEntropy("IndexOfArea", "Features");
```

SdcaMaximumEntropy is the calibrated version of the SDCA algorithm. If you're not interested in the probability of the choice, you can opt for the noncalibrated version.

Switching Back to Text

There's a final missing piece to have in the pipeline. Earlier in the data processing pipeline, the names of the target classes were turned into numbers using the MapValueToKey converter. We now need to add the reverse functionality to the training pipeline so that the predicted numerical value (the index previously assigned to any target class) can be converted back to a human-readable name.

```
// Map the index of the predicted label to the property with the [PredictedLabel] attribute
// in the prediction class
var trainingPipeline = dataPipeline
        .Append(trainer)
        .Append(_mlContext.Transforms.Conversion.MapKeyToValue("PredictedLabel"));
```

A call to MapKeyToValue will do the reverse job.

Evaluating the Model

The SDCA algorithm combines several of the best properties and capabilities of logistic regression and SVM algorithms and, in most cases, is a very good fit for multiclass problems. However, how do you determine if a multiclass model is good enough for the problem at hand? Let's grab some metrics.

```
// Train the model
ITransformer model = pipeline.Fit(trainingDataSet);

// Grab some metrics
var testMetrics = mlContext
        .MulticlassClassification
        .Evaluate(model.Transform(testDataSet));
```

The *Evaluate* method returns a MulticlassClassificationMetrics object. Table 5-6 lists some of the most used metrics reported by the object.

TABLE 5-6 Some Metrics for Multiclass Classification

Property	Description
ConfusionMatrix	Returns the confusion matrix for the classifier
LogLoss	Indicates the mean of the log loss values calculated for each class
LogLossReduction	Indicates the percentage of the advantage the classifier provides over a random prediction
MacroAccuracy	Indicates the average of the F1-score calculated for each class
MicroAccuracy	Indicates the F1-score for all predictions made by the model
PerClassLogLoss	Gets the log-loss of the classifier for each class

Both micro- and macro-accuracy refer to the harmonic mean of precision and recall (F1-score). Micro-accuracy refers to the whole set of predictions, whereas macro-accuracy considers classes individually. In general, micro-accuracy is preferable if you have a large dataset with some relevant degree of class imbalance (that is, many more examples of one class than of other classes). Macro-accuracy, instead, counts more if you are interested in evaluating the model's performance on the various classes, including those with few occurrences in the training dataset.

The LogLoss metric measures the average level of uncertainty about the results of the classifier. The lower the value, the best. The ideally lowest possible value is 0. Figure 5-4 presents some LogLoss values reported for all the classes in the sample dataset. The average is 0.91.

[0]	1.4096851738836109
[1]	1.6006409900381098
[2]	0.73521298067807739
[3]	2.3722157321715533
[4]	0.78698460014512361
[5]	1.0409757032084235
[6]	1.6604941261984392
[7]	1.3512020389213524
[8]	0.96426926218274178
[9]	1.1038087706873752
[10]	1.1138442642132194
[11]	0.99341443005045493
[12]	0.76327409872712026
[13]	1.5166282366622972
[14]	0.31666075446046482

MulticlassClassificationMetrics}
soft.ML.Data.ConfusionMatrix}
1603746643626
8458473203875
9936702910781
0254835738409

PerClassLogLoss	Length = 22
TopKAccuracy	0
TopKPredictionCount	0

FIGURE 5-4 Values of the *LogLoss* metric for all the classes in the sample application

Accuracy refers to the quantity of errors, and loss refers more to the quality of errors and how huge they were. Hence, low macro-accuracy and high loss denote large errors on a lot of data, which is the worst-case scenario. On the contrary, low accuracy but low loss denotes small errors on a lot of data. In case of great accuracy, you have few errors but as large as the loss amount indicates.

Looking at the Confusion Matrix

Yet another tool to evaluate the performance of a classifier is the confusion matrix. The matrix combines predictions and labels on the rows and columns of a square matrix, as shown in Figure 5-5.

		Classes		
		Green	Orange	Red
Predictions	Green	5	2	0
	Orange	3	3	2
	Red	0	1	11

FIGURE 5-5 A sample confusion matrix for a multiclass classifier

The values in the columns (for example, Green) indicate how many times elements in the class have been predicted as any of the values in the rows. The matrix in the figure indicates that an Orange input was recognized twice as Green, three times as Orange, and once as Red. The `MulticlassClassificationMetrics` object exposes a property called `ConfusionMatrix` that gathers all values for such a matrix. In the sample application, the matrix is 22 by 22. The matrix is represented by an ML.NET class named `ConfusionMatrix` with predefined properties to calculate precision and recall on a per-class basis. (See Table 5-7.)

TABLE 5-7 Properties of a Confusion Matrix

Property	Description
Counts	Returns an array of arrays, in which every element refers to a row and contains an array of values for each of the columns
NumberOfClasses	Indicates the dimension of the matrix (number of rows/columns)
PerClassPrecision	Returns an array with the precision calculated for each class
PerClassRecall	Returns an array with the recall calculated for each class

As a reminder, *recall* indicates the percentage of true class positives the model predicts with respect to the total number of actual, real positives found in the dataset for the given class. The *precision*, instead, refers to the percentage of true class positives the model predicts with respect to the total number of positives detected for the given class. For example, suppose a dataset contains images of

10 real cats, but the model only identifies 7 of them as cats. Of these, only 4 are real cats; the other 3 are, say, rabbits mistaken for cats. In this case, the precision of the model is 4/7, whereas the recall is 4/10.

Setting Up a Client Application

In Figure 5-2, we presented a sample application showcasing the binary classifier. The same application is now extended to incorporate some action that triggers the multiclass classifier. (See Figure 5-6.)

Written in ASP.NET, the web page contains an HTML form that posts back to a controller action method which, in turn, ends up invoking the trained model.

```
// Method belonging to a controller class which is injected all necessary prediction engines
public IActionResult SuggestTicketClassification(SubmittedTicket input)
{
    // The _service object is an instance of a helper service class that receives the
    // prediction engine(s) references through the constructor.
    var response = _service.MulticlassPrediction(input);
    return Json(response);
}
```

The response variable is an instance of the TicketPrediction class created by the following code:

```
// This method belongs to a service class invoked from the controller
public TicketPrediction MulticlassPrediction(SubmittedTicket input)
{
    var modelInput = new TicketData
    {
        Title = input.Title,
        Description = input.Description
    };

    // The service class this method belongs received the _ticketEngine object below
    // through the constructor.

    // Predict class
    var prediction = _ticketEngine.Predict("SampleClassify.Ticket", modelInput);
    return prediction;
}
```

The TicketPrediction class is the following:

```
public class TicketPrediction
{
    [ColumnName("Score")]
    public float[] ActualScores { get; set; }

    [ColumnName("PredictedLabel")]
    public string Area { get; set; }
}
```

Serialized to JSON, an instance of TicketPrediction lands in the browser and produces the output of Figure 5-6.

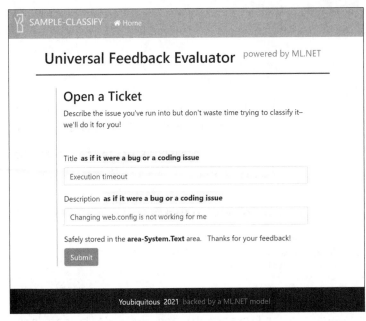

FIGURE 5-6 Multiclass classification in an ASP.NET application

Managing Multiple Prediction Engine Pools

As stated earlier in the book, in a server and multithreaded environment such as ASP.NET using a prediction engine object pool helps performance significantly. Each application pool, however, is strictly defined in terms of input and output classes. What if you have multiple models with different input and output classes?

In Startup.cs, you are not allowed to place multiple distinct calls to the AddPredictionEngine middleware, but you have to resort to following approach:

```
services.AddPredictionEnginePool<SentimentData, SentimentPrediction>()
    .FromFile(modelName: "SampleClassify.Sentiment", filePath: mlSentimentModelPath)
    .Services
    .AddPredictionEnginePool<TicketData, TicketPrediction>()
    .FromFile(modelName: "SampleClassify.Ticket", filePath: mlTicketModelPath);
```

Finally, note that the FromFile method also has one overload that watches the model file path for changes and a companion method—FromUri—which can load the model from a URL.

The ML Devil's Advocate

Together regression and classification cover nearly the whole set of practical problems for which a more intelligent solution might be desirable. Classification, in particular, takes a huge area that encompasses myriad practical problems in the form of binary, multiclass, or even multilabel classification.

As a user, you have a more pleasant experience when the page indicates it understood your input and provides either positive or negative feedback or some automatic (and hopefully faithful) categorization of your tickets. As a developer, it's mostly a matter of getting familiar with a few more classes and methods and taking advantage of the model that someone else (or your team) created. Finally, as a data scientist, it's mostly about the data you have available and how you're able to think about transformations. But here comes the fundamental question—again:

Is this sufficient to say that you're making use of AI in your application? Again, the answer is mixed.

Yes, you're using AI because you're using models trained with machine learning. However, the answer is also "no" because you can do only small things and consequently address only basic tasks with a single shallow learning algorithm.

The Many Faces of Classification

In the end, classification is an easy concept to grasp. It refers to a modeling problem in which you're given sample data and you predict the category it belongs to in a specific context. From a pure modeling perspective, all that classification requires is a training dataset with (really) many examples of inputs and outputs to learn from.

That said, you should be aware that there is no known super theory that explains how to map algorithms and classification problems. Hence, it is generally recommended that everyone start with experiments and discover which algorithm and related configuration leads to the most acceptable performance for the problem at hand.

Everyone? Including experts?

Yes, especially experts do that because they know that nothing is easy, and all you want is modeling input toward a realistically appropriate prediction.

Classification is a very generic term—the more you raise the abstraction level, the more complex the model's classification. Determining whether the text of an email makes it qualify for the spam folder is one thing, but it's quite another to classify an image or a video frame. It's conceptually the same classification task, but the underlying data (and its internal intricacy) is quite different and makes for radically different approaches.

Let's now reconsider the problem of sentiment analysis that we tackled in this chapter with a basic logistic regression algorithm.

That is probably enough if you just want to give some nice visual feedback to a person who leaves a comment on your website (or for a quick and naïve count of good/bad feedback for internal purposes). But what if the entire company is exposed to the quality of automatic sentiment analysis? Think of a customer care service, for example!

Another Perspective on Sentiment Analysis

Sentiment analysis can certainly be solved using a shallow learning algorithm, whether logistic regression trainer or SVM. SVM, in particular, is a great choice if you want a more accurate response with various levels of sentiment, such as poor, mediocre, passable, good, great, or outstanding. Logistic regression is a valid candidate if you're looking for a binary answer, such as good or bad.

In both cases, the quality of the response depends primarily on the size of the training dataset. However, the gears of shallow learning algorithms might not be able to deal properly with rhetorical figures, such as euphemisms, litotes, hyperboles, oxymorons, and in general, anything that is an understatement or overstatement.

At any rate, a clear difference of learning power exists between shallow and deep algorithms. For sure, a neural network has the potential to learn to predict a more accurate response than any other family of algorithms. Sentiment analysis is a delicate matter in which a too sharp response may sometimes be pointless. Therefore, a neural network sounds like a savvier option than a plain classifier when the accuracy of the response is critical for the decision taken based on the response.

The cost of a solution based on neural networks is higher than the cost for a shallow algorithm. But what if you embark on shallow development, and you hardly get the quality you expect? You can insist on changing configuration, tightening screws, and greasing the gears, but all of this would come at some extra cost that just adds up to the total.

There are no certain rules in machine learning. And expecting to find the silver bullet in a regular weapons shop is, well, unrealistic. But even unrealistic things sometimes just happen!

Summary

In this chapter, we presented two ML tasks available in ML.NET: the `BinaryClassification` and `MulticlassClassification` catalogs. After briefly presenting the public API of both objects, we went through the canonical workflow of training and using a machine learning model that takes advantage of the services of the two ML tasks.

In the first part of the chapter, we discussed binary classification and went through data loading, validation, and feature engineering for a sentiment analysis problem. We then presented supported algorithms and their high-level pros and cons. Packaging of the model and using it from within a sample ASP.NET Core application completed the section.

The second part of the chapter was instead dedicated to the multiclass classification problem, and we went through the same workflow and steps for another family of problems.

Finally, the Devil's Advocate section took a deeper look at the sentiment analysis problem, particularly the impact that a poor prediction can have on the decisions that people (such as executives) must make for business reasons. Inevitably, the need for extremely accurate predictions (not strictly required by just any business context) moves practical solutions toward neural networks.

In the next chapter, we tackle clustering.

CHAPTER 6

Clustering Tasks

"It is only prudent never to place complete confidence in that by which we have even once been deceived."

—René Descartes, *Meditations on First Philosophy*, 1641

There are many different approaches to classify data, each with its own pros and cons. ML.NET supports quite a few of these approaches and implements them in native trainers. In Chapter 5, we use logistic regression and the Stochastic Dual Coordinate Ascent (SDCA) algorithm to classify items, but other options, which sometimes are more effective, exist as well—specifically, the Support Vector Machine (SVM) algorithm. SVM and other aforementioned algorithms have one trait in common: they need to know the expected value to predict for each row being processed during training.

However, there are circumstances in which the dataset lacks any preexisting knowledge for a classifier to learn from. Yet, in these circumstances, we sometimes need to group data in possibly homogeneous groups for business reasons. This makes a case for algorithms of unsupervised learning.

Clustering is an unsupervised machine learning technique that attempts to partition data rows into groups (referred to as *clusters*) made by elements reckoned to be in some way similar. The action of clustering develops without any previous knowledge of how the groups should look. In other words, you expect the clustering technique to tell you about groups of possibly related data rows you have in the dataset.

Let's focus on the ML.NET native tools to implement clustering and unsupervised learning.

The Clustering ML Task

In the classification and regression scenarios we examined so far, the resulting model connects input features to an expected outcome to let any sort of structural pattern hidden within the data emerge. Clustering, though, is a different kind of animal.

Unsupervised Learning

In a way, clustering algorithms perform a kind of creative work as they autonomously decide how to split data rows into the specified number of groups. Rows are fitted into a given cluster based on the algorithm's relationships with other data rows. In this context, the term *unsupervised* refers just to the fact that the algorithm proceeds without human supervision and returns a take-or-leave output. Various clustering algorithms depend on the definition of the distance applied to groups of data rows and the size of these groups.

Clustering returns rows partitioned in a given number of clusters, but each of these clusters is left unlabeled and is only identified by index. This means that the (business) reason for that specific way of grouping may not be obvious. It's up to the data science team to figure out what all the rows in each cluster have in common and put any meaningful label on each group.

There are two macro classes of unsupervised algorithms: those that need to receive the number of clusters as a hyperparameter and those that can both partition data rows and determine the ideal number of groups. It is crucial to remark that returned clusters always form a partition, meaning that the entire dataset is covered, and each element belongs to exactly one cluster.

A Look at the Available Training Data

For demonstrating the capabilities of the ML.NET clustering task, we're using a sample dataset available on Kaggle at *https://www.kaggle.com/roshansharma/mall-customers-clustering-analysis*. The dataset comes in the form of a comma-separated CSV file and represents the output of some initial processing of customers' data. Only a few columns have been selected from the raw data store, and aggregated columns have been computed. Still, all customers now belong to a unique group to be appropriately segmented into specific profiles.

Customer Segmentation

Customer segmentation is a canonical marketing activity that consists of dividing customers into groups. The logic behind the segmentation may vary according to a broad range of factors but is always in line with the company's business needs. Segmentation serves the purpose of targeting each group of customers through tailor-made campaigns. The dataset used in this chapter represents the customers of a mall, and customers are described through gender, age, and annual income.

In addition, each customer is assigned a calculated score that indicates the spending capacity. In the dataset, the spending capacity is a numeric value in the 1 to 100 range, where a higher value indicates a higher capacity. This is a good example of some other algorithm applied in advance to the dataset and based on some built-in views on top of the native data store.

Schema of the Data

The following C# class sets a 1:1 correspondence between the rows in the sample CSV file and the properties:

```
public class MallCustomerData
{
    [LoadColumn(0)]
    public int CustomerID { get; set; }
```

```
    [LoadColumn(1)]
    public string GenderText { get; set; }

    [LoadColumn(2)]
    public float Age { get; set; }

    [LoadColumn(3)]
    public float AnnualIncomeInK { get; set; }

    [LoadColumn(4)]
    public float SpendingScore { get; set; }

    [LoadColumn(5)]
    public float Gender { get; set; }
}
```

As you may have noticed, the class has two properties that refer to the gender of the anonymous customer: one is a string column named GenderText, and one is a float column named Gender. Why is that?

Applying Persistent Transformations

The original file available on Kaggle features a single gender column that contains Male and Female string values. (See Figure 6-1.)

1 Male	19	15	39
2 Male	21	15	81
3 Female	20	16	6
4 Female	23	16	77
5 Female	31	17	40
6 Female	22	17	76
7 Female	35	18	6
8 Female	23	18	94
9 Male	64	19	3
10 Female	30	19	72
11 Male	67	19	14
12 Female	35	19	99

FIGURE 6-1 A view of the sample dataset in Microsoft Excel

Clustering algorithms in ML.NET need float values so the original numeric values in the dataset must be turned into floats. Hence, the Male/Female string value must be rendered as a number. However, in this case, it's all about using two different numbers to indicate Male or Female. This is a transformation we can seriously consider making just once directly in the stored dataset instead of dynamically applying it repeatedly to any data processing pipeline. Therefore, we just add one column to the CSV file to render 1 for Male and 2 for Female. Starting from a CSV file, it is as easy as adding an Excel formula to the new column:

```
=IF(B2="Male", 1, 2)
```

The next step is to turn all numeric (integer) values into floats. Again, it's a simple transformation to make in Microsoft Excel. The dataset looks like Figure 6-2.

CustomerID	GenderText	Age	Annual Income (k$)	Spending Score (1-100)	Gender
1.0	Male	19.0	15.0	39.0	1.0
2.0	Male	21.0	15.0	81.0	1.0
3.0	Female	20.0	16.0	6.0	2.0
4.0	Female	23.0	16.0	77.0	2.0
5.0	Female	31.0	17.0	40.0	2.0
6.0	Female	22.0	17.0	76.0	2.0
7.0	Female	35.0	18.0	6.0	2.0
8.0	Female	23.0	18.0	94.0	2.0
9.0	Male	64.0	19.0	3.0	1.0
10.0	Female	30.0	19.0	72.0	2.0
11.0	Male	67.0	19.0	14.0	1.0

FIGURE 6-2 The dataset with float columns and categorized gender information

The same result can be achieved—and sometimes is even more desirable—via code-building a conversion pipeline, as shown here:

```
// Programming conversion of numeric columns into floats
var conversionPipeline = mlContext.Transforms.Conversion.ConvertType(new[]
    {
        new InputOutputColumnPair("GenderAsFloat", "Gender"),
        new InputOutputColumnPair("AgeAsFloat", "Age"),
        new InputOutputColumnPair("AnnualIncomeAsFloat", "AnnualIncomeInK"),
        new InputOutputColumnPair("SpendingScoreAsFloat", "SpendingScore"),
    },
    DataKind.Single);
```

The obtained pipeline must be appended to the training pipeline because it is not directly chainable to other feature engineering transformations you likely need to do, such as with one in particular: adding the Features column.

Modeling Data to Classes

A quick look at Figure 6-2 reveals that two columns in the original dataset may not be strictly needed for training: CustomerID and GenderAsText. The role of the latter has now been taken by the numerical column named Gender. As for CustomerID, that anonymous information about the actual customer may be interesting to maintain in the final clusters but doesn't help the trainer much. In fact, the column carries (anonymized) identity information but no informational content useful to clustering.

Anyway, following is the revised version of the C# class we're using with the ML.NET trainer. Note that the `CustomerID` column, which is not being used for training, retains its original integer type:

```csharp
public class MallCustomerData
{
    [LoadColumn(0)]
    public uint CustomerID { get; set; }

    [LoadColumn(2)]
    public float Age { get; set; }

    [LoadColumn(3)]
    public float AnnualIncomeInK { get; set; }

    [LoadColumn(4)]
    public float SpendingScore { get; set; }

    [LoadColumn(5)]
    public float Gender { get; set; }
}
```

Now, the second column in the original source—GenderAsText—is not mapped and will be ignored.

The selected dataset is not particularly large because it counts just 200 rows. In addition, it's all that we have, and no test dataset is also available. However, it should be noted that clustering is a very special type of problem closer to canonical data mining than to machine learning. Clustering is unsupervised. As a result, a clustering training algorithm won't get you a model you can call later to get a data prediction on input data. A clustering algorithm will just partition data in a way it determines to be appropriate. There's really no need to apply programmatic holdout and extract a dataset for testing or to apply more sophisticated techniques, such as k-fold validation in a clustering scenario. Clustering is just about making a run on the data and examining the results.

In light of this, what's the real purpose of data?

The Real Purpose of Data in Clustering

Most examples out there treat clustering as any other family of machine learning algorithms. Examples, therefore, show how to train and save a model and then how to invoke it later on some input data to get a prediction. One of the tutorials on the ML.NET website does this.

It starts from a very popular small dataset—the Iris dataset—that lists the measurements in centimeters of the length and width of sepals and petals for 50 flowers from 3 species of iris. Interestingly, the Iris dataset was created in 1936 by Ronald Fisher, a British statistician and biologist, to demonstrate the use of measurements in taxonomic problems.

Starting from the Iris dataset, the tutorial on the ML.NET website trains a model using the K-Means algorithm, saves a zip file out of it, and then calls it back passing a sample iris flower. While good for making sense of the core functionalities of the Clustering ML.NET task, the example goes more in the direction of unlabeled multiclass classification than clustering. Used in such a way, the available dataset discovers a fixed number of clusters, and then the model maps input data to one of these clusters identified by a numeric index rather than by name.

It should be clear that for clustering scenarios, the training phase is all you need. Also, it should be clear that the output is not a computation graph to invoke repeatedly. Instead, the output is subsets of the original dataset. Such subsets (clusters) are unlabeled, and it's up to the data science team to make sense of their content and assign each a meaningful label, which will ultimately reduce the starting problem to a multiclass classification scenario.

Clustering is particularly attractive when you end up with large and unstructured datasets to make sense of. At the end of the training, a clustering algorithm has detected similarities between rows and returns clusters. That's it—clustering is always the first step of a longer machine learning pipeline that typically ends in some sort of multiclass classification.

Let's see how to get clusters out of the mall customer data.

Feature Engineering

The inherent simplicity of the sample dataset reduces the data transformation phase to just one action—concatenating the input columns into a single array of numeric values. Here's how to obtain the Features column out of the data in the MallCustomerData class.

```
var pipeline = context.Transforms
        .Concatenate("Features", "Gender", "Age", "AnnualIncomeInK", "SpendingScore");
```

It is worth remarking that in this case, the data transformation pipeline is so short because we applied other possible data transformations directly to the original dataset file. Another reason for a very minimal data transformation pipeline lies in the nature of the problem itself. Clustering is for data segmentation, and the data to act on usually is extracted from some other data store using an Extract-Transform-Load (ETL) procedure. There's no reason why the ETL process should not return data ready-made for machine learning training or very close to the expected machine learning format.

Also, it is worth recalling that having a Features column populated with a numeric array of processing columns is a strict requirement of the training infrastructure of ML.NET. Figure 6-3 shows the value of the Features column during training.

The tree-based view represents the content of the first dataset row with columns such as Age, AnnualIncomeInK, SpendingScore, and Gender. In addition, the figure expands the content of the programmatically added Features column. As you can see, it is a vector of numeric values composed of the aforementioned columns. This vector is what any ML.NET trainer actually works on.

```
▲ ● preViewTransformedData={5 columns, 5 rows}
  ▷ ▦ ColumnView=Length = 5
  ▲ ▦ RowView=Length = 5
    ▲ ● [0]={5 columns}
      ▷ ● [0]={[Age, 19]}
      ▷ ● [1]={[AnnualIncomeInK, 15]}
      ▷ ● [2]={[SpendingScore, 39]}
      ▷ ● [3]={[Gender, 1]}
      ▲ ● [4]={[Features, {Dense vector of size 4}]}
          ▦ Key="Features"
        ▲ ▦ Value={Dense vector of size 4}
            ▦ IsDense=true
            ● Length=4
            ● _count=4
            ● _indices=null
          ▲ ● _values={float[4]}
              ● [0]=1
              ● [1]=19
              ● [2]=15
              ● [3]=39
    ▷ ● [1]={5 columns}
    ▷ ● [2]={5 columns}
    ▷ ● [3]={5 columns}
    ▷ ● [4]={5 columns}
    ▷ ⚙ Static members=
    ▷ ● Results View=Expanding the Results View will enumerate the IEnumerable
  ▷ ▦ Schema={5 columns}
  ▷ ⚙ Static members=
```

FIGURE 6-3 A sneak preview of the Features column during the training phase

Clustering Algorithms

The most popular clustering algorithm is K-Means. A frequently used variation of it is K-Modes. Yet another option is DBSCAN or, better yet, a generalization known as OPTICS.

The K-Means Algorithm

The K-Means algorithm works iteratively moving data rows across K assigned clusters. The purpose of iterations and moves is ensuring that all rows in each cluster fit uniformly around a center point. More specifically, as its initialization step, the algorithm selects K rows and sets each as the center of an empty cluster. The algorithm's jargon refers to the center of the cluster as the *centroid*.

Past the initialization step, remaining rows are iteratively assigned to one of the K clusters. Each row goes in the cluster for which the distance between the row and the centroid is minimal. When all rows have been assigned, K-Means recalculates the new centroid for each cluster. The *centroid* is now intended as the (virtual) data row in which each feature equals the mean of all feature values for all the rows in the cluster. Successive iterations move rows between clusters in such a way that each row still belongs to the cluster with the closest centroid. The algorithm ends after a fixed number of iterations or when no row is moved from the currently assigned cluster. Stop conditions are usually configurable as hyperparameters.

In K-Means, the distance between rows and centroids is expressed as the square of the Euclidean distance between points in an M-dimensional space, where M is the number of features in the dataset. The square is added for computational reasons to ensure a quicker convergence of the minimization function.

K-Means is a relatively seasoned algorithm that has been around since the 1960s. Despite its worst-case scenario complexity, which makes it an exponential NP-hard problem, the algorithm is usually fast and converges to a reasonable output in a polynomial time. However, there's no guarantee that convergence is to the global optimum.

The actual performance of K-Means, and the accuracy of its response, also depends on the initial selection of centroids. For this reason, some implementations run it multiple times with different starting conditions. Choosing initial centroids randomly is common but not certainly the best choice.

The K-Modes Algorithm

Based on the Euclidean distance, the K-Means algorithm requires features expressed through continuous float values. Instead, the K-Modes algorithm also works with categorical values or largely discrete numeric values.

The workflow of the two algorithms is nearly identical except for two aspects. One is the distance function being used. The other is the use of the mode rather than the mean in the definition of new centroids. (The mean is the average of a set of values; the mode is the most common number in a set of values.)

K-Modes measures the distance between centroids and data rows using a variation of the Hamming distance known as *dissimilarity*. In information theory, dissimilarity expresses the distance between two strings of equal length as the number of positions at which the corresponding symbols are different.

The (Right) Value of K

In K-Means and K-Modes, the value of K is a hyperparameter. Yet, picking the most appropriate value is a bit like stabbing in the dark. The ideal value would depend on the nature of the available data. At the same time, though, you use unsupervised learning, especially when you don't know much about the data!

As weird as it may sound, a random value for K is a common start—preferably a small number like 3 that will grow after a few attempts. However, there are some methods with a more solid mathematical foundation to evaluate the feasibility of the number of clusters once a first partition of the dataset has been obtained. One of these is the *elbow* method.

The *elbow* method works by computing the sum of the distances between the points in each cluster and the centroid. The more you grow K, the more the distances shrink because more attraction points (centroids) reduce the distance between rows in each cluster. However, the marginal gain that any additional cluster produces drops at some point, meaning that the elbow is reached, and we're really near the optimal K value for the dataset.

Another approach is the *silhouette* method that uses a metric to estimate how well each data row lies with its peers within the cluster. A value close to 1 means the row likely fits in the ideal cluster; a value close to −1 indicates that the row is probably placed in the wrong cluster. Based on the number of misplaced data rows, you can decide whether to increase the value of K.

The DBSCAN Algorithm

Both K-Means and K-Modes require that the number K of clusters is specified as a hyperparameter. This is often a problem, especially when you have no idea of the number of clusters that may be (reasonably) hidden in the dataset. Another family of algorithms, known as *density* algorithms, can perform clustering without requiring that a fixed number of clusters is set in advance. DBSCAN is the most popular density algorithm; OPTICS (discussed in the next section) is a generalization of DBSCAN that just attempts to fix the major downside of DBSCAN.

Short for Density-Based Spatial Clustering of Applications with Noise, DBSCAN is a relatively recent algorithm first proposed in the late 1990s. At the foundation of density-based clustering is the idea of grouping data rows that lie in a neighborhood defined by a distance. However, even density-based clustering algorithms need a barrier that stops the (inevitable) proliferation of clusters towards the ideal of one row per cluster.

The control that a fixed value of K exercises in K-Means and K-Modes algorithms is exercised in DBSCAN by the minimum number of points each cluster is required to have. During the iterations, rows in clusters with fewer elements than the minimum are considered outliers and moved to other clusters. The minimum number of points is referred to as the density. The value of the density is recommended to stay between three and the number of features in the dataset.

Another viable parameter of density-based algorithms is the *proximity*. Proximity refers to the maximum distance allowed between two data rows to consider them as neighbors and therefore part of the same cluster. In literature proximity is also often referred to as *eps* or *ε*.

It is crucial to note that in DBSCAN, proximity and density parameters can only be set for the entire dataset. This is the root cause of the major downside of DBSCAN. In fact, the algorithm might lose accuracy when set to work on a dataset with large differences in the density of data. (See Figure 6-4.)

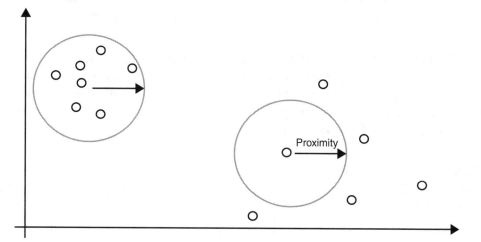

FIGURE 6-4 Representing a dataset with largely different data densities

In Figure 6-4, the gray circle and its radius provide a visual representation of a DBSCAN neighborhood. The radius indicates the proximity. When the dataset has largely sparse values finding the most appropriate (and dataset-wide) value for the parameter of proximity may be hard. From a high-level perspective, the dataset clearly has two groups, but the value of proximity that ideally captures the first is not good to get all the remaining points as a single group. However, growing the parameter of proximity would likely add points to a group that may just be outliers.

> **NOTE** How can we end up with largely different densities in a dataset? It's easier than one may think. For example, it suffices that the sampling rate of some kind of data collection changes at some point. Suddenly, that would generate more (or less) dense sequences of data points. Ideally, you should process different datasets or opt for a different algorithm that can better identify clusters with varying densities.

The OPTICS Algorithm

Short for Ordering Points To Identify the Clustering Structure, the OPTICS algorithm can be seen as a generalization of DBSCAN specifically designed to work around the varying densities drawback. Essentially, it does that by letting the proximity parameter grow dynamically on each cluster until it can reach out at least the predetermined minimum number of points. As a result, in dense regions of data (such as the top-left circle of Figure 6-4) the proximity value will be smaller than in other regions of the dataset.

The concept of proximity (or ε as in DBSCAN) evolves to the concept of *core distance* and is conventionally indicated as ε'. The *core distance* is intended as the smallest distance away from a data row that includes the predetermined minimum number of cluster elements. In other words, core distance is the variable version of the fixed proximity in DBSCAN. Hence, unlike DBSCAN, the OPTICS algorithm only has one mandatory hyperparameter—the density or the minimum number of rows in a cluster.

> **NOTE** Most implementations of OPTICS still require developers to specify a value for the minimum proximity. Although the parameter is not strictly required to guarantee the convergence of the algorithm, having it set to a reasonably small value reduces the algorithm's runtime. The computational complexity of OPTICS is *NlogN*, but it grows to N^2 if the proximity is left unspecified and then assumed to be infinite.

While more accurate in cases of largely variable densities, the OPTICS algorithm is more resource-consuming than DBSCAN. It eats more memory and uses a more expensive logic for nearest neighbor queries. At the same time, it depends only on one hyperparameter.

Another aspect to consider about OPTICS is that it doesn't return an array of row collections. Instead, it merely extracts an ordered sequence of reachability distances whose interpretation is left to the developer or, more likely, to the data science team. Technically, the reachability distance is the maximum of the core distance and the distance between two rows.

Composing the Training Pipeline

The choice of the trainer is usually a delicate step because, as an ML.NET engineer, you have many choices from IntelliSense and often limited knowledge about the internals of the various algorithms and the impact that available data may have on each of them. Data science skills are required to make a savvy choice.

However, as far as clustering in ML.NET is concerned, things are much easier because the offering of algorithms is limited to just one. While the number of supported algorithms will likely increase in the future, the current downside is that if the only supported algorithm (K-Means) doesn't work well, you have to code it on your own, perhaps starting from some open-source implementation. As an alternative, you can build and train a model in Python using scikit-learn (where more clustering algorithms are available) and import it in ML.NET through the NimbusML module.

> **NOTE** NimbusML is a Python library that provides bindings for ML.NET, thus enabling smooth integration of scikit-learn pipelines into ML.NET code. Therefore, by means of NimbusML, you have access to the whole set of algorithms in scikit-learn, including those for clustering that are missing in the native ML.NET packages.

Running the K-Means Algorithm

It doesn't take that many lines of code to run K-Means over a dataset. You need to get an instance of the selected trainer object and append it to the data processing pipeline, as shown here:

```
// Configure the pipeline with data transformations and trainer
var trainer = mlContext.Clustering.Trainers.KMeans("Features", numberOfClusters: 5);
var pipeline = mlContext.Transforms
    .Concatenate("Features", "Gender", "Age", "AnnualIncomeInK", "SpendingScore")
    .Append(trainer);
```

Invoking the Fit method on the pipeline generates the trained model. If you intend to save it to a zip file, you just add the same code used in past chapters:

```
var model = pipeline.Fit(dataset);
mlContext.Model.Save(model, dataset.Schema, modelPath);
```

We've repeatedly mentioned that training algorithms are driven by hyperparameters. However, we haven't provided an example of how hyperparameters can be configured. Each ML.NET trainer has an overloaded constructor that accepts an Options class. The KMeans trainer is no exception. Interestingly, the list of hyperparameters is not limited to known parametric input of the general algorithm (clusters, tolerance, iterations), but also includes configurable parameters specific to the ML.NET internal implementation of trainers (memory budget, threads).

K-Means Options in ML.NET

In our sample code, the K-Means trainer is explicitly passed two parameters: the name of the feature column and the desired number of clusters. However, more parameters are available as listed in the `KMeansTrainer.Options` class. Values in the code below refer to the default configuration of the class and the actual values being passed to the trainer if not otherwise specified.

```
// Default options for K-Means in ML.NET
var kmo = new KMeansTrainer.Options
{
        NumberOfClusters = 5,
        FeatureColumnName = "Features",
        MaximumNumberOfIterations = 1000,
        InitializationAlgorithm = KMeansTrainer.InitializationAlgorithm.KMeansPlusPlus,
        OptimizationTolerance = (float) Math.Pow(10, -7),
        AccelerationMemoryBudgetMb = 4096,
        NumberOfThreads = null,
        ExampleWeightColumnName = null
};
var trainer = mlContext.Clustering.Trainers.KMeans(kmo);
```

Let's find out more about each single option parameter.

As mentioned, `FeatureColumnName` sets the name of the aptly created column containing each row's input values to be taken into account for training the model. The `NumberOfClusters` property refers to the desired number of clusters. The `MaximumNumberOfIterations` property sets an unsurmountable, upper limit to the iterations, after which the K-Means algorithm has to stop and return the current configuration of clusters. The `InitializationAlgorithm` parameter indicates how initial centroids are chosen. ML.NET offers three options for the `InitializationAlgorithm`, as shown in Table 6-1.

TABLE 6-1 Supported K-Means initialization algorithms

Algorithm	Description
KMeansPlusPlus	Default value; refers to the KMeans++ algorithm proposed in 2007 and is considered the most popular and reliable to make the most out of the traditional K-Means. It is demonstrated that the method reshapes K-Means to make it deliver a solution that is at most only O(log K) worse than the optimal solution.
KMeansYinyang	Refers to an even more recent algorithm (proposed in 2015 by a Microsoft Research team). The Yinyang algorithm delivers a significant performance gain, the key of which is the initial clustering of centroids that makes a good deal of subsequent distance computations unnecessary.
Random	Initial centroids are selected randomly. This might lead to potentially bad approximations with respect to the optimal clustering.

The `OptimizationTolerance` parameter refers to the accepted tolerance that would ensure the convergence of the trainer. The algorithm ends after the maximum number of iterations or when no data rows need to be moved because they are sufficiently close to the centroid. The optimization tolerance sets the minimum accepted distance.

The `AccelerationMemoryBudgetMb` property represents the maximum amount of memory to reserve for speeding up the algorithm. The `NumberOfThreads` property is a nullable integer referring to the number of threads to use and gives a measure of allowed lock-free parallelism. By default, trainers figure it out automatically.

Finally, the `ExampleWeightColumnName` refers to the name of an optional column that ML.NET allows you to specify to assign a specific coefficient (weight) to each data column in the dataset. In this way, you can tell the algorithm to give more (or less) relevance to some specific columns of the dataset.

Setting Up a Client Application

By design, in ML.NET, all training pipelines return a chain of transformers good for serialization and later calls. This pattern is great for scenarios like regression and classification but not for clustering. In clustering, we're not typically interested in serializing a set of transformations to replicate later on unseen input data. Instead, we're mainly interested in one-off processing of the dataset that returns a fixed number of partitions based on some detected similarity among the rows.

In other words, the typical output of a clustering algorithm is a list of files that forms a partition of the original dataset. In ML.NET, some extra code is required to get this.

Inspecting the Transformed Dataset

Unlike the other chapters in this book, the sample code for this chapter won't be a web application. Instead, the sample code is just the trainer program we're discussing here. It takes an input dataset and creates many text files partitioning the original dataset into the specified number of clusters.

```
// Runs K-Means and returns the transformed dataset
var transformedDataView = pipeline.Fit(dataset).Transform(dataset);
```

The code above first builds a model (chain of transformers trained on the given dataset) and then applies the obtained transformations to the same input dataset. The output is a lazy object you can turn into a familiar .NET enumerable collection.

```
var enumerable = mlContext.Data
    .CreateEnumerable<MallCustomerPrediction>(transformedDataView, reuseRowObject: false)
    .ToList();
```

Figure 6-5 shows a sneak preview of the data stored in the `transformedDataView` variable of type `IDataView`.

The actual type of the `transformedDataView` variable is `ClusteringScorer`—an internal type of ML.NET that implements `IDataView`. The two schema properties you see in Figure 6-5 are the `DataViewSchema` type. Interestingly, after running K-Means on the given customer's dataset, the output schema contains eight columns—the five defined in the `MallCustomersData` class plus `Features`, and the two output columns generated by the K-Means algorithm (`PredictedLabel` and `Score`). All these columns will be bounded by the properties of any output prediction class.

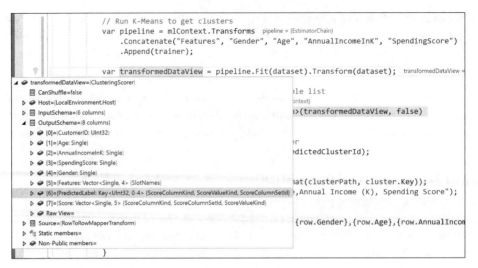

```
            // Run K-Means to get clusters
            var pipeline = mlContext.Transforms   pipeline = {EstimatorChain}
                .Concatenate("Features", "Gender", "Age", "AnnualIncomeInK", "SpendingScore")
                .Append(trainer);

            var transformedDataView = pipeline.Fit(dataset).Transform(dataset);   transformedDataView =
```

transformedDataView={ClusteringScorer}
- CanShuffle=false   le list
- ▷ ● Host={LocalEnvironment.Host}   ntext}
- ▷ ▥ InputSchema={6 columns}   }>(transformedDataView, false)
- ▲ ▥ OutputSchema={8 columns}
  - ▷ ● [0]={CustomerID: UInt32}
  - ▷ ● [1]={Age: Single}   er
  - ▷ ● [2]={AnnualIncomeInK: Single}   dictedClusterId);
  - ▷ ● [3]={SpendingScore: Single}
  - ▷ ● [4]={Gender: Single}
  - ▷ ● [5]={Features: Vector<Single, 4> {SlotNames}   at(clusterPath, cluster.Key));
  - ▷ ● [6]={PredictedLabel: Key<UInt32, 0-4> {ScoreColumnKind, ScoreValueKind, ScoreColumnSetId} ,Annual Income (K), Spending Score");
  - ▷ ● [7]={Score: Vector<Single, 5> {ScoreColumnKind, ScoreColumnSetId, ScoreValueKind}
  - ▷ ● Raw View=
- ▷ ▥ Source={RowToRowMapperTransform}   {row.Gender},{row.Age},{row.AnnualIncom
- ▷ ⁛ Static members=
- ▷ ● Non-Public members=
```
            }
```

FIGURE 6-5 The schema of transformed data view

Binding Output Columns to a C# Class

The following code shows our C# class used to capture the rows of the transformed dataset:

```csharp
public class MallCustomerPrediction
{
    [KeyType(5)]          // 5 is the number of clusters
    [ColumnName("PredictedLabel")]
    public uint PredictedClusterId;

    [ColumnName("Score")]
    public float[] Distances;

    // Copy columns from source data (automatically bound to source data)
    public uint CustomerID { get; set; }
    public float Gender { get; set; }
    public float Age { get; set; }
    public float AnnualIncomeInK { get; set; }
    public float SpendingScore { get; set; }
}
```

The autogenerated PredictedLabel column is mapped to the (custom) PredictedClusterId property, whereas the other autogenerated column Score maps to Distances. All other columns map one to one to the output columns as in the schema in Figure 6-5.

The KeyType attribute instructs the ML.NET training engine to consider the marked integer property as theKeyDataViewType—a special type of enum ranging from 1 to the specified number. In this case, the upper bound is the number of requested clusters. In our example, the PredictedClusterId property takes values in the range 1 to 5.

Saving Clusters to Separate Files

The next step is to enable our code to access the transformed data and manipulate it as easily and effectively as possible with .NET enumerable collections and LINQ. Here's how to extract an `IEnumerable` collection from the transformed dataset:

```
// Turn the transformed model into a .NET enumerable list
var enumerable = mlContext.Data
    .CreateEnumerable<MallCustomerPrediction>(transformedDataView, reuseRowObject: false)
    .ToList();
```

At this point, using the grouping capabilities of LINQ, we can easily obtain distinct datasets, one per cluster, ready to save to disk as text or CSV files:

```
// Create one CSV file per identified cluster
var clusters = enumerable.GroupBy(r => r.PredictedClusterId);
foreach (var cluster in clusters)
{
    var writer = File.CreateText(string.Format(clusterPath, cluster.Key));
    writer.WriteLine($"CustomerID, Gender, Age, Annual Income (K), Spending Score");
    foreach (var row in cluster)
    {
        writer.WriteLine($"{row.CustomerID}, {row.Gender}, {row.Age}, {row.AnnualIncomeInK},
                         {row.SpendingScore}");
    }

    writer.Close();
}
```

Figure 6-6 shows the output folder when the training program ends.

Name	Date modified	Type
Mall-Customers-Cluster-1.txt	4/7/2021 12:23 PM	Text Document
Mall-Customers-Cluster-2.txt	4/7/2021 12:23 PM	Text Document
Mall-Customers-Cluster-3.txt	4/7/2021 12:23 PM	Text Document
Mall-Customers-Cluster-4.txt	4/7/2021 12:23 PM	Text Document
Mall-Customers-Cluster-5.txt	4/7/2021 12:23 PM	Text Document

FIGURE 6-6 The output folder of the training folder with freshly created cluster files

What happens if you run clustering multiple times on the same dataset and with the same hyperparameters? The partition remains the same, but the indexes of the clusters may be shuffled. Figure 6-7 shows the content of one of the cluster files created by the training program.

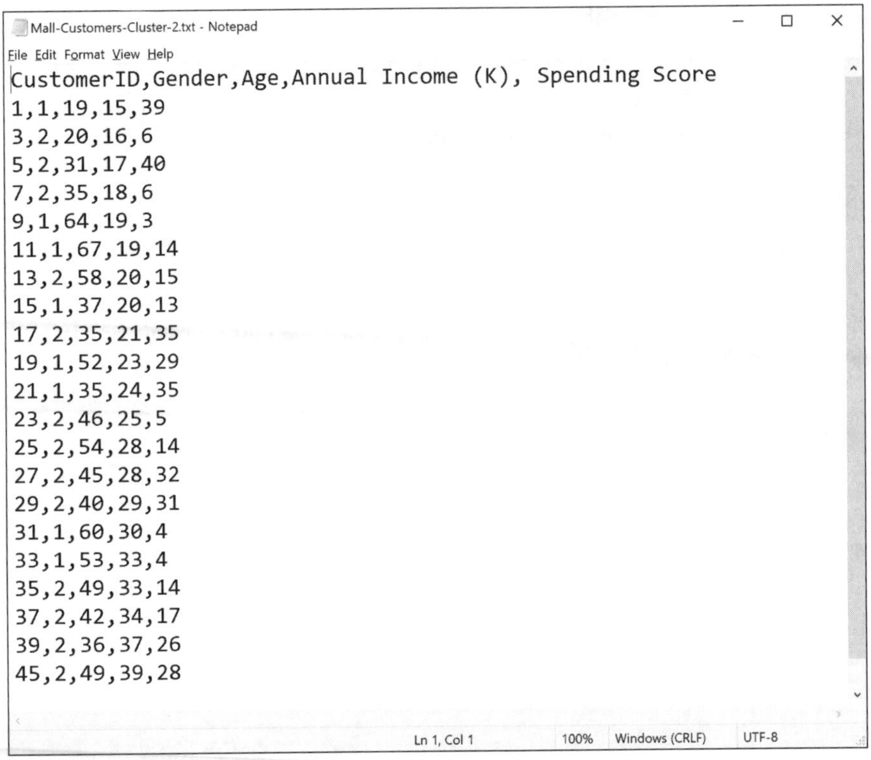
Mall-Customers-Cluster-2.txt - Notepad

File Edit Format View Help

```
CustomerID,Gender,Age,Annual Income (K), Spending Score
1,1,19,15,39
3,2,20,16,6
5,2,31,17,40
7,2,35,18,6
9,1,64,19,3
11,1,67,19,14
13,2,58,20,15
15,1,37,20,13
17,2,35,21,35
19,1,52,23,29
21,1,35,24,35
23,2,46,25,5
25,2,54,28,14
27,2,45,28,32
29,2,40,29,31
31,1,60,30,4
33,1,53,33,4
35,2,49,33,14
37,2,42,34,17
39,2,36,37,26
45,2,49,39,28
```

Ln 1, Col 1 | 100% | Windows (CRLF) | UTF-8

FIGURE 6-7 A sample cluster file created by the K-Means algorithm

The ML Devil's Advocate

To make our usual counter-exam of the clustering task, let's just start from the five text files listed in Figure 6-6, each containing a subset of the original dataset as created by the K-Means algorithm.

Clustering Is Always the First Step

As most datasets in the real world are—at least initially—large, sparse, and poorly structured, clustering is an effective tool for marketing and business analysts to perform surface-level scans of data and to mine data insights. As the sample dataset used in this chapter proves, clustering excels at profiling customers, whether for spending capacity, demographics, or geographical location.

Clustering has virtually infinite fields of applications in domains ranging from market segmentations to social network analysis, from detection of any sort of anomalies to document grouping and, in general, in any applications where filtering, grouping, and/or ranking of data is required.

By the rule of thumb, if you land on machine learning, then inevitably, at some point, you'll be using clustering. Even though ML.NET presents clustering as one algorithmic task, the reality is that clustering is different from all other tasks such as regression, classification, ranking, and the like. From a business perspective, clustering is in a way closer to data preparation than it is a prediction for a specific problem. In this regard, it is mostly the means, and rarely the end, of a machine learning task.

Although clustering may belong to any real-world machine learning pipeline, it is often only the first step of a longer workflow. We already said (and will repeat it here): There's no such thing as a single algorithm trained and put in production in the real world. Even problems that can be easily matched to one well-known task (for example, regression, anomaly detection, or classification) in the real world requires a multistep pipeline and the involvement of multiple machine learning modules. One of these is almost always a clustering module.

Want an example?

Figure 6-6 presents five text files created from an initial dataset. The original dataset has therefore been split into five subsets. Presumably, K-Means detected relevant similarities in the data rows placed in each subset. Yet, each subset is unlabeled and only identified by index. The content of each cluster should be carefully analyzed from a business perspective, and appropriate labels should be defined to reflect the actual content. At that point, you have a fully labeled dataset ready for a canonical form of supervised learning.

Unsupervised Reduction of the Dataset

The practical problem that clustering addresses is helping make sense of large and unstructured data. So now imagine you have a very large dataset with plans to run it on some canonical forms of supervised learning. The humongous size of the dataset is a big obstacle. You might not have sufficient computer power or the time it could take to train such a huge block of data.

This is where unsupervised learning comes into play.

Other techniques exist side by side with clustering to simplify the dataset's structure —for example, cutting down the number of features (columns) and/or the number of rows.

Reducing the Number of Features

There are two nonexclusive approaches to reduce the number of features in a dataset: feature selection and feature extraction. Feature selection comprises a set of techniques aimed at *selecting* columns of data that look more relevant. Feature extraction, instead, is about merging more columns into one or adding new columns that better represent the same information than a few existing ones.

When there is no reliable domain knowledge to state the limited value of some features, you can use a number of techniques to evaluate the relevance of a given feature algorithmically:

- **Heatmaps** A heatmap shows the correlation between a feature and the target value the model is expected to predict. A low correlation might indicate that the feature can be safely dropped.

- **Variance threshold**   Variance threshold addresses features whose values always fall into a limited range of values. Columns whose variance falls below a given threshold can be flagged for removal.

- **Correlation analysis**   Measures the level of correlation of two features. If they look particularly correlated, then the same model accuracy can be obtained by keeping only one of the two.

Sometimes, though, a deeper refactoring is necessary to go beyond the simple removal of a few columns. Feature extraction focuses on the need to keep information constant while reducing the number of columns that carry it. Here are a few specific techniques:

- **Grouping of sparse data**   When a column has categorical content, you might want to merge some of the distinct options into a larger category.

- **Computed features**   You may decide that the information spread over two or more columns can be safely represented by a new column with a new set of values, and you replace all such columns with a new one. For example, imagine you have columns with the cost and time of a taxi ride. You may decide that a new column may effectively represent the same information that is valuable in a given scenario at hand. Therefore, you may replace cost and time with a categorical value, such as short-, medium-, or long-range.

- **Dimensionality reduction**   It's the umbrella term for a number of data transformation techniques aimed at algorithmically compressing two or more columns into one. An extremely popular technique is Principal Component Analysis (PCA), which essentially projects the dataset originally sitting in an N-dimensional space to a space with a smaller number of dimensions. Note, though, that dimensionality reduction is not simply about dropping some of the least relevant columns. Instead, the projection algorithm tries to linearly combine multiple columns to render the same information through a smaller number of columns. It's clearly lossy transformation, but hopefully, it's not painfully impacting the prediction capabilities of the resulting model.

Using Clusters to Reduce Rows

If the dataset is too large for effective processing, how can you cut rows from it without altering the actual knowledge in the dataset?

You can make a pass of K-Means (or another unsupervised algorithm) on the dataset and get a number of clusters of rows. The success record of K-Means guarantees that data in the clusters are sufficiently homogeneous. Then, you build a new, smaller dataset by picking a few rows from each cluster. This ensures you get a smaller dataset with the same level of homogeneity as the original one.

Summary

In this chapter, we discussed unsupervised learning and presented and commented on a number of clustering algorithms. Of the various known (classes of) algorithms, only the K-Means algorithm is natively supported by ML.NET.

More importantly, we stressed the role that unsupervised learning plays in machine learning projects. Clustering is not directly the solution to a business problem but, more often than not, it is only a preliminary step of a longer and more sophisticated machine learning pipeline. In light of this, most of the tutorials and examples that train a clustering model and then use it as a plain classifier, just don't make sense. Although they can still make predictions, they do not actually solve any real-world problems.

The most common scenario for clustering is to run a surface-level analysis of a dataset, get unlabeled clusters of presumably homogeneous rows, make sense of the content, add a label column, and reformulate the original problem as an instance of multiclass classification.

Clustering is not free of issues.

For example, dealing with large number of dimensions and a large number of data rows can make any solution overwhelmingly problematic because of time complexity. In addition, the method's effectiveness depends on the definition of the "distance." Subsequently, a deep knowledge of the domain is required. Finally, the results of the clustering algorithm (often arbitrary) must be interpreted by experts and can be interpreted in different ways by different people.

CHAPTER 7

Anomaly Detection Tasks

"Truths of this kind should be drawn from notions rather than from notations".
—*Carl Friedrich Gauss, Disquisitiones Arithmeticae, 1801*

In data mining and machine learning, anomaly detection refers to the steps necessary to identify unusual occurrences of items in an amount of data that might be quite large. At the same time, many high-level business problems can be formulated as instances of the core anomaly detection problem, such as detecting bots in web pages, spotting outliers in sales reports, flagging suspicious fraudulent behaviors, and monitoring the health of industrial machines. Furthermore, in machine learning, anomaly detection is also used to remove outliers from a dataset to augment the accuracy of a model being trained on it.

In a nutshell, anomaly detection is the umbrella term for a class of machine learning methods and algorithms aimed at solving—directly or as part of a more sophisticated pipeline—a number of complex real-world problems. In ML.NET, these methods are grouped under the programming interface of the `AnomalyDetection` catalog.

In this chapter, we just focus only on anomaly detection and introduce concepts such as spikes and change points. This chapter is tightly related to Chapter 8, where we discuss time series analysis.

What Is an Anomaly?

While "anomaly detection" is the moniker for a specific class of machine learning methods, the common definition of "anomaly detection" leads to a variety of domain-specific problems—often in a restricted and very specific business context, such as fraud detection, predictive maintenance, or unusual activities like bots and cyberattacks.

However, such (complex) business problems can hardly be solved by picking and training a single (numerical) algorithm from a catalog. More realistically, such problems sometimes find a solution in a pipeline of neural networks and sometimes are reformulated (and then solved) as regression or classification problems.

Therefore, the meaning of the expression "anomaly detection" is prone to a broader interpretation than are the names of other machine learning tasks such as "regression" or "classification." On the one hand, anomaly detection is the umbrella that covers a number of statistical techniques to

119

spot anomalous values in a column of data. On the other hand, in the collective imagination, anomaly detection refers to concrete business problems. Being aware of these two levels of abstraction is crucial to finding effective solutions to business problems.

All this said, let's focus on the mathematical techniques known to identify spikes and outliers in a given dataset.

General Approaches to Detect Anomalies

Anomalies found in an otherwise regular flow of data are not necessarily the post-mortem sign of an occurred incident. They can also be the indicator of some new trend in data, such as the functioning of a machine (indicating a possible upcoming fault) or the behavior of customers (denoting a possible business opportunity).

A precondition to detecting anomalies is the availability of a large dataset that tracks the operational performance of systems and/or machines. An anomaly in this volume of data is any significant deviation of logged data from the usual pattern.

Time Series Data

A time series is a series of values captured sequentially at successive (and possibly equidistant) points in time. Examples of time series are the audit log of a software service, intraday values of a stock in an exchange market, or the historical status of critical indicators in a mechanical component, such as a pump or turbine. At its core, each record in a time series is made of two data items: the value and the time it refers to.

What is a deviation from the usual pattern? And more importantly, how do we define the "usual pattern"?

The Usual Pattern

For a baseline to make educated guesses from time-series data, it should be initially set to define what is meant by normal behavior in the specific business context. Normally, this is done through one or more Key Performance Indicators (KPI). A KPI is any measurable value determined to be helpful to demonstrate the effectiveness of a business activity. Anomalies are recorded deviations from the expected value of a KPI at a given point in time.

A KPI, however, is more than just numbers in a given range. A KPI needs context to be effective. The number of sales, for example, is normally a good indicator of the health of the business. However, a number that is just above average is not good for each day of the year. For example, sales that are just a bit over average on Black Friday aren't necessarily a good sign and likely aren't following the expected trend.

Therefore, the "usual pattern" is not simply a min/max pair of lines, with everything outside the range being considered unusual. Deep analysis of time series data should also be able to recognize expected cyclical occurrences of data, such as a significant growth of sales at certain times of the year.

A per standard usage, I've been marking this tailor-made, but this nonstandard usage has been pretty consistent throughout. anomaly detection software system should be aware of KPIs, and because it knows the information in time series data, it should catch true outliers in KPIs and report various levels of alarms. Machine learning is not strictly needed to do effective anomaly detection. Expert systems (and manually crafted decision trees) might easily do the job. If small quantities of data are involved, simple statistical methods (such as what lies outside the interquartile range)—and even an expert human eye—can be enough to report anomalies effectively.

Unfortunately, though, data can deviate from the usual pattern in different ways, and businesses need to react promptly to moving trends—creating a need for automated anomaly detection tools.

Classification of Outliers

Broadly speaking, anomalies (or outliers) can be classified into three different groups:

- **Point outliers**   The simplest and most intuitive scenario is when a single instance of data is caught too far off from the rest of the dataset. For example, an exceptionally high consumption of electricity or a not-so-common amount spent on a credit card are point outliers.

- **Contextual outliers**   Suppose you have a vacation home you live in only in the summer. The consumption of electricity is very low most of the year and higher for a few weeks, say, in July. If you blindly focus only on numbers, then a significantly higher summer consumption looks odd. However, it is normal if you consider that someone is living in the house at that time. Another example of a contextual outlier is the sales of a grocery shop during the year. An average of $200 per customer per day might be considered normal in the holiday season but not during the rest of the year. More generally, outliers can be context-specific and follow seasonal patterns.

- **Collective outliers**   Collective outliers refer to data items that, taken individually, are neither point nor contextual outliers. However, if considered as a collection, they look unusual and deviate remarkably from the other data items within the dataset.

Figure 7-1 offers a graphical representation of the various types of outliers. Point outliers are clearly visible spikes in an otherwise regular line chart. A contextual outlier breaks the regularity of some repeating pattern in the line chart. As in the Contextual Outlier section of the figure, an unexpected low point appears where a significantly higher was expected, well rendered by the grayed segment. Finally, let's focus on the collectinve outlier section. All values plotted fall in an acceptable range and don't even abruptly break a repeating pattern. The problem, however, is that out-of-schema values last for too long, and the temporal amplitude of the deviation makes it an anomalous situation.

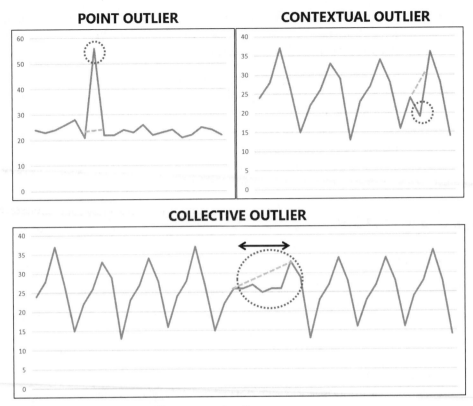

FIGURE 7-1 Graphical view of different types of outliers

> **NOTE** The dashed gray lines you can see in Figure 7-1 are not simply a visual aid to help you make sense of why an outlier was detected. They also provide a rather intuitive explanation of why anomaly detection algorithms mark certain values as outliers. Algorithms track the expected value internally and measure the deviation!

Statistical Techniques

Time series datasets are built by sampling data very frequently. For example, the sensors embedded in industrial machines (such as turbines, pumps, and elevators) save their state at least every few minutes. Typically, the state is made by a few dozen signals. Each signal makes for a distinct time series. How would you go through this mass of data?

There are a number of statistical methods to spot irregularities in a time series quickly. In the end, it's all about identifying the data points that deviate by a certain quantity from one of many well-known statistical properties of a distribution, such as the mean, median, or mode. (As a reminder, the *mean* is the average of values in a data series, the *mode* is the value that appears more often, and the *median* is the middle number in a sorted series.)

However, static observation of data is not necessarily accurate because data values can be subject to random, short-term fluctuations because of occasional working conditions and unpredictable electronic glitches. A *moving average* is a type of data analysis that doesn't look at point values but computes the average across multiple data points. When you have established the amplitude of the moving window—namely the number of sequential data points to consider—the resulting time series delivers a more stable view of the data because it smooths short-term fluctuations and highlights long-term fluctuations.

There are different types of moving averages. The simplest just uses the arithmetic mean of values detected in the established window of time. More sophisticated types of moving averages assign some weights to more recent values. This is the case for the exponential moving average.

> **NOTE** A data trend is an indicator of how values increase/decrease over time in a time series, whether linearly, exponentially, or stabilizing at some point (damped trend).

Machine Learning Approaches

Beyond basic statistical techniques, any approach to anomaly detection falls in the realm of machine learning and hits supervised or unsupervised learning.

Supervised Classification

As we've seen in Chapter 5, "Classification Tasks," supervised classification (whether binary or multi-class) starts from the foundation of having one label column in the dataset that determines the truth. An anomaly detection–specific problem can be formulated as a binary or multiclass classification problem as long as a dataset exists with labels that clarify what should be intended as normal and what *is* abnormal. It goes without saying that a basic normal/abnormal label makes for a binary classification instance, whereas the presence of more types of abnormal behavior makes for a multiclass classification instance.

Another supervised approach to anomaly detection passes through density-based exploration algorithms, the most popular of which is K-nearest neighbor (KNN). KNN assumes that similar data items lie together in a relatively small neighborhood. Hence, the distance between data items (whatever measure of a distance is appropriate for the type of data) is significantly higher for data items that represent an abnormal status.

> **NOTE** The K-nearest neighbor algorithm finds its natural fit in the context of recommendation problems. For this reason, we'll return to it in much greater detail in Chapter 9, "Recommendation Tasks," which is entirely devoted to the most effective techniques for suggesting relevant items to users.

Unsupervised Clustering

When no prior knowledge of the data exists, and it is impossible (or just impractical) to label data items as normal or abnormal, an unsupervised learning approach is in order. In Chapter 6, "Clustering Tasks," we presented K-Means and discussed other clustering, density-based algorithms. In the context of clustering, an outlier is a data item that doesn't fall into any identified clusters.

Local Outlier Factor (LOF) is an interesting variation of density-based algorithms specifically devised to capture outliers. Conceptually based on the same principles of DBSCAN and OPTICS (see Chapter 6), LOF labels a data item as an outlier if the item is farther from its neighbors than the average distance between every other pair of neighbors (see Figure 7-2).

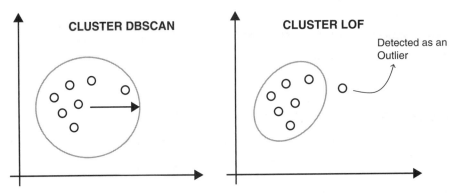

FIGURE 7-2 DBSCAN and LOF clusters around the same set of data points

The same set of data items is rendered in Figure 7-2 with a cluster as computed by DBSCAN and LOF. As you can see, DBSCAN includes all points falling with a radius of a globally set length in the cluster. As a result, no outliers are detected. Instead, LOF defines a cluster as made by all the data items that are close enough to form a very dense agglomerate. As a result, just one data item slightly farther from all the others is flagged as being a potential outlier. In other words, DBSCAN works on data globally, whereas LOF works locally and can be (in some cases) much more precise than DBSCAN or OPTICS. At the same time, the same figure clearly raises the doubt as to whether the point detected as an outlier should really be considered as such. As usual, it depends!

Isolation Forest should be applied. This approach assumes the data has a static distribution, which statistical models can describe, and flags the data points with values that are not within the approved range of the distribution as outliers. The most popular ML algorithms applicable to this approach include K-means clustering, proximity-based techniques (such as Gaussian/Elliptic Envelope), Isolation Forest (a class of the decision tree-based method), and One Class Support Vector Machine (SVM).

Semi-supervised Learning

Algorithms that start from a known notion of normality but lack an accurate definition of abnormality also fall under the umbrella of semi-supervised learning. The dataset might contain labels for data items regarded as normal and might miss labels for other items that might be normal.

In general, semi-supervised learning applied to anomaly detection consists of first running a canonical supervised algorithm to spot what is normal, followed by an unsupervised method (such as K-Means) that separates normal items from the rest. Therefore, the semi-supervised approach works well in abundant normal data, but it's very hard to find abnormal data. A real-world example of this is fault detection in industrial machines. Technically, these scenarios are referred to as *noise removal* or *novelty detection*.

To be precise, there is a difference between noise removal and novelty detection. The former refers to the process of cleaning the dataset from unwanted or patently abnormal observations that in a real-world monitoring system can be due to malfunctioning or occasional electronic peaks. Novelty detection is more concerned with discovering very rare patterns in data or, even better, the appearance of previously never observed data patterns.

A popular algorithm for such forms of semi-supervised learning is the One Class Support Vector Machine (OCSVM), which is a special (unsupervised) variation of a famous supervised algorithm—the Support Vector Machine (SVM). The logic employed by OCSVM departs from the logic of SVM. Instead of looking for a hyperplane to split the dataset in two—leaving the maximum possible margin between subspaces—it uses the concept of a hypersphere to include the maximum possible data points. All remaining points are flagged as outliers.

The Anomaly Detection ML Task

In the rest of this chapter, we'll focus on the built-in features of ML.NET, which is tailored to face anomaly detection problems. In particular, we'll look at some of the methods exposed by the AnomalyDetection catalog. In this chapter, we'll focus on detecting spikes (point anomalies) and change points, meaning when the behavior of a time series changes significantly.

> **NOTE** Until now, we haven't mentioned *change points,* so let's define it now. In statistics, a change point is where the behavior of a time series changes significantly and, more importantly, persistently. A change point is not simply an outlier and not even a collective outlier. Outliers are anomalous observations, even repeated over a certain amount of time, after which the time series returns to its previous pattern. Instead, a change point sets a definitive deviation from a previously recognized pattern. In change point detection, different approaches are used for offline detection (post-mortem analysis) and online detection (stream analysis).

A Look at the Available Training Data

In this chapter, we'll be using a popular time series dataset packed with three years of total shampoo sales. It is very similar to the dataset used by one of the ML.NET anomaly detection tutorials.

> **NOTE** Originally created by Rob Hyndman, Professor of Statistics at Monash University, Australia, the dataset can be found at *https://github.com/FinYang/tsdl/blob/master/data-raw/data/shampoo.dat*. Note that the same GitHub repository contains an amazing number of other time-series datasets.

Univariate and Multivariate Time Series

In any time-series datasets, all data items (such as observations) are ordered by the time they occurred. The order is immutable and part of the informational content. Typically, a time series has two columns—time and value. These simple time series are referred to as *univariate* time series.

Univariate time series are easy to plot, and the resulting chart intuitively and clearly indicates the data trends and clues of possible seasonality. Figure 7-3 shows the line chart directly built from the value of columns of the sample shampoo dataset. As you can see, this univariate time series shows a linearly growing trend and shows a seasonal pattern because of the succession of higher and lower values.

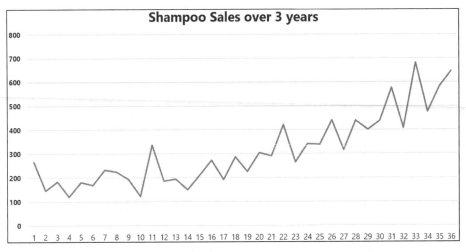

FIGURE 7-3 Line chart of the shampoo sales dataset

A multivariate time series is a time series in which multiple values are recorded over time at equidistant intervals. Wind turbine monitoring is a good example of a multivariate time series when data such as weather temperature and pressure, wind speed and direction, salinity and humidity, plus a ton of other mechanical parameters are dumped every few seconds. Realistically, it can be over 50 different signals often captured every 10 to 30 seconds.

Techniques to deal with multivariate time series need to be much more sophisticated than with univariate series because each observed signal depends not only on its past values but also on other signals. The issue is not just the horizontal complexity that can result from intra-signal dependencies, especially with multivariate time series. The higher relevance of (cross signal) changes that can occur over subsequent observations also is an issue. For example, a stop in a turbine is a singular point anomaly. However, in order to effectively predict when a similar turbine could fail, you might want to look also at how multiple related values have changed in the past hour to determine the recorded stop. Consider that for a wind turbine, the interval to look should be no smaller than a couple of hours.

The majority of anomaly detection of real-world problems (such as the prediction of faults in industrial machines, effective scheduling of maintenance work, suspicious financial transactions, and detection of cyberattacks) are based on large multivariate time series. A multivariate time series is the natural sweet spot of a neural network.

Schema of the Data

The univariate time series of shampoo sales comes in the form of a CSV file. Table 7-1 shows the first few rows in a tabular format for ease of reading.

TABLE 7-1 Top rows of the shampoo sales dataset

Month	Sales
1-Y1	266
2-Y1	145.9
3-Y1	183.1
4-Y1	119.3
5-Y1	180.3

To represent the content of a data row, we used the following straightforward C# class:

```
public class SalesData
{
    [LoadColumn(0)]
    public string Month { get; set; }

    [LoadColumn(1)]
    public float Sales { get; set; }
}
```

Each public property binds to the ordinal column in the original CSV file via the LoadColumn attribute.

Loading Data and Feature Engineering

ML.NET solutions for anomaly detection work a bit differently from other examples we have seen in the previous chapters. In particular, you hardly need to apply column transformations via feature engineering techniques. In our example, we might have felt the need for some data transformation to turn possible integer source values in the series into floats.

All we need to do here is load the source dataset into an IDataView descriptor and move on to the training phase.

```
IDataView timeSeries = mlContext.Data.LoadFromTextFile<SalesData>(
    _salesDataRelativePath, hasHeader: true, separatorChar: ',');
```

It helps to recall that the content of an `IDataView` object can also be set by reading from a database source or from any of the `IEnumerable` collections, such as JSON data that is read from a local or remote endpoint.

Composing the Training Pipeline

As mentioned, anomaly detection is the process of detecting those points within a given time series where the value doesn't go well with the others. What we intend by "doesn't go well" and "others" makes a whole world of a difference in specific instances of the problem. We'll return to this in a moment.

Meanwhile, the class below describes the response from ML.NET algorithms after running on a time-series dataset.

```
public class SalesPrediction
{
    [VectorType(3)]
    public double[] Prediction { get; set; }
}
```

Essentially, the response from an ML.NET anomaly detector contains at least three values, all stored in the `Prediction` property array of the response class. One is a 0/1 value (referred to as an *alert*) to indicate whether the specific value should be considered an outlier. The *p-value* indicates the probability that the current value is an outlier. A third value being returned is the actual raw value (referred to as *score*).

Let's see what we can do to detect spikes and change points using the ML.NET tools.

> **NOTE** There's no specific reason why the predictions should flow into an array of doubles instead of being distinct properties. The ML.NET design dictates this.

Detecting Spikes

A spike is a point outlier, namely a temporary peak value (high or low) in an otherwise standard data flow. The simplest way to detect a spike is by scanning the time-series values, looking at the density of the values. The preparatory work for calculating density estimations is performed by the method `DetectIidSpike`. Note that this is an extension method in the `Transforms` catalog that requires the additional `Microsoft.ML.TimeSeries` NuGet package to be installed.

The `IID` in the name stands for independent and identically distributed random variables, meaning that the values in the time series are assumed to be independent from one another and equally spaced in their sampling rate. The following code returns an estimator that sets the grounds for calculating density estimations necessary for getting spikes.

```
var spikeEstimator = mlContext.Transforms.DetectIidSpike("Prediction", "Sales", 95d, 9);
```

The method doesn't do any physical work on any physical data yet. It just receives the name of the output column to be added to the predictions and the column's name in the input dataset containing time-series values.

As for the final two numeric values, the former (95) is a double value in the 0–100 range that refers to the requested level of confidence you want from the library for any detected spike. The latter parameter (9) is the size of the sliding window to be used for computing the probability that the given row is a spike. With a value of 9, the probability (p-value) refers to a moving slice of 9 values.

The DetectIidSpike method also accepts a fifth parameter, an enumerated value from AnomalySide. The enum accepts Negative, Positive, and TwoSided (default), meaning that both negative or positive spikes should be detected.

```
// Trains the estimator on the schema of the actual data being passed
ITransformer detector = spikeEstimator.Fit(timeSeries);
```

One more transformation step is required in which the internal structure of the spike estimator is further modified based on the schema of the data it will be called to work on. Note that this particular implementation of spike detection is not really a supervised form of learning. No trainer goes through canonical training and testing steps to produce a model that will be invoked later to predict new data. It looks more like an unsupervised pass on the time series to identify spikes.

The call to the Fit method shown earlier can be dramatically simplified by not passing the real time series; instead, pass an empty data view. In fact, the method doesn't work on data; instead, it just needs to know about the data schema. To save some memory during the run, we can pass an empty enumerable object.

```
// Create an empty, schema-only dataview
var emptyView = mlContext.Data.LoadFromEnumerable(new List<SalesData>());

// Get a further modified transformer
ITransformer detector = spikeEstimator.Fit(emptyView);
```

We're now ready to make a run on the actual time-series values. The returned data view contains the additional column with estimations for alerts and p-values.

```
var transformedData = detector.Transform(timeSeries);
```

For the sake of further analysis, we can even save the data view to a text file in much the same way we did in Chapter 6 for the clusters of a K-Means algorithm.

```
// Extract a .NET enumerable from the data view
var analyzedSeries = mlContext
    .Data
    .CreateEnumerable<SalesPrediction>(transformedData, reuseRowObject: false);

// Save the output to a TXT file
var filename = string.Format(outputPath, "spikes");
var writer = File.CreateText(filename);
writer.WriteLine($"Value\tAlert\tP-value");
foreach (var row in analyzedSeries)
```

```
{
    writer.WriteLine($"{row.Prediction[1]:f2}\t{row.Prediction[0]}\t{row.Prediction[2]:F2}");
}
writer.Close();
```

Figure 7-4 shows the content of the text file with detected spikes. The file is made of three columns for the actual value, and a 0/1 flag for whether the row has been detected as a spike. The final column indicates the confidence the detector has about the 0/1 alert. The value is a probability distribution, and the closer it is to 0, the more likely the row is to be regarded as a spike by the detector.

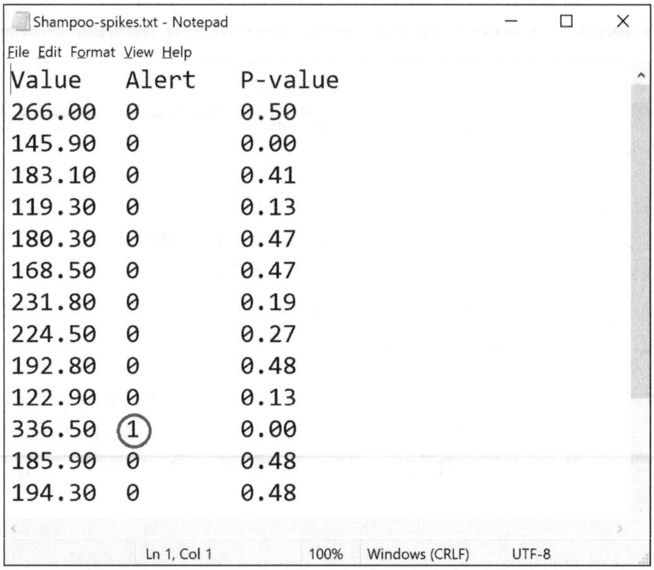

Value	Alert	P-value
266.00	0	0.50
145.90	0	0.00
183.10	0	0.41
119.30	0	0.13
180.30	0	0.47
168.50	0	0.47
231.80	0	0.19
224.50	0	0.27
192.80	0	0.48
122.90	0	0.13
336.50	1	0.00
185.90	0	0.48
194.30	0	0.48

FIGURE 7-4 Dump of the spike detection process

Detecting Change Points

In a time series, an occasional burst of the curve might simply be the final effect of a technical glitch, such as the temporary failure of an electronic sensor. An occasional burst, though, is just occasional. What if a spike lasts over several time intervals? There are two possibilities. One is that at some point, the values return to flow as before. The other possibility is that values tend to repeat and remain around the spike—this is a persistent change in the flow and the sign of a different data trend. This latter situation is referred to as a *change point*.

A change point that persists for too long, though, might be the root cause of some relevant damage. For example, the temperature of a wind turbine generator that is reported too hot for too long may be the sign of overheating, which can take the cooling system down and even result in fire. When the generator fails, no power is produced, which possibly costs the wind farm operator good revenues.

A software module that monitors the time series of the internal temperature of the generator and can spot change points is immensely helpful to many businesses. Let's see how ML.NET addresses the problem.

The structure of the change point detector is nearly identical to the spike detector above. First and foremost, you get an estimator to set the grounds for calculating change points:

```
var cpEstimator = mlContext.Transforms.DetectIidChangePoint("Prediction", "Sales", 95d, 9);
```

The numeric values are the same as with spikes. The remaining code is identical:

```
IidChangePointDetector detector = cpEstimator.Fit(emptyView);
var transformedData = detector.Transform(timeSeries);
var analyzedSeries = mlContext
    .Data
    .CreateEnumerable<SalesPrediction>(transformedData, reuseRowObject: false);
```

Figure 7-5 shows the output from the text file created after making a pass on the time-series data.

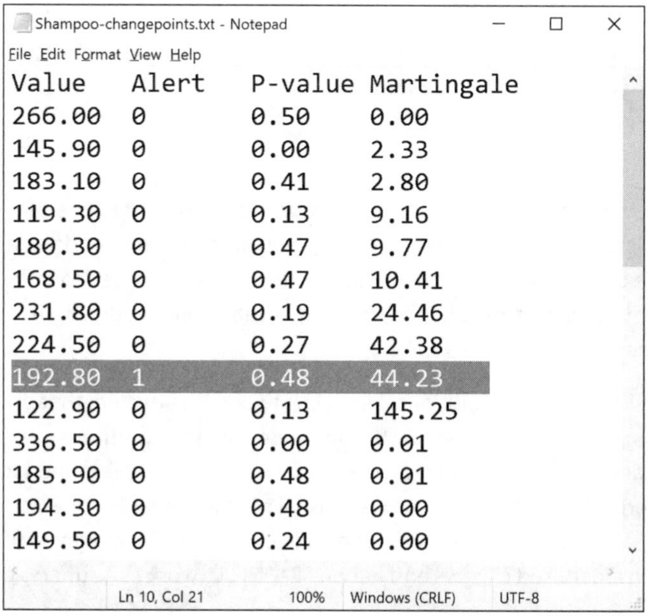

Value	Alert	P-value	Martingale
266.00	0	0.50	0.00
145.90	0	0.00	2.33
183.10	0	0.41	2.80
119.30	0	0.13	9.16
180.30	0	0.47	9.77
168.50	0	0.47	10.41
231.80	0	0.19	24.46
224.50	0	0.27	42.38
192.80	1	0.48	44.23
122.90	0	0.13	145.25
336.50	0	0.00	0.01
185.90	0	0.48	0.01
194.30	0	0.48	0.00
149.50	0	0.24	0.00

FIGURE 7-5 Dump of the change point detection process

The change point detector also returns a fourth column with the Martingale score. Built upon the p-value, the Martingale score detects a change of distribution over a sequence of independently and identically distributed values. The calculated value beyond a computed threshold is used internally to decide whether a candidate point is really a change point. The method DetectIidChangePoint also takes two additional parameters (with respect to our example above) to configure the Martingale scorer. One parameter is an enum value for the scorer type (the default is MartingaleType.Power), and the other is a threshold parameter (the default is 0.1) for the Martingale power method.

Using the SSA Method

The spike and change point detectors we used (based on IID) are not particularly good at capturing the seasonality of data. In other words, a spike is a spike regardless. Another transformation method exists in the same NuGet package `Microsoft.ML.TimeSeries` and is called `DetectSpikeBySsa`.

Short for Singular Spectrum Analysis, SSA decomposes the time series into various components: trend, seasonality, and noise. In addition, it attempts to forecast the future values of the time series. SSA performs spectral analysis on the time series to discover any periodicities. In doing so, it first transforms data internally, moving from a time-based representation to a to frequency-based one. A time-based representation shows how a signal changes over time. A frequency-based representation, instead, shows how the signal is distributed over a range of frequencies. A frequency-domain analysis is particularly useful for spotting the cyclic behavior of a signal. The Fourier transform is a function commonly used to convert from time to frequency domain.

ML.NET provides SSA for spike detection as well as change point detection. In the latter case, the transformation method is called `DetectChangePointBySsa`.

Using the SR-CNN Service

SR-CNN refers to a dedicated service built at Microsoft for continuous observation of a time series and instantaneous alerts in case of anomalies. The method focuses on point anomalies but works in a more traditional way compared to all the detectors considered so far. In other words, you need to train the model based on the SR-CNN algorithm (as wrapped by the method), create a prediction engine, and pass live data to get a response whether the value is a spike or not.

SR-CNN stands for Spectral Residual and Convolutional Neural Network. It's a system that processes data in two steps. First, the input data is grouped by the SR unsupervised algorithm (using the Fast Fourier Transform internally), and then the output is processed by a CNN that is pretrained to work on visual saliency detection problems in a supervised way. Visual saliency detection is a computer vision step aimed at finding salient objects in an image. Specifically, the service assigns artificially generated anomaly labels to the unsupervised clusters and has an SR-CNN to work as a supervised algorithm.

There are two key innovations in this approach. One is reducing the time-series anomaly detection problem to the visual saliency detection problem. The other is pipelining the unsupervised SR algorithm to a pretrained supervised CNN good at saliency detection problems.

The code to use in ML.NET is below:

```
var estimator = mlContext.Transforms.DetectAnomalyBySrCnn("Predictions", "Sales");
var model = estimator.Fit(timeSeries);
```

A number of hyperparameters can be specified as the sliding window's size to generate a saliency map for the series, the number of points to add to the back of the training window, and the threshold to determine anomalies.

Using Randomized PCA

Principal component analysis (PCA) is a learning process aimed at identifying the principal features of a dataset in order to reduce the complexity and dimensionality of a dataset. Typically, after running PCA, you get a smaller dataset of fewer new columns obtained through some sort of mathematical combination of original columns. In ML.NET, the RandomizedPca trainer is the implementation of a PCA algorithm that uses the Singular Value Decomposition (SVD) technique (with a random number generator) to decompose a matrix into a lower rank matrix.

Applied to machine learning, SVD (a linear algebra algorithm) has the effect of reducing the training time series to a subset of salient facts. The trainer saves in the model three pieces of information. One is the projection matrix that will be used to transpose any input data from the original space to the lower-dimensional space of salient facts. In addition, the trainer stores the two vectors in the original and reduced spaces representing the normality. These vectors are essentially made of columns' mean values in the two spaces. When the model is invoked in production on a set of live values, the model first projects the input values into the reduced space where salient facts are condensed. An anomaly score is then computed, measuring and mathematically combining the distances between input and mean in the original and reduced space. The higher the anomaly score in the 0–1 interval, the more likely it is an outlier. By default, the threshold value is 0.5. (See Figure 7-6.)

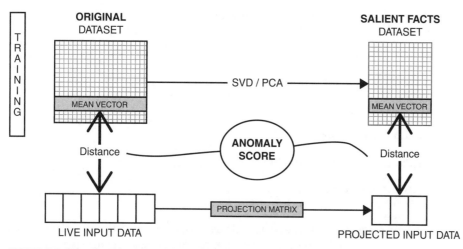

FIGURE 7-6 Overall architecture of the Randomized PCA trainer

Unlike most of the DetectXxx methods considered so far—which are extension methods of the Transforms catalog—RandomizedPca is a method on the Trainers catalog of the AnomalyDetection task. To use the RandomizedPca method, you follow a programming approach identical to what we have seen for classification and regression tasks. First, you identify a dataset; next, you build a data processing pipeline, add a trainer to it, and fit the method. The saved model is then deployed to production, and a prediction engine is built out of it to predict anomalies on live data.

> **NOTE** RandomizedPca, as well as the other approaches discussed in this chapter, are all forms of unsupervised learning. However, as we'll see in the upcoming "The ML Devil's Advocate" section, anomaly detection can also be approached and solved using a form of supervised learning.

Setting Up a Client Application

The spike and change point detectors we have seen can be easily integrated—as is—in a client application that receives a series of data from some external source. Plain detectors work easily on static sequences of data (such as historical data analysis). Trained models (such as those created with SR-CNN) work better for real-time analysis.

Our sample ASP.NET Core application will work on the same static time series of three years of shampoo sales, render it as a line chart, and highlight spikes and change points on demand. The sample application features a controller class with three methods like this:

```
public IActionResult Plain()
{
    return Json(ChartService.FromFile(_timeSeriesPath,
            "Shampoo Sales 3y"));
}
public IActionResult Spikes()
{
    return Json(ChartService.FromFile(_timeSeriesPath,
            "Shampoo Sales 3y",
            AlertType.Spike));
}
public IActionResult ChangePoints()
{
    return Json(ChartService.FromFile(_timeSeriesPath,
            "Shampoo Sales 3y",
            AlertType.ChangePoint));
}
```

The Plain method reads the time series data and builds a chart-friendly data transfer object. Similarly, the Spikes and ChangePoints methods read the time series and calculate the alert points, which are then embedded in the JSON response.

On the frontend, a line chart object backed by the Chart JS library plots the data as provided by the transfer object below.

```
public class ChartDescriptor
{
    public IList<string> Labels { get; set; }
    public IList<float> Values { get; set; }
    public IList<int> Alerts { get; set; }
    public string Title { get; set; }
}
```

The collections Labels and Values are used to plot the chart, whereas Alerts indicates the points to highlight.

Here's a glimpse of the FromFile method above that reads the time series and calculates spikes and change points using the detectors seen earlier in the chapter.

```
public static ChartDescriptor FromFile(string path,
        string title = "---", AlertType alertType = AlertType.None)
{
    var cd = new ChartDescriptor {Title = title};
    var lines = File.ReadAllLines(path).AsQueryable().Skip(1).ToArray();

    var salesData = new List<SalesData>();

    foreach (var l in lines)
    {
        var tokens = l.Split(',');
        var month = tokens[0];
        var sales = float.Parse(tokens[1]);
        var sd = new SalesData {Month = month, Sales = sales};

        salesData.Add(sd);
        cd.Labels.Add(month);
        cd.Values.Add(sales);
    }

    // Detect alerts
    switch (alertType)
    {
        case AlertType.Spike:
            cd.Alerts = AnomalyService.GetSpikes(salesData);
            break;
        case AlertType.ChangePoint:
            cd.Alerts = AnomalyService.GetChangePoints(salesData);
            break;
        default:
            return cd;
    }
    return cd;
}
```

The code is intuitive: after reading the lines of the time series. The FromFile method splits each line in column values (month and sales) and creates further data shapes. Independent arrays are required for charting labels and values, and a list of reference SalesData objects is required to extract spikes and change points from the detector.

Hidden in the folds of the AnomalyService helper class, we have the same core code we presented earlier in the chapter. Here's a sample method.

```
public static IList<int> GetSpikes(IList<SalesData> series)
{
    var alerts = new List<int>();
    alerts.AddRange(FindSpikes(series));
    return alerts;
}
```

```
private static IList<int> FindSpikes(IList<SalesData> series)
{
    var mlContext = new MLContext();
    var emptyView = mlContext.Data.LoadFromEnumerable(new List<SalesData>());
    var spikeEstimator = mlContext.Transforms
                .DetectIidSpike("Prediction", "Sales", 95d, 9, AnomalySide.TwoSided);
    var dataview = mlContext.Data.LoadFromEnumerable(series);
    var detector = spikeEstimator.Fit(emptyView);
    var transformedData = detector.Transform(dataview);
    var analyzedSeries = mlContext
            .Data
            .CreateEnumerable<SalesPrediction>(transformedData, reuseRowObject: false);

    // LINQ query the indexes of alert rows
    var alerts = analyzedSeries
        .Select((r, i) => new {Row = r, Index = i})
        .Where(r => r.Row.Prediction[0] > 0)
        .Select(r => r.Index)
        .ToArray();

    return alerts;
}
```

Figure 7-7 shows the sample application in action. By clicking any of the three buttons, you get three different views of the same time series.

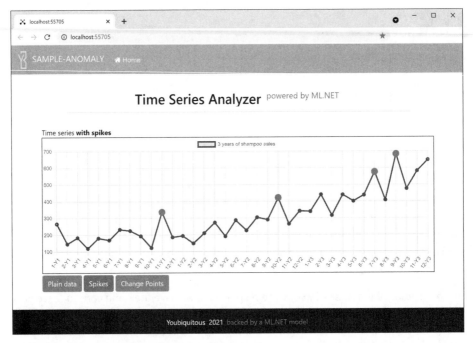

FIGURE 7-7 Detected spikes on the time series

The ML Devil's Advocate

Anomaly detection is really one of the sweetest spots for machine learning. Many real-world problems can be effectively formulated as anomaly detection instances, though at various levels of abstraction. The level of abstraction is crucial.

In this chapter, we have discussed alert detectors and trainers that operate on a time series and return a 0/1 answer associated with a probability. Is this dry 0/1 response good enough in the specific business domain? With reference to Figure 7-7, is knowing the position of spikes as in the chart sufficient for the purposes of the business? Is it insightful enough? Is it a definitive answer or just the input to a pipeline of machine learning components?

The bottom line is that anomaly detection is not a single machine learning problem with just a few algorithms to choose from and train. More often, it is about predicting (or just recognizing) an anomalous sequence of values that appear over a given window of time

In general, we can distinguish three different macro areas of influence for anomaly detection:

- Monitoring the performance of industrial systems (regardless of whether we're talking about power plants or IT departments)

- Monitoring the flow of business transactions (such as sales or financial operations)

- Checking the quality of products (such as manufacturing or web sites)

Another critical parameter to consider is whether the analysis to spot anomalies is conducted over historical or real-time data. A statistical-oriented solution method is preferable for historical data, whereas machine learning methods are recommended for live data.

Let's delve a bit deeper in a couple of real-world problems.

Predictive Maintenance

Industrial machines are expected to work uninterruptedly, and every second of work produces revenues—directly or indirectly. So, if a machine breaks, you want any damage repaired as soon as possible. This means rushing to send technicians on site, have them inspect the device carefully, diagnose the fault, possibly order new hardware, and most importantly, deploy the hardware on site. Now, what if it happens on a rough winter day in a power plant located in the mountains?

The biggest challenge with predictive maintenance is that dozens of different signals are logged every few seconds. It's a huge volume of data and correlated signals to be tracked.

Beyond Condition-based Analysis

IoT sensors make it possible to track the status of components in mechanical and electronic systems. For the industry, this means shifting from dummy calendar-based maintenance to condition-based maintenance. It's not enough, though. The major drawback of condition-based maintenance is that any sensor reports just one signal, even though many physical components may contribute to it. Hence, a reliable model would be desirable that can quantify the risk of failure for a machine in any moment in time. In a nutshell, the model must be able to correlate multiple signals and monitor a number of business rules and KPIs.

This can be achieved via a dynamically configurable expert system that relies on human expertise but is also an attractive field for machine learning. When it comes to machine learning, though, it becomes critical to define a clear objective. You want the machine to learn about what, exactly?

Here are a few options: minimizing downtime and/or production losses, optimizing operation scheduling and/or stock of spare parts, and avoiding major damages. As you can see, what was generically called "anomaly detection" has become predictive maintenance and then one of the other five options (neglecting combinations thereof).

Regression or Classification?

Let's suppose we're interested in trying machine learning to minimize downtime and keep the system up and running as long as possible. The perspective of the problem changes: is it better formulated as a regression or classification instance?

- **Regression**   Given a number of real-time signals captured every N second, the model will predict how much time is left before the device fails.

- **Classification**   Given a number of real-time signals captured every N second, the model will classify the device as subject to fail, break down, or work normally in the next prefixed amount of time.

At a glance, predicting the remaining useful life seems like it is much more accurate information to have, but it requires a lot of data, especially when it comes to failures because the system needs to learn, from numbers, what can cause a failure. The problem is that the number of failures is usually very small (remember, novelty detection), and collecting the decent number of instances that can drive a machine learning process takes time (years).

On the other hand, getting to know the state of the device in a fixed future window of time can return a greater accuracy with less data. From a business perspective, this might be acceptable because it gives the status of your devices in the near future and the margin to intervene.

Whether classification or regression, though, the use of a sophisticated neural network for getting answers is realistically necessary. For example, you might want to compact the definition of a good state to a smaller chunk of information, which is what auto-encoder neural networks do. Predictive maintenance is a tough problem that can only be approached per domain, no matter the abundance of tutorials out there showing in 1,000 words how to predict a mechanical failure.

> **NOTE** The goal of our "ML Devil's Advocate" section is to raise the doubt that it is one thing is to solve problems on paper and get acceptable numbers from training, but it is quite another to get numbers that are useful and realistic.

Fraudulent Financial Operations

In this context, a credit card payment is not the same as a money transfer operation. In the former scenario, the purpose is to detect the theft and abuse of credit card details. The latter, instead, is typically aimed at spotting money laundering operations. A fraudulent credit card operation has more of a canonical anomaly because it typically involves any of the following: unusual goods, unusual places, unusual amounts. A fraudulent financial transaction has a more blurred definition. It's not a spot operation but should be seen correlated to other operations. In addition, the response about a financial transaction must be based on public or private block lists, the response of existing bank expert systems, and directives expressed by local and international laws. However, both scenarios share a common solution architecture.

Structure of the Response

The response of the transaction validator is not typically a blind 0/1. More likely, the system returns the likelihood that the input transaction falls in one of multiple possible states. So far, it looks like a classification instance. But there should be much more.

The response will often go through an automatic but human-controlled workflow, namely an algorithm crafted to be comprehensible and updatable by humans. The workflow will drive the response to a Boolean state: approved/suspect. In the end, the client system that consumes the machine learning pipeline will actually get some 0/1 flag, but that is never the response of a plain anomaly detection algorithm.

Facts of a Common Solution

A fraud detection system plugs into the existing flow of live operations. If the final response is positive, it just lets the incoming transaction pass and be processed as usual. Otherwise, the transaction can be run as usual but still be flagged as suspicious or be routed to an alternate pipeline that is reserved for strongly suspicious transactions.

Inside the fraud detection black box, it's reasonable to find a network of neural networks with different layers and characteristics. The black box ultimately responsible for the final response will be likely fed input parameters resulting from three main sources in addition to the actual data of the transaction:

- **Recommender system**   A relatively simple neural network, or even a simpler chain of shallow learning algorithms, that skims across the surface of transactions and provides a first, possibly naïve, response to the fundamental question, "Is this transaction fraudulent?" This piece of information, which can be just rated as the layman's opinion, is one more piece of input contributing to the final output. The combined use of shallow and deep learning algorithms is a common pattern for problems that need to look at data from many angles to find an ideal yet articulated answer.

- **Expert system(s)**   Any existing expert system(s) that have been on duty for years and are still able to provide a valuable opinion for the overall system to crunch.

- **Encoders** An encoder is a type of neural network that encodes large information in a compact but highly representative format. Encoders are used to codify laws, block lists, and other similar information to be taken into account while rating the transaction.

These three sources represent facts that the system has processed along with live data. Finally, the core engine of the fraud detection system can be devised as a graph of neural networks of probably different types.

Summary

Anomaly detection flags unexpected and unusual events in a set of data. The issue is going from the abstract definition of anomaly detection down to an actual machine learning project for real-world problems that may have a huge impact on various businesses: finance, manufacturing, energy and general industry, health, and intrusion detection, to name a few.

In this chapter, we've first discussed a few general approaches to detect anomalies and introduced time series data and concepts like the outlier and different types of outliers. Then, we moved to revise the common ways to approach anomaly detection using machine learning. Finally, we opened up Visual Studio and used the tools of ML.NET to detect spikes and change points in a historical time series.

As for the live analysis of data, well, that's a different story, and a trained model is required. However, as the "ML Devil's Advocate" section mentioned, any realistic anomaly detection system—especially one that processes real-time data—is complex machinery that needs be crafted case by case.

In the next chapter, we'll discuss time series, but this time, we'll talk about forecasting and detecting data trends.

CHAPTER 8

Forecasting Tasks

"Complete chaos is impossible."

—*Theodore Motzkin, talking about Ramsey's theory, 1951*

In Chapter 7, where we discussed spotting anomalous values in data series, we introduced the concept of time series. As a reminder, a time series is a sequence of values captured at successive, ideally equidistant points in time. Therefore, a time series is a discrete (as opposed to continuous) collection of values. The wind speed values reported every 30 seconds by the anemometer installed on a specific wind turbine in a specific farm is a good example of a time series.

There are two types of information that can be extracted from a time series. One type of information is spikes and change points, namely anomalous values. A spike indicates a measurement that differs too much from the others; a change point is a point when the flow of data starts changing direction. The other type of information that can be extracted is what we cover in this chapter: extrapolating values and predicting future data trends.

Predicting the Future

Predicting the future is a delicate art whose roots date back to 2000 BCE when Babylon soothsayers observed maggots' (naturally trained) movements in the rotten livers of dead animals to make predictions.

You can't be too generic about what you would like to know when it comes to forecasts. Moreover, you must also be very specific about the expected horizon of the prediction. For example, do you want sales forecasts for one specific product or an entire line of products? Do you want those forecasts taken at a specific outlet or in a geographical region? Do you want those forecasts to be based on daily or monthly data? And for how far in advance do you want these forecasts? One month? One year? A few hours? Precise answers are necessary.

Simple Forecasting Methods

Using machine learning for forecasting values is a more and more popular option these days, but from a pure business perspective, it's far from being the only option. Well beyond the naivety of inspecting a sheep's liver or listening to the rantings of a likely intoxicated oracle in the Delphi's temple, a few mathematical methods exist to attempt forecasts that are simple and relatively effective.

One is the average method, which consists of taking the average of the historical data for the time horizon of choice (the mean value of the last six months). Taking the value of the last observation is another even simpler method that is surprisingly effective, especially for some financial time series.

Yet another method that works well for strongly seasonal data is taking the last observed value from the same time of the year. For example, why should you consume a significantly different amount of electricity this summer compared to the last one? Assuming the consumption will be the same is a good starting point that all energy utilities use to estimate your needs and charge you in advance.

Mathematical Foundation of Forecasting

To make more accurate guesses about the future values of a time series, it is necessary to separate the time series into components. The decomposition of a time series has the ultimate purpose of bringing hidden trends and cyclic behavior to light while filtering out noisy and dirty data. The following sections discuss a few technical attributes of a time series that deserve more attention.

Trends and Cycles

In time-series data, a trend indicates a long-term, structural change of direction of the observed values. When it happens, you see values that start increasing or decreasing in a way that can be linear or non-linear and more or less slow. The point in time when the change of direction begins is referred to as a change point.

There might be multiple trends over time, though. One trend might range from time T1 to time T2 and be growing, while another trend might occur later and be declining. Such fluctuations that repeat over time indicate cyclic behavior. A cycle encompasses multiple trends.

In the real world, cycles are typically bound to economic or business conditions. For example, in a sports scenario, a cycle can be the performance of a great team of players over a few years—going up slowly, reaching the peak, staying around the peak, and then decreasing. Although domain and context-specific, the duration of a cycle is generally no less than two years.

Seasonality

Seasonality refers to a pattern that fully describes a periodic fluctuation of values, such as higher sales in the holiday season or low electricity consumption during the night. Seasonality is a special type of cyclic behavior. In particular, there are two key differences:

First off, seasonality is any predictable fluctuation of values that regularly repeats over a period. Second, a seasonal fluctuation is periodic, whereas a cycle might not be of some fixed length, and guessing its peaks and troughs might not be obvious. Put another way, each cycle is unique and has its own period and peak values. On the contrary, a season has peaks and troughs, but they are regular and predictable. A season is a cycle that repeats time after time.

Stationarity

Stationarity is another mathematical piece of information that's useful to know about a time series. It indicates the fluctuation of key statistical attributes such as mean or variance. In particular, a time series is said to be stationary if the two properties are nearly constant over time. Put another way, a time series is stationary if the observed values do not depend on the time at which they have been observed.

A stationary time series has no long-term patterns such as trends or seasons, and its values are laid out around some horizontal line. Minimal cycles are still possible—but with nearly constant variance (the squared distance of values from the mean).

Why is stationarity crucial?

The very same idea of forecasting starts from the assumption that some sort of continuity exists between values of today and values to predict for tomorrow. If surrounding conditions might change between today and tomorrow, then observed values will depend on the observation time. This makes reliable forecasts impossible to obtain by definition, and the best you can get is a guess.

The something that remains constant over time is usually combinations of individual signal values in the series. One way to have the desired invariance that enables forecasts is to have the mean and variance constant and independent of time (stationarity).

A non-stationary time series can be turned into a stationary one by applying differencing techniques. Differencing consists of computing the differences between consecutive observations. (See Figure 8-1.)

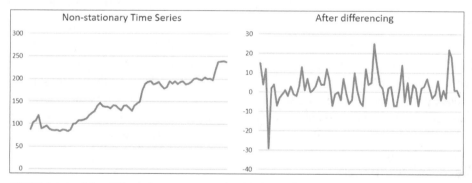

FIGURE 8-1 Applying differencing to a non-stationary time series

The leftmost chart plots the absolute values of the time series, whereas the rightmost chart plots the difference between two consecutive points in the series. The original time series is not stationary and counts a few increasing trends. The chart on the right—after differencing was applied—has its values nearly constantly laid out around a horizontal line. Differencing helps stabilize the mean of a time series, eliminating (or just reducing) trends and seasonality.

Common Decomposition Algorithms

To make sense of the values in a time series, the time series must be decomposed in a number of components—trend (and cycles), seasonality, and the remainder part. In a way, we can represent the time series as shown below:

$$y_t = S_t + T_t + R_t$$

In the formula, y_t the element indicates the whole time series at time t. The other elements in the formula refer to the seasonal, trend, and remainder component, respectively.

A number of methods exist to decompose a time series and have been in the works for about a century now. For example, the X-11 method is an iterative process based on moving averages that decomposes a time series into trend/cycle, seasonal, and irregular components for quarterly and monthly data. Another method is STL, short for Seasonal and Trend decomposition using the Loess method. Unlike X-11, STL can handle any type of seasonality and is not limited to quarterly and monthly data.

A more advanced decomposition method is based on the Singular Spectrum Analysis (SSA) algorithm. We already met the SSA acronym in the past chapter, but we'll say more about the internals of the algorithm here. Interestingly, in ML.NET, spikes, change points, and forecasts share the same algorithmic foundation—the SSA algorithm.

The SSA Algorithm

SSA works by decomposing any time series into its trend and seasonal, oscillatory components. The work is accomplished through two main steps: decomposition and subsequent reconstruction of the time series.

> **NOTE** The following two sections attempt to provide a mathematical description of the SSA algorithm. Admittedly, it's a very high-level (and compact) explanation that might sound obscure if you're looking for details. In this case, you might want to take a look at *https://www.researchgate.net/publication/260124592_Singular_Spectrum_Analysis_for_Time_Series*.

The Decomposition Step

The time series is first mapped to a matrix called the trajectory matrix. The building of the matrix contributes a parameter known as the `window length`, which ultimately determines the size of the matrix. The window length is a hyperparameter usually assigned based on experience. The choice of the window length depends on the size of the time series and the specific analysis to perform. The window length impacts the quality of the decomposition. Figure 8-2 shows a sample trajectory matrix for a window length of K and a time series size of N.

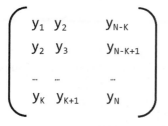

FIGURE 8-2 A sample trajectory matrix for a window length of K

A common value for the window length is N/4, where N is the number of elements in the time series, but it's been recommended that the value is as large as possible but never larger than N/2. The larger the window length is, the longer cycles can be resolved. On the other hand, a value that is too large value might capture too few cycles.

The trajectory matrix is further processed using the Singular Value Decomposition (SVD) method. In particular, the SVD applied to the trajectory matrix multiplied by its transposed matrix (rows and columns swapped) yields a collection of K eigenvectors and related eigenvalues.

This becomes the input of the reconstruction step of the algorithm.

> **NOTE** An `eigenvector` of a linear transformation (a function between vectorial spaces) is a nonzero vector that changes at most by a scalar factor when the transformation is applied to it. The scalar factor is called `eigenvalue`.

The Reconstruction Step

Starting from the calculated eigenvectors, the algorithm attempts to create a new matrix that represents a valid approximation of the original trajectory matrix representative of the original time series. In particular, a subset of eigenvectors is selected, and the number is another critical hyperparameter to define.

The new matrix contains an embedded time series similar to the structure of Figure 8-2. The embedded time series, however, is not the original one but takes into account principal values.

At a higher level of abstraction, the algorithm has done a plain transformation of the original time series from a time-based space to a frequency-based space where values indicate how often certain values are found.

Now, the interesting thing is that the values of the reconstructed matrix satisfy some linear formula according to the net effect that the next element of a time series results from a linear transformation of all previous values. In the end, this is the mechanism that yields forecasting capabilities.

The Forecast ML Task

SSA is a very flexible algorithm that can be employed to decompose a time series into trend and cyclic components to make forecasts but also to identify change points and outliers. In Chapter 7, "Anomaly Detection Tasks," we just explored these two latter capabilities. Now, let's proceed with forecasting. In particular, we'll look at some of the methods exposed by the Forecasting catalog.

Note that in order to use ML.NET forecasting capabilities, you should install the additional Microsoft.ML.TimeSeries NuGet package.

> **NOTE** For this chapter, we'll follow the same approach used in previous chapters: reusing the same dataset presented by the official ML.NET documentation or a very close one. We do this for two reasons: to make it simpler for the reader to follow and to move easily across the steps. The added value we strive to provide is in the comments, where we can provide more detail.

A Look at the Available Data

In the ML.NET official documentation, forecasting is illustrated by resorting to a dataset created by Hadi Fanaee-T and Joao Gama in 2013. The actual data refers to a two-year usage log of a bike-sharing system (Capital Bikeshare) active in the Washington, D.C. area. The dataset is particularly appropriate because of the time interval it covers—the full two-year life cycle of the system.

The Actual Database

The original dataset on which the aforementioned scientists built their analysis also included columns to reflect seasonal and environmental factors such as weather conditions, weekdays, and holidays. We're using here a simplified version that counts only date and total rentals in the day. The information about the year has been hot-encoded to an enumeration value (0 for the first year, 1 for the second year). Any preliminary work has been done already, and all we have is an MDF database file ready to be attached in a SQL Server local or network instance.

> **NOTE** Reducing to use a simplified version of the dataset is good for showing the training step, but admittedly, it lowers the whole example to the level of a toy application. As you'll see later, we won't even be using the year information for the purpose of predictions.

The sample DailyDemand.mdf file available for download opened up in Visual Studio 2019, as shown in Figure 8-3. It is made of a single table, the Rentals table, with three columns.

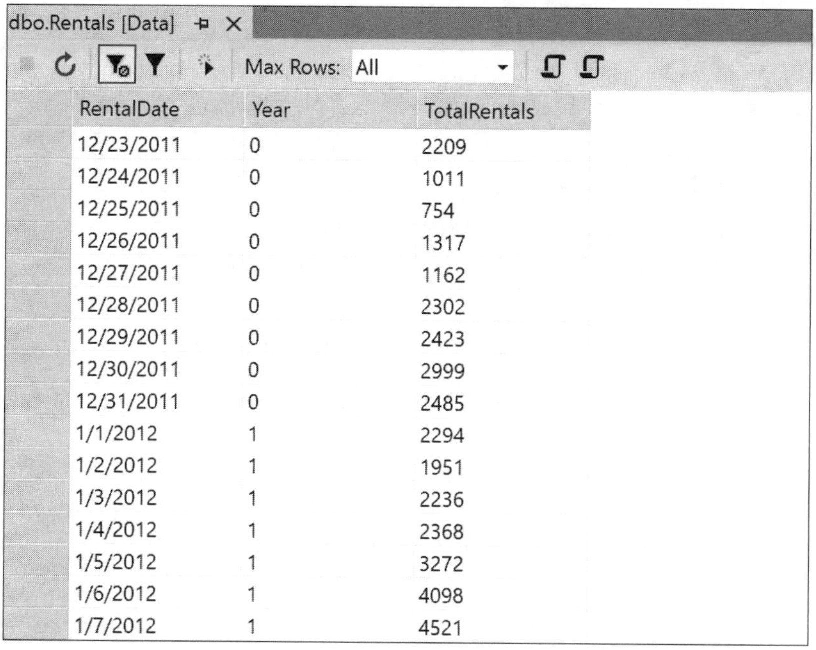

RentalDate	Year	TotalRentals
12/23/2011	0	2209
12/24/2011	0	1011
12/25/2011	0	754
12/26/2011	0	1317
12/27/2011	0	1162
12/28/2011	0	2302
12/29/2011	0	2423
12/30/2011	0	2999
12/31/2011	0	2485
1/1/2012	1	2294
1/2/2012	1	1951
1/3/2012	1	2236
1/4/2012	1	2368
1/5/2012	1	3272
1/6/2012	1	4098
1/7/2012	1	4521

FIGURE 8-3 A view of the MDF sample dataset in Visual Studio 2019

Helper Classes

The following C# class is used to model the individual rows of the dataset.

```
public class RentalData
{
    public DateTime RentalDate { get; set; }
    public float Year { get; set; }
    public float TotalRentals { get; set; }
}
```

The forecast model will ultimately return a response modeled after the following C# class:

```
public class RentalPrediction
{
    public float[] ForecastedRentals { get; set; }
    public float[] LowerBoundRentals { get; set; }
    public float[] UpperBoundRentals { get; set; }
}
```

Each member of the `RentalPrediction` class is defined as an array because it is expected to contain values (exact, lower, and upper) for all the days in the forecasted period.

Let's turn to the building of the training pipeline.

Composing the Training Pipeline

We need to train a model for a forecasting problem and then deploy it to the production environment. The overall approach is similar to what we have done in the past chapters for regression and classification.

Loading Data from a Database Source

We hinted already at ML.NET being able to load data into a data view from a database source. We also showed some code snippets, but now it's different as we're doing it in a real application.

```
var mlContext = new MLContext();
DatabaseLoader loader = mlContext.Data.CreateDatabaseLoader<RentalData>();
```

The code above creates an instance of the loader object capable of running a query on the source and returns a data view of RentalData objects. Here's the actual SQL query:

```
var query = "SELECT RentalDate,
                    CAST(Year as REAL) as Year,
                    CAST(TotalRentals as REAL) as TotalRentals
             FROM Rentals";
```

Query command and connection string are encapsulated in a dedicated DatabaseSource object.

```
DatabaseSource dbSource = new DatabaseSource(
          SqlClientFactory.Instance,
          _connectionString,
          query);
```

Needless to say, you need to reference in the project some client database NuGet package. Specifically, here you need the System.Data.SqlClient NuGet package. You only need this as we're silently assuming that we use a local DB file. If the database is attached to an instance of SQL Server—and you plan to use an O/RM to deal with it—then you also need to reference the package of the O/RM of choice (such as Entity Framework, Dapper, and so on). Here's the connection string we're using:

```
private static readonly string _connectionString =
    $"Data Source=(LocalDB)\\MSSQLLocalDB;AttachDbFilename={_dataPath};
      Integrated Security=True;";
```

Finally, here's how you get the data view wrapper for the content of the dataset.

```
IDataView dataView = loader.Load(dbSource);
```

At this point, the data view references the entire dataset, two years of bike rentals data.

Separating Training and Testing Data

Should we use the whole dataset to train? Should we opt for a manual 80/20 split or perhaps go for a cross-validation approach? In the end, our current dataset is two full years, so it's not bad to take the first year for training and the second year for testing.

```
IDataView year1 = mlContext.Data.FilterRowsByColumn(dataView, "Year", upperBound: 1);
IDataView year2 = mlContext.Data.FilterRowsByColumn(dataView, "Year", lowerBound: 1);
```

The `FilterRowsByColumn` method is a facility provided by the data view object to slice the rows of the view between a lower (inclusive) and upper bound (exclusive) value. It works only on numeric columns.

Applying the Algorithm

Curiously, in ML.NET, the `Trainers` collection of the `Forecasting` catalog is empty and doesn't list any method. However, when installing the additional time-series package, you get an extension method called `ForecastBySsa` directly exposed out of the catalog. SSA is the only trainer available for forecasting problems. Here's how to append it to the training pipeline.

```
var forecastingPipeline = mlContext.Forecasting.ForecastBySsa(
    outputColumnName: "ForecastedRentals",
    inputColumnName: "TotalRentals",
    windowSize: 7,
    seriesLength: 30,
    trainSize: 365,
    horizon: 5,
    confidenceLevel: 0.95f,
    confidenceLowerBoundColumn: "LowerBoundRentals",
    confidenceUpperBoundColumn: "UpperBoundRentals");
```

As you can see, there are quite a few parameters to specify and make sense of. Some of them map easily to some concepts of the general SSA algorithm we summarized earlier. Table 8-1 details the purpose of the parameters used in the example.

TABLE 8-1 Parameters of ForecastBySsa

Parameter	Description
outputColumnName	Name of the dataset column that will receive the forecasts of the model.
inputColumnName	Name of the dataset column that will provide the input to the model.
windowSize	The size of the window length required for building the trajectory matrix.
seriesLength	The number of data points that are used when performing a forecast.
trainSize	The total number of points in the time series used for training.
Horizon	The time horizon to aim at. In this case, it indicates the number of days in advance for which we want the model to forecast rentals (for example, the next five days).
confidenceLevel	0–1 value denoting the target confidence level to aim at during forecasting. The confidence level refers to the certainty with which you can take the predicted value being between lower- and upper-bound.
confidenceLowerBoundColumn	Name of the output column that will receive lower values of the forecast. If not specified, the confidence intervals will not be calculated.
confidenceUpperBoundColumn	Name of the output column that will receive upper values of the forecast. If not specified, the confidence intervals will not be calculated.

The pipeline above will decompose the whole 365-day time series assuming a reasonable seasonal cycle of 7 days as per the value of the windowSize parameter. Instead, the value of the seriesLength parameter sets that values in the last 30 days should be used for any predictions. Finally, the horizon parameter set to 5 indicates that the model will be able to make a forecast for the next 5 days.

The parameter windowSize is the most important to tune the accuracy of the model and should be carefully chosen for each scenario. Its value depends on the seasonal cycle known (or expected) to be in the time series. Typically, you start the training of the algorithm using the largest window size that is representative of the seasonal business cycle for your scenario.

For example, if the business cycle is known to have weekly periods, and the data is collected daily as in the presented time series, then 7 might be an acceptable value. At any rate, the actual seasonality found in the data is less important than the way the model is expected to work. An ideal window size is 30 rather than 90 if the real data has, say, a quarter seasonality, but we're interested in looking at data monthly.

> **NOTE** Generally, you should refer to time periods instead of days. Here, we can safely talk about days because they're implicit given the content of the dataset. If time-series values were taken every hour, then the time period would have been the hour.

Other parameters can be specified as well. In particular, there are three more parameters related to each other. They all refer to the desired rank of the subspace used to reconstruct the time series after decomposition. More technically, the rank refers to the number of eigenvectors being picked up. One parameter sets the method for choosing the value. The enum RankSelectionMethod gives value to the parameter rankSelectionMethod. Feasible values are Fixed, Fast, or Exact (default). If set to Fixed, the rank parameter also must be specified to indicate the number of eigenvectors. If omitted, the actual value of rank becomes maxRank, which, in turn, if not specified, defaults to windowSize - 1. If the rank method is not fixed, it is automatically determined based on prediction error minimization.

Another optional parameter is whether the model being built should be adaptive and stabilized. The adaptive flag forces the ML.NET trainer to pick up a special, adaptive version of the SSA algorithm. Stabilization, instead, refers to an internal characteristic of the algorithm and how it treats values used to reconstruct the time series.

Saving and Evaluating the Model

The training pipeline is then fitted on the training dataset and produces an output transformer that is ready to be saved to a ZIP file on disk.

```
// Training time series can be what we called year1 earlier
SsaForecastingTransformer model = forecastingPipeline.Fit(trainTimeSeries);
mlContext.Model.Save(model, trainTimeSeries.Schema, outputPath);
```

Here's a quick analysis of the performance of the model.

```
// Build up a data view of the test data
// Testing time series can be what we called year2 earlier
IDataView predictions = model.Transform(testData)

// Extracting an enumerable list of actual values from the test dataset
IEnumerable<float> actual = mlContext.Data
    .CreateEnumerable<RentalData>(testData, true)
    .Select(observed => observed.TotalRentals);

// Extracting an enumerable of values predicted by the model for test data
IEnumerable<float> forecast = mlContext.Data
    .CreateEnumerable<RentalPrediction>(predictions, true)
    .Select(prediction => prediction.ForecastedRentals[0]);
```

To compare errors—namely, the difference between actual and predicted values—we use the code below. What we do is take the rentals in the test dataset (second year of real data) and compare each value, day by day, to the prediction obtained from the model trained on the time series of the first year.

```
var metrics = actual.Zip(forecast,
                    (actualValue, forecastValue) => actualValue - forecastValue)
                .ToArray();
```

The method `Zip` is defined on any `IEnumerable` object that applies a specified function to the corresponding elements of two sequences, producing a sequence of the results. The `metrics` array usually contains the difference between the actual and predicted values.

```
var meanAbsError = metrics.Average(error => Math.Abs(error));
var squaredMeanError = Math.Sqrt(metrics.Average(error => Math.Pow(error, 2)));
```

To examine the outcome and evaluate the quality of the model, you can look at the mean absolute error and/or the root mean squared error.

Setting Up a Client Application

So, now we have trained a model and have saved it to a disk that is ready to be deployed to production. However, how would you consume a forecasting model in a client application? Looking at past chapters, we should be able to create a pool of prediction engines, get one instance for each request, trigger it, collect any response, and refresh the user interface.

Sounds easy, doesn't it? Unfortunately, the devil is in the details.

Forecasting Is a Highly Dynamic Task

As our sample dataset contains bike rentals data for 2011 and 2012, let's say we spent the first day of 2013 training the model, and on January 2, we internally deployed a new admin application. The application shows the charts of past years and offers to make predictions for the next five days.

The first time we click the button, we get predictions until January 7. What happens if we click the button 10 times the same day and then click it 10 more times the next day? How do we learn from what happened in the first days of January?

A forecasting model needs some sort of state to be kept and updated over time. In addition, we should be ready to provide the trained model with the starting day of the horizon. More importantly, we need to be ready to provide the latest values we know so that we get a more accurate prediction. Our question to the model should be like this: "Given these most recent rental values and your knowledge of the business gained during training, what can we expect for the next five days?"

Next, we should find a way to update the model so that it incorporates the most recent observations in the internal state and is ready to use for future predictions.

Creating a Time Series Engine

The web client application will load the model any time it is requested to forecast. The following code belongs to the controller responsible for carrying the forecasting task.

```
DataViewSchema schema;
_model = new MLContext().Model.Load(modelPath, out schema);
```

The returned ITransformer exposes a new method we have never met before—an extension method added by the time series NuGet package.

```
var mlContext = new MLContext();
var forecastEngine = _model.CreateTimeSeriesEngine<RentalData, RentalPrediction>(mlContext);
```

The forecast engine can be seen as a wrapper around the trained model. It can be used to make plain predictions, but it also can update the embedded model with newer information.

```
var predictions = forecastEngine.Predict();
```

The interesting thing about the previous line of code is that the model does its job and returns a forecast for the default horizon. The time series the forecasts are based on is just the one used for training. So, in our example, no matter what day you ask the engine to make the forecast, any prediction will be based no later than 2012 because that is the time range in the sample data. Forecasts make sense in a continuous flow of data. You contribute new observations to the system and make the time series longer. The engine then returns predictions based on the latest entries. For this to happen, though, a new concept must be introduced—the checkpoint.

Creating Checkpoints

In machine learning, particularly in neural networks, a checkpoint refers to taking a snapshot of the system and its internal state. When applied to forecasting, a checkpoint refers to updating the model with a new observation.

The sample application has a textbox where the user enters the number of the latest bike rentals for the day. The page calls back an endpoint that controls the forecast engine.

```
// Make a prediction based on latest observation
var predictions = forecastEngine.Predict(latest, horizon);
```

The engine is called to make a forecast based on the latest value and for the specified horizon (say, five days). The variable predictions are an instance of the RentalPrediction class the model was trained on. It has a property ForecastRentals, which is an array of float values, one for each day on the horizon.

The method will likely want to save the observation back to some database and have an updated time series, which can be used for whatever purpose, including retraining the model at some point.

```
// Save model back and return
forecastEngine.CheckPoint(mlContext, _modelPath);
```

Finally, the controller endpoint will update the state of the current model with the latest observation and save it back to the same ZIP file where it was originally loaded. This is the result of calling the method CheckPoint.

The net effect is that the model can take into account any new value, and after any value is recorded, new fresher forecasts are returned. Figure 8-4 gives an idea of the achievements.

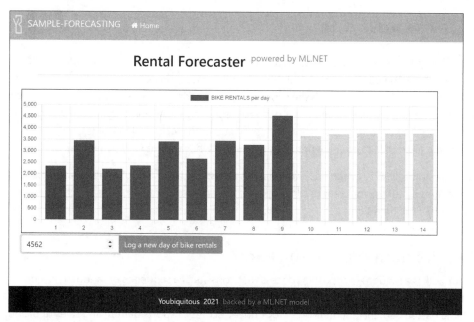

FIGURE 8-4 A sample client application using the forecast engine

The darker bars refer to the latest values of bike rentals based on which the engine offered forecasts. Lighter bars refer to predicted values. Each bar is for one day. The checkpoint allows us to keep the model uptodate without retraining from scratch. Without checkpoints, any forecast would be the same after the first hit of the model following any initial training.

> **NOTE** In a neural network context, the checkpoint is a snapshot of the internal state of the network. In this context, it can also be seen as a form of reinforced learning—not a full retraining from new data but a way to calculate more accurate coefficients for more accurate predictions.

The Discount Factor

In forecasting, the initially trained model must be updated regularly with new data points. How should the engine value dynamically add points? In the ML.NET implementation, the SSA algorithm also supports a discountFactor optional parameter. You should see it as one more row in Table 8-1.

The discountFactor parameter is a float value and falls in the 0–1 interval. The default value is 1. The parameter sets the weight to be assigned to online updates (new logged observations) compared to those taken into account in the originally trained model.

The ML Devil's Advocate

The SSA algorithm was born for processing a single value over time, but extensions of it exist for dealing with multivariate time series. In ML.NET, the implementation of SSA only allows you to deal with a single time series, even though the support for multivariate time series might come in the near future. Frankly, single time series analysis is not very useful in the vast majority of real-world applications, including financial and industrial scenarios. In fact, both stocks and machines are subject to the changes of a myriad of factors and working components whose status vary dynamically.

Therefore, this ML.NET section has two main warnings: The first is about multivariate time series, and the other is about the inherent predictability of the time series. Let's just start with the inherent predictability of the time series.

Nota a Random Walk in the Park?

A random walk is a random (stochastic) process that consists of a sequence of randomly occurring values that are modeled through a time series. Random here should be intended as the lack of a clearly predictable pattern. So, the fluctuation of stock prices, scores of sports games, and sales of products can be all approximated as random walks.

Now a random walk is unpredictable by definition, and there's no form of learning built on any sort of historical data that can reliably predict future values of a random walk sequence. The interesting thing is that most real-world time series are random walks, but predictions on their future values are still attempted in some way.

The bottom line is that machine learning is not magic, especially when we consider forecasting. Any model you put in production should be carefully verified, and any results it delivers should be treated very skeptically.

So, what about the evaluation of the model against test data?

Common metrics such as R-squared might even configure a good match, but this does not necessarily indicate good prediction powers for random walks. You can make a few quick tests on the time series to see if it can be considered a random walk.

If any correlation between two successive data points tends to be zero over time and the last observed value is still the best prediction you can have, then the odds are that the time series is really a random walk. Furthermore, if you switch to a differencing view—where differences between two points are plotted rather than absolute values—this still doesn't deliver a clearly learnable model. This just reinforces the idea that you have a random walk and, therefore, it is impossible to predict.

Other Approaches to Time Series

Beyond the SSA algorithm and its multivariate flavor that you can see well explained at https://bit.ly/3eQZj8x, there are other methods to approach forecasting in the case of time series. A common starting point is using a special type of neural network called LSTM (Long Short-Term Memory).

As we'll see in more detail in Chapter 11, an LSTM is a neural network capable of maintaining and using some internal state so that it can output values based on both input features and the current state. An LSTM neural network is quite appealing here for its innate ability to learn from sequences of data. LSTMs were developed in the late 1990s to deal with time-series data.

However, every time series is a different project and its own scenario, so using a basic neural network might also be reasonable, though a neural network is not necessarily more accurate on a random walk sequence than a much simpler tree-based random forest algorithm.

Back in the 1950s, researchers at Rand Corporation developed a new method (the Delphi method) to make forecasts in the absence of sufficient data. They did it for a specific military problem, and the actual method was never implemented in software. However, the core idea revived forty years later in the foundational concept behind random forests: a group forecast is generally more accurate than any forecast from individuals.

This is what a random forest actually does. A random decision forest is made of a multitude of individual decision trees, and the final response is given by the mean of the responses predicted by the individual trees.

All this said, let's figure out the key design challenges for a real-world prediction system that forecast the number of megawatts being generated on the following days by a wind (or solar) farm.

Energy Production Prediction

There are three important sources of data that can be used to arrange an energy production forecast algorithm:

- Punctual weather forecasts

- Power plant data in the form of multivariate time series for each turbine (or inverter)

- Company's expertise and knowledge

Quite surprisingly, the most delicate of all these sources is weather forecasts. The most commoditized, instead, is power plant data. People expertise is the most valuable.

Extremely Accurate Weather Forecasts

All the weather forecasts we find on web sites and mobile apps result from a standard mathematical model of the atmosphere and oceans and refer to a coordinate system that divides the globe into a 3D grid. The precision of forecasts strictly depends on the size of the cell being used.

The default (and cheapest) size of the cell makes the precision of weather forecasts acceptable for the news but not for the more delicate scenario of forecasting energy production. Default forecasts are based on 30-kilometer square of cells, but commercial choices exist that restrict to a square of fewer than 3 kilometers. It's much better, but still not enough for production forecasts.

Despite the cell size, the point is that the forecast is more accurate if the model can effectively predict, say, the wind flow (speed, direction, gust) near the ground and the turbine. However, this information is hard to get via physical models because of the typically complex terrain where wind turbines are located. A similar—though less impactful problem—exists for irradiation and solar plants.

Real-world forecasting solutions must necessarily build a probabilistic model on top of high-resolution weather forecasts in order to make quite accurate predictions for specific geographical points. The probabilistic model uses measurements of historical weather data for each specific point of interest. At worst, there is one point for each physical wind turbine. In fact, the wind can be very different at different heights. In particular, at 80 meters, the nature of the terrain, valleys, or trees can create different conditions and effects, thus increasing or decreasing speed and changing gust and direction. And different conditions might exist even for nearby turbines.

Collecting Power Plant Data

Real-time and historical records of effective production for each generation unit (such as wind turbines or inverters for solar plants) are the second type of information needed for a production forecast system. As mentioned, this data is today near to being a true commodity.

Power plant data is collected via monitoring whether through custom and commercial IoT devices, SCADA tools, and various sensor data. The information is collected and cataloged by dedicated monitoring applications and turns out to be a huge amount of time series data showing the power output of units and functional parameters.

A comprehensive model for a production forecast can be completed without a specific client's knowledge. However, to predict the production level of a given turbine, the direct knowledge of operators and technicians can't be ignored because it can explain the whys and wherefores of a particular set of outliers or the relevance of a set of feature values that are crucial to engineer a machine learning model that predicts numbers effectively.

The Forecasting Pipeline

Production forecast is a predictive problem but can hardly be reduced to a multi-linear form of regression trained on historical data. To be honest, multi-linear regression can even be a solution but accuracy of prediction is not guaranteed. In this way, historical data can tell how much a unit might produce if historically tracked hardware and weather conditions persist.

What if one of the generation units unexpectedly slows down or even stops working? No matter what the regressor might state, you're not getting any megawatts from that generation unit. What if the weather changes and you actually get different sun or wind conditions? But there's more.

How often should you (re)train the model if weather forecasts change? How would you normalize weather information to reduce the impact on you of inaccurate forecasts that suggested, say, a much stronger wind than you're getting? And what if the power curve you use to calculate the expected performance of the turbine, and then the exact amount of energy produced, is inaccurate?

There are so many intricate aspects to consider that linear regression and more sophisticated regression algorithms such as Naïve Bayes, Random Forests, or Support Vector Machine might be unreliable overall. Maybe neural networks are the answer? An LSTM network is a viable approach here, but training a neural network is a huge and expensive task. How often should you adjust and retrain the model in a system so strictly dependent on real-time and volatile data (such as weather and telemetry data)? Can you afford it?

It turns out that the engine of a renewable energy production forecaster is more effective if given a design fairly different from that of a canonical machine learning model. In fact, most commercial products out there tend to use a lean pipeline where training is minimal, but processing of live data occurs for every forecast. This approach is acceptable from a performance point of view if a proper hardware and software platform provides sufficient computing power, which is the case for most cloud platforms and, where it applies, for on-premise data centers of involved utilities.

Overall, in renewable energy production, forecasting is considered to be a relatively exact science even though the approaches to making actual predictions may differ across vendors and companies. If you're a utility and need to predict how much your power plant will produce, you can find a valid solution in the marketplace.

Summary

Forecasting is not the same as, say, regression. Both approaches are called to make predictions, but the time factor is much more relevant in forecasting than in regression. Time series are representative of a continuous flow of data, and incoming data points are relevant as much as input features.

Historical data is important, but even more important is understanding the nature of the actual data in depth to figure out how much causality exists between values. There's no generally agreed-upon solution that works for forecasting, though the SSA algorithm we presented here is one of the most advanced that doesn't involve the design of some ad hoc neural network. More often than not, a forecast problem is tightly coupled to its surrounding business context that requires multiple data sources and a dedicated, business-specific pipeline to be solved appropriately.

Just because you usually want predictions for the sake of the business, you don't want just one prediction; you want a really accurate one. No certainties exist for the simple reason that the real world is full of random walks, and random walks, by definition, are unpredictable. For the same reason, the idea that you can then make some accurate prediction work using a single univariate time series sounds quite naïve.

Hence, even when you think you have a model that seems to give accurate answers, well, you'd better stay skeptical and look for real matches before you claim you solved the problem. Metrics in forecasting is a number and not necessarily a solid and reliable number.

CHAPTER 9

Recommendation Tasks

"The determination of the value of an item must not be based on its price, but rather on the utility it ultimately yields."
  —Daniel Bernoulli, *Exposition of a New Theory on the Measurement of Risk, 1738*

An old quote attributed to St. Francis of Assisi says that the ideal way to approach life is to start by doing what's necessary and moving later to what's possible. Skipping over the final statement that by doing so, one would suddenly be doing the impossible, it's inevitable to see here some sort of implicit ranking applied to the things of life.

When you have a large volume of data to make sense of, you have to start somewhere and just starting from the beginning is not always an option because no end and no beginning is often obvious to find. Motivational speech apart, this chapter is about the core task of learning to rank available data items in order to extract and/or predict insightful information.

A number of web-based services we consume every day make intensive use of ranking functions—from search to e-commerce and from media entertainment to social feeds. In a way, the core task of ranking has been shaped to the form we'll be discussing shortly by the need to work well when classifying data items by relevance and spotting related items in an incredibly large volume of continuously growing data.

Two similar terms find their place in this context: ranking and recommendation. Both refer to different but closely related tasks. We could even see recommendation as the system frontend and ranking as the system backend that is globally aimed at learning and communicating the actual relevance of processed data.

Inside Information Retrieval Systems

Ranking and recommendation find their sweet spots in any kind of information retrieval system. You find ranking in Google's page classifications and TripAdvisor's ratings, Amazon's suggestions, and Instagram's advertising. As harsh as it might sound, no web search you ever perform today results from the pure matching of features; instead, it's always a result of rank-filtered lists of fewer relevant items. On the other hand, the massive amount of available raw data would make it impossible to even plan pure feature match research.

Machine learning has become a formidable tool for lending attribute-weighted relevance to data items in order to guess the hidden sentiment of data, settle down collaboratively gathered feedback, and present realistically interesting opportunities to potential consumers.

The mechanics that are commonly referred to through the interchangeably used terms of ranking and recommendation are actually articulated in three distinct functions—ranking, recommendation, and collaborative filtering—each with slightly different training needs and goals. Figure 9-1 shows how the three functions relate to each other. Ranking functionality is leveraged to some extent by recommendation and collaborative filtering.

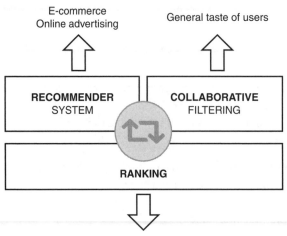

FIGURE 9-1 Connection graph of ranking, recommendation and collaborative filtering

The Basic Art of Ranking

Ranking is the most basic task used as a sort of backend engine on top of which both the recommender and collaborative filtering systems thrive. The results are from the output of a ranking algorithm, regardless of the recommendation you get as a consumer or the product or service you find on the marketplace.

Therefore, the ranking is the core engine of top-level modules such as recommender systems that provide users with an ordered list of items. Typically, a ranking algorithm is a supervised algorithm that learns to produce a score for each item in the dataset. Depending on the algorithm's configuration, the final score might just define the relevance as a binary entity (relevant/not relevant), or it might use a broader form of judgment through a numerical or ordinal score.

Typically, training data is made of data items with some partial order specified in binary or numerical form. The trained model's ultimate goal is to assign a score to an unseen item and order an unseen list of data items by relevance.

The critical point of ranking algorithms is to discover and properly handle the mutual relationship between items that have structural context, as well as handle the role of users' preferences and/or the specific intents in the context. A blind scoring function that applies to each item while ignoring the context will not be very useful in real-world scenarios.

The Flexible Art of Recommendation

A recommendation is a personalized form of ranking that produces a list of products or services expected to align with the user's preferences and intents in the application context. The recommendation comes from some historical rating or activity data collected for the user. Anytime you get a "you may like this, too" kind of message from an online service, you can be sure that you unknowingly interacted with a recommender system built in the backend of the site or app you were using.

Ranking Versus Recommendation

The key difference between ranking and recommendation lies in the fact that ranking is global, whereas recommendation is mostly personal. Ranking tends to address ratings aggregated over large populations of users and produces a kind of general-purpose rating. Recommendation tends to override the default ranking for the specifically recognized preferences and intents of each user.

A ranking algorithm uses a search query that is provided by users who know what they are looking for. A ranking algorithm extracts information from what users actually search for. Recommender systems, on the other hand, work without explicit input from the user and attempt to provide information the user wouldn't have found otherwise. Recommender systems are primarily used in e-commerce applications.

Another difference between ranking and recommendation is that ranking algorithms normally put more relevant items at the top of the list. Instead, the overall notion of relevance is different in a recommendation system where the goal is to find items that are related to other items while not being too similar. In fact, a good recommender system would not typically suggest the top thriller books if you bought one of the top thrillers, but it would propose related books that might have a number of common aspects. For example, if you bought a legal thriller book, you might be given suggestions for other equally suspenseful and plot-driven books with some bearing to the legal domain.

More concretely, if you give the Amazon's recommender reason to believe you're interested in, say, domain-driven design, Amazon would also propose a bunch of books on microservices, event-driven systems, and design patterns, along with books that seem to offer domain-driven design coverage from a different angle. In a nutshell, a recommender still uses ranking, but the scoring function is much more sophisticated as it doesn't count pure relevance but aims at a broader and diversified idea of relevance.

Personalization

Ranking and recommendation move on distinct lines that intersect in some way. Google, for example, started as a general-purpose page ranker 20 years ago. but at some point, it started slowly but steadily moving toward becoming a personal recommender service. Hence, personalization is a key factor in a recommender system, and an emphasis on personalization makes a system more exposed to more sparse data.

Typically, personalization is achieved in two steps. First, filtering methods decompose data items in features, and then the consumer activity is matched to a number of those features. For example, a book can be featurized by author, genre, leading character, and year of release. This information is then matched to consumer browsing or buying history to find out how many books of that author, those genres, that year the customer has shown interest in. Interestingly, in a content-filtering recommender system, no user personal information (such as gender, nationality, or age) is used.

> **NOTE** A recommender system is personal by definition, but what about ranking? When we get a ranking, are we sure it is valid globally, at least for a given domain? Is it biased in some way? In which way? More, is it deliberately biased? As you can see, this way of reasoning will soon lead to AI ethics. At the same time, when we add the capability to control what's ranked (and how it's ranked), we move away from ranking and get into personalization, where no idea of generality exists by definition.

The Delicate Art of Collaborative Filtering

A content-filtered recommender relies heavily on any known past activity of the user within the host system, whether an e-commerce site, media platform, or social network. This scenario presents a clear drawback: final recommendations may be inaccurate for inactive users because of a lack of core information to match to data features. However, new users are problematic to handle, too, because a content-based filtering system would experience the same lack of information for both inactive and new users. (This is also known as the *cold start problem*.)

Collaborative filtering is a method specifically designed to address both limitations above. It does that by turning the principle of content filtering upside down and heavily leveraging cross-user information. More generally, we can consider collaborative filtering as a special form of a recommendation system that is best suited to scenarios where user data is known, such as age, gender, earnings, occupation, and residence, but there's a shortage of user-specific activity within the host platform.

Unlike a classic content-based recommendation system, a collaborative recommender attempts to predict how much a given consumer might be interested in an item based on other consumers' previous interest in the same item. Essentially, such a recommender uses some heuristics to predict a user's rating for an item, starting from the ratings of other users who have similar personal traits, such as age, gender, earnings, and so on.

Finally, note that collaborative filtering is not free of issues when it comes to data. In fact, less popular items with only a few ratings risk being inaccurately mapped to users.

The ML Recommendation Task

A common example to make sense of recommenders is taking a list of movies and predicting which of them would be of interest to a given user. Or, the other way around, when any user logs in, the system presents a list of movies that might be interesting to watch. At its core, it is a matter of getting a software module that is capable of taking a user ID and a movie ID and scoring the match between the two. If the score turns out to be higher than a fixed threshold, then the movie makes it to the list of recommendations; otherwise, it will just be ignored.

In order to go through the following example, you will need to install an extra NuGet package on top of the default ML.NET library. From the NuGet frontend, you pick up the package named `Microsoft.ML.Recommender`.

A Look at the Available Data

The sample application we discuss here covers a canonical use case for a recommendation system: Predict if a user is going to like a given movie that they haven't watched yet. Technically, the recommender works by estimating the user's movie rating and voting for "like" if the rating exceeds a fixed satisfaction threshold.

The data we'll work on in the example is a CSV text file made of a few comma-separated columns, including user ID, movie ID, rating in the 1 through 5 interval, and time of the rating. The dataset comes from the repository of ML.NET samples and contains a collection of about 100,000 ratings. The database is fully anonymized, and both movies and users are identified with a numeric ID. As a side note, the number of distinct users is in the order of a few hundred; the number of distinct movies is in the order of a few thousand.

Schema of the Data

The C# class that describes the features we're considering for recommendation is shown below. The property we want the model to predict is `Rating`. We also ignore the `Timestamp` column in the dataset.

```
public class RatingData
{
    [LoadColumn(0)]
    public float UserId;

    [LoadColumn(1)]
    public float MovieId;

    [LoadColumn(2)]
    public float Rating;
}
```

Figure 9-2 shows a glimpse of the source dataset in Microsoft Excel.

	A	B	C	D
1	userId	movieId	rating	timestamp
2	1	1	4	964982703
3	1	3	4	964981247
4	1	6	4	964982224
5	1	47	5	964983815
6	1	50	5	964982931
7	1	70	3	964982400
8	1	101	5	964980868
9	1	110	4	964982176
10	1	151	5	964984041
11	1	157	5	964984100
12	1	163	5	964983650
13	1	216	5	964981208
14	1	223	3	964980985
15	1	231	5	964981179

FIGURE 9-2 An interior view of the dataset used for the movie recommender system

The UserId and MovieId columns identify users and movies anonymously, whereas the Rating column indicates the level of satisfaction the given user expressed about the given movie in a scale that ranges from 1 (poor) to 5 (excellent). It goes without saying that any client application calling into the finalized model will have to provide a real user ID and a real movie ID from the same production database where the data to train the model originally came. Typically, a recommender system works on a per-user basis. Therefore, the users whose movie preferences have been used for training should be the same for which movie predictions are requested (with the obvious exception being new users of the system and new and unrated movies in the catalog). In this case, it becomes a matter of guesswork.

Selecting Columns of Data

In our example, the timestamp column still found in the dataset is ignored by the model because we decided counting the time of rating was not relevant. Remember, though, that this is only a demo. In a real-world scenario, the time of rating might be used to assign a different weight to each row. For example, you might want to count different ratings from last year versus the ratings made two or more years ago.

The dataset's timestamp column reports a UNIX epoch date (number of seconds elapsed since January 1, 1970). If you go through the sample dataset, you find that it covers ratings until about 2017. Hence, you might want to give more relevance to those entered after, say, 2014.

> **IMPORTANT** In each of our "ML Devil's Advocate" chapter sections, we stress the difference in the scale of complexity between easy-to-arrange-and-explain demos (including these) and real-world business scenarios. The simple change is that adding a different weight to older and newer dates could make the solution significantly more complex. The extra layer of complexity could range from an additional data transformation step on top of a shallow learning algorithm (such as matrix factorization that we'll be using here) to using a tailormade neural network.

A Bit of Feature Engineering

Loading the data into a new ML.NET data context is in no way different from what we have seen in previous examples. You can use file or database loaders depending on the actual storage location of the data. In this case, we'll proceed with a CSV text file:

```
var filePath = ...;
var mlContext = new MLContext();
var dataView = mlContext.Data.LoadFromTextFile<RatingData>(filePath,
                        hasHeader: true, separatorChar: ',');
```

Using the training dataset shown in Figure 9-2, there's not much to do with feature engineering. However, in a real-world system, the user ID and movie ID are not always plain numbers. If they're expressed as alphanumeric strings, then you need to map those unique strings to numbers.

```
private IEstimator<ITransformer> ComposeDataProcessingPipeline(MLContext mlContext)
{
    IEstimator<ITransformer> pipeline = mlContext
        .Transforms
        .Conversion
        .MapValueToKey(outputColumnName: "userIdEncoded", inputColumnName: "UserId")
        .Append(context
            .Transforms
            .Conversion
            .MapValueToKey(outputColumnName: "movieIdEncoded", inputColumnName: "MovieId"));

    // More stuff possibly goes here.
    // For example, making small values smaller and high values higher

    return pipeline;
}
```

Note that if you run the above code on the dataset of Figure 9-2, you get two identical copies of the `UserId` and `MovieId` columns. However, if ID columns were text-based, you get two equivalent numeric columns more comfortably processed by any algorithm.

Relevance by Date

The column `Timestamp` in Figure 9-2 presents apparently weird numbers. As mentioned, they represent dates saved as UNIX epochs, namely the number of seconds after the UNIX's Big Bang of the digital world—January 1, 1970. In .NET, the `DateTimeOffset` class lets you easily convert dates to and from the UNIX representation, which, incidentally, is the same used in JavaScript.

What if you want to give more relevance to more recent ratings and disregard older ones? First and foremost, it's not a trivial issue to address, and there's not much you can do using a shallow learning algorithm for training. We'll say more on the relevance of rating by date later in the "ML Devil's Advocate" section. For now, suffice it to say that if you decide that ratings older than a specific date are irrelevant, you can just rule them out with a data filter. The code below sets Jan 1, 2014, as a UNIX date.

```
// Numeric timestamp threshold for Jan 1, 2014
var unix2014 = new DateTimeOffset(2014, 1, 1, 0, 0, 0, TimeSpan.Zero);
var after2014 = unix2014.ToUnixTimeSeconds();
```

The `IDataView`'s method `FilterRowsByColumn` allows you to keep only those rows following a given date. Here's an example.

```
var filteredData = mlContext
            .Data
            .FilterRowsByColumn(dataView, "Timestamp", after2014);
```

It is worth noting that this approach just reduces the number of rows eligible for training. It doesn't really attribute a different weight to each rating based on age. As mentioned, that's a far more wicked problem to tackle.

Composing the Training Pipeline

We now need to choose a trainer and append it to the ML.NET learning pipeline in order to train the model and evaluate its results. Which algorithm should we start with?

The Matrix Factorization Algorithm

A common (collaborative filtering) algorithm for recommender systems is Matrix Factorization (MF). The algorithm works on a dataset like the one used here by decomposing the entire matrix of user/movie interaction into the product of the two lower-ranked matrices. The lowest-ranked dimension of these two matrices is one of the algorithm's hyperparameters.

In ML.NET, you find an implementation of the MF algorithm that we'll be using here. The ML.NET code for the training and testing pipelines is shown below:

```
private static void TrainEvaluateSaveModel(MLContext mlContext,
    IDataView trainingDataView,
    IDataView testDataView,
    IEstimator<ITransformer> dataProcessPipeline,
    string modelPath)
{
    var options = new MatrixFactorizationTrainer.Options
```

```
{
    MatrixColumnIndexColumnName = "userIdEncoded",
    MatrixRowIndexColumnName = "movieIdEncoded",
    LabelColumnName = "Rating",
    NumberOfIterations = 20,
    ApproximationRank = 300
};

// Training
var trainer = mlContext.Recommendation().Trainers.MatrixFactorization(options);
var trainingPipeline = dataProcessPipeline.Append(trainer);
var model = trainingPipeline.Fit(trainingDataView);

// Evaluate model
var prediction = model.Transform(testDataView);
var metrics = mlContext.Regression.Evaluate(prediction,
        labelColumnName: "Rating",
        scoreColumnName: "Score");

Console.WriteLine("MSE... : " + metrics.RootMeanSquaredError);
Console.WriteLine("R2.....: " + metrics.RSquared);

// Save the trained model to a .ZIP file
mlContext.Model.Save(model, trainingDataView.Schema, modelPath);
}
```

We set the MF trainer to work on data rows represented as triplets of values such as user ID, movie ID, and known rating. We also set two hyperparameters, such as the maximum number of iterations to run until returning and the rank of the approximation matrices to use for internal purposes. More precisely, if the dataset is $M \times N$ then the algorithm internally builds two approximation matrices to express the original dataset as a product of matrices: $M \times k$ and $k \times N$ in size, where k is the approximation rank provided.

> **NOTE** On an historical note, the MF family of algorithms gained popularity back in the early 2000s during the Netflix prize challenge. Netflix set up the challenge in 2006 as an attempt to find a way to improve the accuracy of watch suggestions made to users. Put another way: The challenge was about predictions of how much someone would have enjoyed watching a given movie. The 1-million-dollar prize was awarded to a combined team from various research institutes globally known as BellKor's Pragmatic Chaos team. The algorithm they proposed is a rather sophisticated variation of a classic MF algorithm that uses an Ensemble approach to train multiple MF models simultaneously and applies a non-linear blending to make the final decision.

Any Missing Pieces?

In a nutshell, the algorithm does the following. First, it gets a user and a movie and looks for other users in the dataset that rated the same movies the given user rated. If the user has not rated the specified movie, but any of the other users with similar preferences did, then an average of the available ratings is taken. What if there are no ratings whatsoever (such as a new and inactive user and/or a new and unpopular movie)? Frankly, in this case, it's not much different from tossing a coin. Yet, it can be acceptable for a media platform or a web site. In the end, it's a mere suggestion!

If you want to (try to) be as accurate as possible, an ad hoc algorithm must be arranged that likely connects various pieces in a cascade. Therefore, it's not simply about training an algorithm; it's about building, testing, and finally, training a learning machine.

Evaluating the Model

Recommender systems pose a challenge when splitting up the available data into training and test datasets. In this example, we started with predefined datasets and didn't perform any splitting on our own, but in general, you have a list of ratings (such as participants for the Netflix prize could count on 100 million ratings back in 2006) and must make a typical 80/20 split manually.

For a recommender system, you should always reason in terms of user/movie pairs and pick them randomly from the well of data. You mustn't select users or movies individually at random. The issue is that if a user is found only in the test dataset, the trained model might be unable to accurately predict the preferences of a user it knows nothing about. This leads us to consider ranking and recommendation problems that make it unique in the machine learning landscape. You always need information about the user; the actual production prediction should be effectively based on a personal time series of ratings rather than on a model that has been generically trained to predict preferences. As the name itself suggests, a recommender system is up close and personal. Training must reflect that, and generally, the whole idea of collaborative filtering is about using provided ratings to predict the rating a user would give to movies they haven't watched yet.

The actual performance of a recommender system depends on the (limited) sparseness of the user/movie matrix being built internally. Often, this matrix (all movies and all users) is fairly sparse, with lots of empty spaces for all those users who haven't rated a movie. However, many other aspects contribute to the effectiveness of a recommender system. Any platform (media, e-commerce, or social) you recommend on is unique and is subject to different parameters. In this regard, reading some technical reports of the Netflix prize challenge algorithms would be highly instructive. You need to come up with ways to handle aspects like human bias, tendency to enter bulk ratings, and subsequent temporal memory effects. For example, days after watching a movie, a user might only remember what they liked most and then skip rating what they watched but didn't enjoy. (We'll return to this point later in the "ML Devil's Advocate" section.)

The most common way to give a passing evaluation to a recommendation algorithm is the root mean square error (RMSE), namely the mean from the sum over the squared error of known entries in the test set (distance between the predicted and expected). The smaller the value, the better the alleged performance. Here's code to get predictions out of the test dataset and calculate regression metrics (which delivers R-squared and RMSE values) using the Rating source column as the truth and the column Score as the container of the computed prediction.

```
var predictions = model.Transform(testDataView);
var metrics = mlContext.Regression.Evaluate(predictions, "Rating", "Score");
```

Where does Score come from?

Actually, in this chapter, we haven't yet mentioned the C# class that the MF algorithm uses to return computed predictions.

```
public class RatingPrediction
{
    public float Label { get; set; }
    public float Score { get; set; }
}
```

As a curiosity, the algorithm that won the Netflix prize scored an RMSE of 0.8567 on the test dataset.

Other Algorithms

A possible reading of the final stage of the Netflix prize (which ran for three consecutive years ending in 2009) is that matrix factorization, while not perfect, is probably the best performing algorithm in terms of both physical performance and accuracy. Which are alternatives?

K-Nearest Neighbors (KNN) is an excellent starting point for the development of a recommender system. In itself, KNN separates the rows in a dataset into several clusters and is an unsupervised method. Applied to a recommender system, it turns out that its outcome can be used to infer the cluster where new data points may fall in. KNN makes no assumptions about the distribution of data but just measures the distance between items to spot possible similarities. KNN calculates the distance between the movie to consider and all other movies in the database and returns the top K movies that the employed distance reported as nearby and then similar.

> **IMPORTANT** KNN is powerful, especially in this context of recommenders but leaves an open point. Which parameters can you really use to compute the distance? It can only be fragments of information about the movie itself, things like category, actors, director, year, and the like.

The effectiveness of a KNN method is strictly dependent on the effectiveness of the selected distance function. The classic choice of a Euclidean distance might not be optimal in recommenders with a high degree of sparseness, and a cosine distance might be preferable sometimes (or something different as the actual quality of data might suggest). In a way, the challenge is improving KNN so that also scales well with very large datasets like those commonly involved with recommenders.

Anyway, one of the facts that surfaced clearly from the Netflix challenge as a way to improve the accuracy of a recommender system, beyond optimization in the computational aspects of the training process, is the idea of using ensemble methods. In machine learning, ensemble refers to a few classes of algorithms that generate a predictive model from the combination of multiple learning techniques. Essentially, they group weak learners together to form one stronger learner.

> **NOTE** Generally, there seems to be agreement on the fact that matrix factorization techniques can be trained efficiently, and predictions can be generated more quickly than with KNN or other methods such as a Restricted Boltzman Machine (RBM). Also, the integration of additional data features and filters on the data is easier.

Setting Up a Client Application

There are many different ways in which one can create a recommender. For example, should the recommender return a list of suggestions (say, top 5) of movies the user may want to see? Should this happen as soon as the user has finished watching a movie and/or when they log in to the system? Or should the system predict how much the user is going to enjoy a given movie they have not watched yet? It's a mere matter of what the business demands. Our example supports the latter scenario, but supporting the former is a matter of adding some more work and access to the database of users and movies.

Skeleton of the App

The sample web application follows the same pattern we have seen in past chapters. It has a prediction engine picked up from the pool of engines and injected into the controller:

```
public class RateController : Controller
{
    private readonly RatingService _service;

    public RateController(PredictionEnginePool<RatingData, RatingPrediction> ratingEngine)
    {
        _service = new RatingService(ratingEngine);
    }

    // ...
}
```

The `RatingService` class does the job of calling the model from the data it has received from the frontend.

```
public RatingPredictionInfo Recommend(UserMovieInput input)
{
    var modelInput = new RatingData {MovieId = input.MovieId, UserId = input.UserId};

    // Predict movie rating
    var prediction = _ratingEngine.Predict("SampleRanking.Recommender", modelInput);

    // Cut some decimals
    var score = (float) Math.Round(prediction.Score, 2);

    // ...
}
```

The model we trained can only return a movie rating for a given user. The Score variable in the snippet above is the predicted rating the user would give to the movie and is a number in the 1..5 interval.

The User Interface

The sample page contains an HTML form through which user ID and movie ID are collected. Admittedly, the user interface you can see in Figure 9-3 is fairly scanty and just uses input fields to accept ID values. In a realistic scenario, you likely have a drop-down menu for the movies with titles displayed and hidden IDs. The user ID instead would likely result from the currently logged-in user. At any rate, the two pieces of input data in the figure can be assumed to be always available.

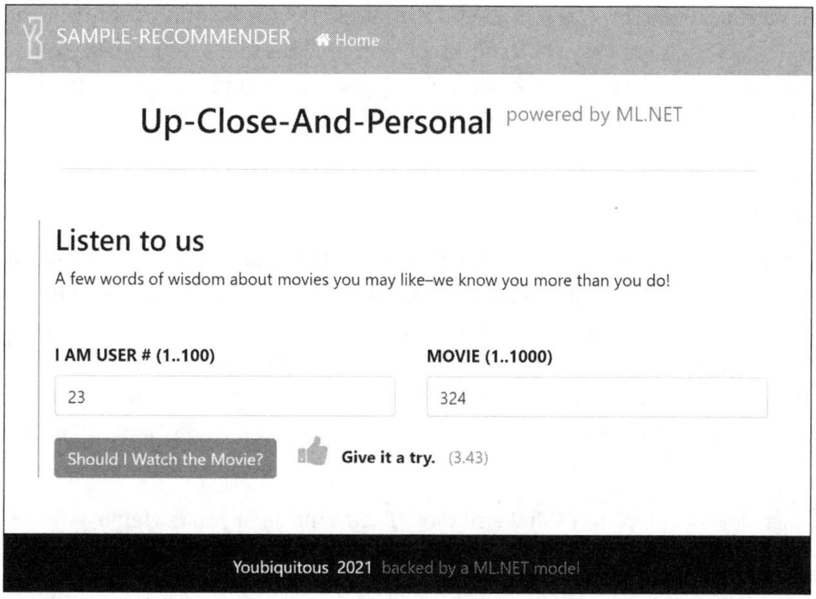

FIGURE 9-3 A sample movie recommender in action

User and movie IDs are posted to a controller endpoint and processed as discussed before. The result is a float number representing the predicted level of preference. How should we present the raw response to the user? The following code provides a human-readable version of the computed score.

```
if (prediction.Score >= 0 && prediction.Score <= 1.5)
    info.HumanReadableScore = new HumanScore {Text = "You'd rather skip this!",
                                              Style = "fa fa-2x fa-thumbs-down"};
else if (prediction.Score <= 2.74)
    info.HumanReadableScore = new HumanScore {Text = "Give it a try, but may not like it",
                                              Style = "fa fa-2x fa-thumbs-down"};
```

```
else if (prediction.Score <= 4.0)
    info.HumanReadableScore = new HumanScore {Text = "Give it a try.",
                                              Style = "fa fa-2x fa-thumbs-up"};
else
    info.HumanReadableScore = new HumanScore {Text = "You're going to LOVE this movie.",
                                              Style = "fa fa-2x fa-heart"};
```

The class HumanScore is a plain data-transfer object with only two string properties (Text and Style) created just for the purposes of the user interface.

ML Devil's Advocate

Even though matrix factorization is likely the most effective algorithm for collaborative filtering, building up a recommender system is not easy. It can be so complex at times that a rather naïve solution is often regarded as more than acceptable. In the end, it's all about how accurate you need to be in your specific context. Let's start from the aforementioned Netflix challenge.

If You're Like Netflix

If you have to design a recommender system expected to generate an average of 30 billion predictions per day, you must be at the top. You must be able to penetrate the mind of individuals and try to read the content. It's a matter of business survival; it's just what can help you make the difference with competitors. More, it has to become your unique, distinctive trait. Therefore, you can even set up a public competition and challenge participants to improve by 10 percent or more the best result you currently have. You're not just interested in a better solution; you want it to be significantly better than anything you may have.

Isn't it what we just played with so far? What else should you consider if you're Netflix?

All models based on collaborative filtering ultimately try to capture the sense of interactions taking place between users and movies (in general, items to recommend). Each user is different, however, and each may be subject to a form of bias. For example, some users may show a systematic tendency to give ratings higher (or lower) than others for the same effective feelings. This is an aspect of rating that you want to moderate if you're Netflix. This likely means that you want to organize the prediction around a user-specific time series that only comprehends real user-movies interaction. In this case, the scale of rating is likely the same across the entire dataset. It may mean grouping users and training multiple models or perhaps keeping clusters of movies created via KNN and finding a match between global and user-specific clusters. One way to do this is using an auto-encoder neural network to reduce user and movie information to a new, smaller representation. This encoder will convey personal user information (gender, age, profession, and residence) and movie facts (director, year, and genre). The user representation might even be further enriched with previous ratings to form an expression for the user that is as comprehensive of all aspects of the user being a consumer of the media platform.

Another aspect you want to look at is bulk rating. Users don't typically rate right at the end of the movie. Sometimes several days separate the actual watching experience and the rating. It is generally believed (and psychology confirms) that even when doing bulk rating, users still tend to express their natural preferences. The issue here is that you may experience asymmetry in the number of ratings per movie. Typically, a movie for which strong feedback is provided (whether positive or negative) is remembered longer and consequently tends to get more reviews. As a result, some movies end up with fewer ratings, thus creating a discrepancy in the available dataset.

Yet another aspect is when users share the same account. Over time, ratings for the same user might not follow a recognizable pattern, or they might follow multiple patterns. Furthermore, it should also be taken into account that users might change their moods and preferences over time, so their ratings follow different patterns even when they do not share the account. Should the algorithm consider the same ratings provided years before? Should you remove those old ratings from the count? There's no obvious answer, and to some extent, all answers are good. It depends on who you are and what you're going to build.

What If You're Not Like Netflix?

If your business is economically centered on what users do with your suggestions (watch more stuff, buy more things, or do more work) then accuracy is a key element, and you should also take into account every single wrinkle that may alter the data you own. Otherwise, more naïve solutions are acceptable as well. In this case, you may even avoid machine learning altogether and opt for an expert system.

To put it another way, it's like the level of accuracy you need from a regression algorithm that attempts to predict the cost of a taxi ride. If you're a competing and compelling ride-hailing company, predicting near-exact prices is a must. In other business scenarios, it might still be helpful to offer a cost prediction, but a less accurate prediction is also acceptable. In Chapter 4, "Prediction Tasks," we found out that once trained, the algorithm produces a prediction model whose results work well for New York (where the dataset originated) but are still acceptable for Rome, too, once you have changed USD for EUR. Again, it's all about expectations.

Anyway, for recommenders, if you need to go beyond naivety, it might be fairly complex. And do not forget that Netflix put up its challenge more than 15 years ago! It's vision, not just technology.

Summary

Terms like "ranking" (or "search ranking") and "recommenders" are sometimes used interchangeably, and the difference between the two is often blurred. While both algorithms are trying to present items in a sorted way, there are some key differences between these two terms. In particular, a recommender system collects data from many users to guess the preferences of each user. A ranking system measures the relevance of documents in an information retrieval system of any kind. A recommender won't receive any input from the user; a ranker will.

Both systems try to help users of a system to get what they're looking for. Both systems (especially recommenders) suffer from a possible lack of interpretation of the results. The interesting thing is that users have no way to check the quality of the suggestion other than by following it. In doing so, though, they break the core statement that a recommendation (or a suggested document) is good (or relevant for the search). However, adding explainability is problematic and is still a subject of deep research. Probably for this reason, in the whole spectrum of ranking solutions across the industry, you might jump from naïve to fairly sophisticated solutions with nothing left in the middle.

With the next chapter, our tour of ML.NET tasks comes to its end. The next chapter is again about classification, but it's a very special type of classification: image classification.

CHAPTER 10

Image Classification Tasks

"Speculations? I have none. I am resting on certainties."

—Michael Faraday

The saying, "A picture is worth a thousand words," works well for humans, but its application is much more complicated in software. Humans feature highly parallel brains capable of carrying extremely complex operations instantaneously. For computers, certain operations—standing their current internal architecture—require much more effort and/or a lot of training. The quintessential example is recognizing what's featured in an image. This macro area can be further split into at least two more specific areas: image classification and object detection.

Image classification aims at automatically classifying images into one or more categories based on the content represented. Conceptually, it's no different from the classification task we discussed in Chapter 5, except that we don't have a number of feature columns for classification algorithms to work on to extract similarities. An image is a different kind of animal and requires a different kind of environment to be processed.

Object detection is the primary form of computer vision and refers to the ability to recognize the object featured in the image (or video frame) in much the same way a human brain would do.

Dealing with images in machine learning poses a crucial problem. Realistically, no team outside IT giants can start from scratch. First, it's deep learning, and no straight algorithm exists for it. Second, you need to set up a neural network with certain characteristics (we'll tackle neural networks in the next chapter) and train it for hundreds of hours on millions of images. It's a relevant computational cost that no individual and not even the majority of teams can easily pay.

The way out—fully supported by ML.NET—is to use a sort of shortcut known as transfer learning or retraining. Though not perfect, it works acceptably well.

Transfer Learning

Both image classification and object detection are commonly tackled in custom applications taking publicly available, pre-trained models for image processing and retraining them to achieve a more specific purpose. This is the approach we'll demonstrate in this chapter.

Popular Image Processing Neural Networks

Transfer learning requires a foundation model to build on. As far as images are concerned, the most popular model is Inception. In particular, Inception v3 is an image recognition model that has proven already capable of offering significant accuracy. The model was built and refined over the years and now sets the ground for solid computer vision implementation. The paper describing the internal architecture of Inception can be found here: *https://arxiv.org/pdf/1512.00567.pdf*.

Inception has been trained on the ImageNet dataset available at *https://image-net.org/download.php*. The dataset contains over 1,200,000 images and recognizes more than 1,000 object classes. In other words, it means that the Inception model is sufficiently capable of recognizing over a thousand common-use objects and entities in submitted images. The power of transfer learning lies just in the ease through which you can extend the core capabilities of Inception to fit your needs. You also save hours of training—typically by one order of magnitude. You must be aware of what you intend to achieve and on which images. The cost of adapting Inception to your needs is affordable to nearly everyone.

Other Image Neural Networks

Inception is only the most popular image processing predefined neural network. Other networks exist for you to choose and build your own tailormade solution. All these networks support retraining, so in the end, it's about defining your objectives, pursuing them, and leveraging the programmability of such neural networks.

The following link groups a few links to image processing neural networks alternatives to Inception.

https://tfhub.dev/s?module-type=image-feature-vector&tf-version=tf2

Most of them have been initially trained on the ImageNet database. Each neural network features an alternative internal neural architecture which ends up in different costs of training and, from the user perspective, in different levels of accuracy in recognizing images.

Without further ado, let's see how to work with Inception in an ML.NET-based C# application.

Transfer Learning via Composition

Transfer Learning can take place in either of two ways. One way is through the ML Image Classification task; the other is via explicit model composition. The ML Image Classification task hides most of the underlying details, whereas the composition approach requires that a new explicit model is built on top of the results of the pretrained model. Let's tackle composition first.

As mentioned, model composition performs nearly the same tasks as the ML Image Classification task except that it makes most of the steps explicit, whereas the task cuts them off by convention or parameterization. In the model composition scenario, first, the application loads the prebuilt Inception model in the training pipeline. Second, it turns the problem into a more manageable canonical classification problem like the one we looked at in Chapter 5, "Classification Tasks." To put it another way, the preloaded Inception model allows you to extract image-related features that can then be worked on as plain classification matter.

The Transfer Learning Pattern in ML.NET

In order to unleash the power of image classification and transfer learning in ML.NET, you need to install a few additional NuGet packages in the .NET solution. In particular,

- `Microsoft.ML.ImageAnalytics`

- `SciSharp.TensorFlow.Redist`

- `Microsoft.ML.TensorFlow`

Inception is a neural network model built with TensorFlow, which is one of the most popular frameworks for such tasks. You need the bits of the model and the ML.NET bindings necessary for the ML.NET framework to interact with the model and the TensorFlow framework. Figure 10.1 shows the overall connecting parts. Ultimately, the custom application code will receive the retrained ML.NET model built from the Inception binaries and ML.NET bindings.

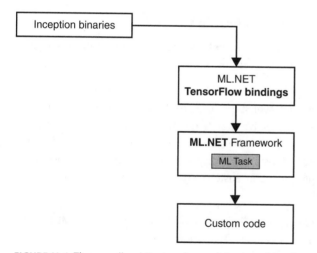

FIGURE 10-1 The overall architecture for model composition from TensorFlow models in ML.NET

The top of the chain is the source-trained model as it comes from the Inception project. It's a free download of files to be incorporated into the ML.NET training project. The additional NuGet packages referenced above provide the bindings between the native TensorFlow framework (the framework used to build Inception) and the host ML.NET framework (the framework used to build the new retrained model). Instead, the `ImageAnalytics` Nuget package contains just the facilities to operate the image classification task in ML.NET.

Overall Purpose of the New Image Classifier

The idea is fairly simple: Use the trained model (Inception) to extract features from the custom image dataset and turn it into suitable input for a classical machine learning algorithm such as a multiclass classifier. The final goal is building a dedicated, far simpler image classifier that can tag images with one of a few categories. The net result of such a transfer learning operation is performing a plain multiclass classification except that it takes place on top of images rather than text.

> **NOTE** Building your own neural network for processing images is realistically out of the question for small teams. An image processing tool is a complex and tailor-made neural network that results from the composition of multiple types of neural networks combined through connectors of many types. This is not exactly an exercise you can run for fun. To experiment with neural networks, you need to resort to dedicated frameworks like Tensor-Flow or PyTorch. There's also a tentative roadmap to offer neural network building infra-structure in future versions of ML.NET as well.

Mapping to a Canonical Classification Problem

In order to analyze the content of an image, a neural network builds a mathematical represen-tation of the image—let's call it an *encoding* of the image.

This representation travels across the layers of the network and gets more precise at every step. When the encoding reaches the final layer, it gets used to classify the original image within the prefixed tags of the network. When we use a large pre-trained network, we can safely assume that the encoding that makes it to the final layer effectively offers a consistent representation of the processed image. Transfer learning just overrides the way the encoding is mapped to tags. In a transfer learning scenario, custom tags are used instead of the tags originally supported by the network.

In model composition, the override of the final layer is explicitly coded; with the ML Image Classification task, it's conducted via parameters and configuration.

A Look at the Available Data

Any transfer learning project has two blocks of input data—one is the trained model, and the other is the (few) sample images to classify. To use the Inception model as the trained model, you need to get ahold of the model files and save them in one of the folders of the ML.NET project.

The download URL for the latest version of the Inception model is *https://bit.ly/2ShnXSA*. When you unzip the file, you find the serialized model—a Protobuf .pb binary file—and a couple of text files. One is the license, and the other is the list of the 1,000 categories that the model can recognize in a submitted image.

Let's build our necessary C# tools.

The Sample Image Dataset

The following C# class defines the typical data row in our training dataset. As mentioned, there are two string properties.

```
public class ImageData
{
    [LoadColumn(0)]
    public string ImagePath;

    [LoadColumn(1)]
    public string Label;
}
```

In a transfer learning scenario, you don't need to put a large dataset on the table. You are relying on a fully trained and fully functional model; a dozen images may be enough for a quick demo, a thousand (or, better, a few thousand) are sufficient for a more detailed composed model. Here's an example of a dataset. It takes the form of a TSV (tab-separated) text file. One column refers to the sample image file and the second column is about the expected category.

```
veggie.jpg        food
pizza.jpg         food
pizza2.jpg        food
teddy2.jpg        toy
teddy3.jpg        toy
teddy4.jpg        toy
toaster.jpg       appliance
toaster2.png      appliance
```

We load this file into the pipeline using the familiar `LoadFromTextFile` method on the Data catalog.

```
var mlContext = new MLContext();
var data = mlContext.Data.LoadFromTextFile<ImageData>(trainingDataPath);
```

As in the multiclass example seen in Chapter 5, we need to map the names of the class to predict unique numbers. Any model—and neural networks are no exception—can only work on numbers! The dataset column to turn into numbers is `Label`—the second column, as seen in the `ImageData` class declaration. The name for the new column is `LabelKey`.

```
// Add new column LabelKey with a numeric value for each distinct value in column Label
var converter1 = mlContext.Transforms.Conversion.MapValueToKey("LabelKey", "Label");
```

This is only the first step of our data transformation process. More work is required to add all necessary transformations that will enable the TensorFlow model to work properly.

Making Necessary Image Transformations

The image classifier we are building is not natively able to deal with images. It will rely on the Inception Model library for that. However, for this to happen, the training dataset must also include image information in a format that the underlying neural network can understand.

By referencing the `Microsoft.ML.ImageAnalytics` NuGet package, you have access to three estimators tailormade for the Inception Model. The first transformation, carried by the `LoadImages` method, adds a new feature to the dataset named `input`. The content of this column is then iteratively transformed by the chained action of the remaining estimators.

```
// Create dedicated estimators for the Inception Model
var loading = mlContext
    .Transforms
    .LoadImages("input", _trainImagesFolder, "ImagePath");
var resizing = mlContext
    .Transforms
    .ResizeImages("input",
                InceptionSettings.ImageWidth,
                InceptionSettings.ImageHeight,
                "input");
var extracting = mlContext
                .Transforms
                .ExtractPixels("input",
                    null,
                    ImagePixelExtractingEstimator.ColorBits.Rgb,
                    ImagePixelExtractingEstimator.ColorsOrder.ARGB);
```

The `LoadImages` estimator uses the content of the `ImagePath` column to locate the image and load its bitmap into the new Input feature. The `ResizeImages` estimator resizes the bitmap in the `Input` feature, and the `ExtractPixels` estimator extracts color information. At the end of the chain, the originally added Input feature contains pixel information about the image loaded from the path specified by the `ImagePath` column. The net effect is shown in Figure 10-2.

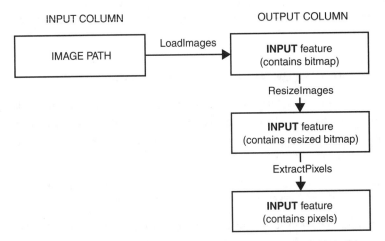

FIGURE 10-2 Image-specific transformations to invoke the Inception Model

Composing the Training Pipeline

Now, let's compose the training infrastructure for the final custom image classifier. First, we need to append the TensorFlow model to the ML.NET pipeline, and then we bring in the specific trainer we intend to use for the multiclass classification.

Adding the TensorFlow Model to the Pipeline

The TensorFlow model to import is saved as a file somewhere in the project. To load it into the ML.NET pipeline, all that's required is knowing the path and calling the LoadTensorFlowModel method from the Model catalog.

```
var inceptionPipeline = mlContext
    .Model
    .LoadTensorFlowModel(tfModelPath)
    .ScoreTensorFlowModel(new[] { "softmax2_pre_activation" }, new[] { "input" }, true);
```

The ScoreTensorFlowModel method invokes the previously loaded TensorFlow model by passing an array of output columns and a set of input columns. In the specific example, each array is made by one column. The output column is softmax2_pre_activation. (The name of the column depends on the actual network used, which in this case is Inception.) The input column is input. (The input column has been obtained after the image transformations above.) These two columns form the output and input of the TensorFlow pre-trained model. Via the input column, the model receives the images to process, and via softmax2_pre_activation column, it returns the output of the neural network on those images.

Retraining the TensorFlow Model

The final step consists of taking the output of the Inception Model library and further using it for our goal of building a custom image classifier. To do so, we need to add the same operations we have seen earlier in the multiclass classification example.

```
var trainer = mlContext
        .MulticlassClassification
        .Trainers
        .LbfgsMaximumEntropy("LabelKey", "softmax2_pre_activation");
var converter2 = mlContext
        .Transforms
        .Conversion
        .MapKeyToValue("PredictedLabelValue", "PredictedLabel");

// Build up the whole pipeline
var trainingPipeline = converter1
    .Append(loading)
    .Append(resizing)
    .Append(extracting)
    .Append(inceptionPipeline)
    .Append(trainer)
    .Append(converter2)
    .AppendCacheCheckpoint(mlContext);

// Train and save the model
var model = trainingPipeline.Fit(data);
mlContext.Model.Save(model, dataViewTraining.Schema, _modelPath);
```

We opt for using the LbfgsMaximumEntropy classification algorithm. The algorithm takes the name of the column it will fill with the response. It is the aptly created numeric column, LabelKey.

It also takes the name of the column it will use as its input. In this case, it gets the output of the TensorFlow model as the input.

According to documentation, the algorithm returns a response that is made of an index named PredictedLabel and an array of float values, each indicating the score for any of the possible classes. This property is named Score. The class index is not enough for us, though, and that's why we turn the index into a string value using the call to MapKeyToValue. As a result, the response of the model can be mapped to the following C# class.

```
public class ImagePrediction
{
    public float[] Score;
    public string PredictedLabelValue;
}
```

So in the end, we call the composed model, pass an ImageData object and receive back an ImagePrediction object.

Setting Up a Client Application

An image classifier sample client application will silently accept (or retrieve) images and add proper tags from a finite short list of labels. A possible real-world example could be a frontend application where users are asked to upload headshots, document photos, and personal photos to share with other users. An easy-to-use user interface could allow users to just upload photos in no special order and with whatever name. A machine learning module under the hood could then properly categorize the uploaded pictures. This is the scenario that we'll address in this chapter.

Skeleton of the App

The web application we're building follows the same pattern we have seen in past chapters. A prediction engine is picked up from the pool of engines and injected into the controller along with the web host container object:

```
public class ImageController : Controller
{
    private readonly ImageService _service;
    private readonly IWebHostEnvironment _env;

    public ImageController(PredictionEnginePool<ImageData, ImagePrediction> imgClassifierEngine,
                        IWebHostEnvironment env)
    {
        _service = new ImageService(imgClassifierEngine);
        _env = env;
    }

    // ...
}
```

The `ImageService` class does the job of calling the model from the data it has received from the frontend via the HTML file uploader.

```
public async Task<IActionResult> Suggest(IFormFile imageFile)
{
    if (imageFile == null)
        return null;
    // Save the image locally to the server
    var filePath = $"{_env.WebRootPath}\\uploads\\{imageFile.FileName}";
    await using var fs = System.IO.File.Create(filePath);
    await imageFile.CopyToAsync(fs);
    fs.Close();

    // Prepares a call to the model
    var input = new ClassifiedImage {ImageFile = filePath};
    var response = _service.Predict(input);
    return Json(response);
}
```

The model we trained can only recognize three categories of pictures: food, appliances, and toys. Admittedly, the number of images used in the sample code is ridiculously small; therefore, expect some funny responses until you retrain it with at least a few hundred additional relevant images. You can even change the target classes to whatever works for you (such as headshots and documents).

```
public class ClassifiedImage
{
    // Source picture
    public string ImageFile { get; set; }

    // Predicted class
    public string TargetClass { get; set; }

    // Score for each possible class (ie, food, toys, appliance)
    public float[] Score { get; set;

    // Web-based URL of the server-side image for rendering purposes
    public string ImageUrl { get; set; }
}
```

The class above renders the response made available to the client and displayed in the user interface.

The User Interface

The sample page contains an HTML form through which users can upload an image. The backend will classify the image and return the target class, as well as the URL to the server-side stored image for rendering purposes. Needless to say, saving the image as a file on the server is arbitrary. More likely, you would have saved it to some blob storage and tagged the file with the response of the model.

> **NOTE** Saving the image server-side builds a free database of images for future retraining. In particular, you can find an interactive way to ask the users to comment on whether the image was categorized well.

Figure 10-3 shows the index page of the sample application. Note that in the client project, you need to reference the same three additional NuGet packages you referenced in the trainer project: `Microsoft.ML.ImageAnalytics`, `Microsoft.ML.TensorFlow`, and `SciSharp.TensorFlow.Redist`.

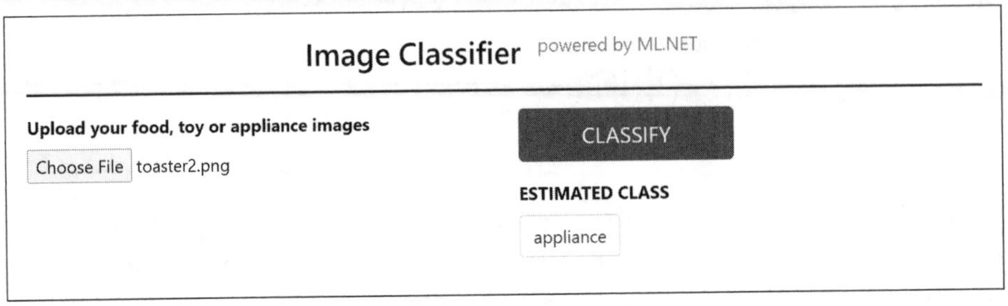
Image Classifier
powered by ML.NET
Upload your food, toy or appliance images
Choose File
toaster2.png
CLASSIFY
ESTIMATED CLASS
appliance

FIGURE 10-3 The sample application using the image classifier model

The ML Image Classification Task

Model composition was the first way provided by ML.NET to do transfer learning. Later, the team added a new native transfer learning method. It's still a matter of transferring knowledge from one model to another, which takes a fraction of the time to train and work. However, with native transfer learning, no explicit composition of the pipeline is required via C# code. Instead, all the magic takes place via the Image Classification API, which makes use of TensorFlow.NET, a low-level library that provides C# bindings for the TensorFlow C++ API.

The Image Classification API

Internally, the Image Classification API conducts the training process by loading a pre-trained TensorFlow model and then retraining as commanded by the programmer. The activity of the Image Classification API is therefore articulated in two steps:

- Bottleneck phase
- Training phase

Altogether, both phases deliver the same service we described earlier through model composition.

The Bottleneck Phase

The name "bottleneck" informally identifies the penultimate layer of a neural network. The API works through the pre-trained model up to the penultimate layer. There, it injects some custom code for the required custom form of training. The bottleneck phase does the job we described earlier on the pixels of the input images and runs images through the preliminary, frozen layers of the neural network.

The term "frozen" here means that preliminary neural network layers are used as in production, and no training occurs on them. Only training (actually, retraining) takes place in the new final layer.

The nice thing about the Image Classification API is that it is designed to work with multiple image analysis pre-trained models and not just Inception. The denser the number of frozen layers, the more accurate the preliminary image analysis is. This analysis extracts lower-level features from the submitted images, which are then finalized later in the overridden layer. It should also be noted that more layers require more computation, and performance can be further improved by adding a cache layer.

The Training Phase

During the training phase of a new image classifier, the pre-trained model works as it would do in a production environment. The output values computed by the bottleneck layer are used as input to retrain the final, custom layer of the model. Note that this process is iterative and runs for the number of times specified as a parameter to the API.

During each run, both loss and accuracy are evaluated, and appropriate, automatic adjustments are made with the purpose of improving the quality of the final result. The interesting thing is that the output is twofold. You get both a ZIP file which represents the native format of ML.NET, and a Protobuf (.pb) file, which represents a TensorFlow source model. This makes it possible to re-import the ML.NET trained model outside ML.NET and use it natively in, say, Python environments.

Using the Image Classification API

Here's some code that shows the use of the image classification API:

```
var pipeline = mlContext
    .MulticlassClassification
    .Trainers
    .ImageClassification(classifierOptions)
    .Append(mlContext.Transforms.Conversion.MapKeyToValue("PredictedLabel"));
ITransformer trainedModel = pipeline.Fit(trainSet);
```

As you can see, the code is much more compact, and many details we've run through with the model composition example are now incorporated in the `ImageClassification` task. Let's have a look at the parameters you can pass to the task.

```
var classifierOptions = new ImageClassificationTrainer.Options()
{
    FeatureColumnName = "Image",
    LabelColumnName = "LabelAsKey",
    Arch = ImageClassificationTrainer.Architecture.InceptionV3,
```

```
        ReuseTrainSetBottleneckCachedValues = true,
        ReuseValidationSetBottleneckCachedValues = true
};
```

The most relevant parameter is `Arch`, which refers to the underlying neural network to use for the bottleneck phase. Multiple public image classifiers are supported as shown in Figure 10-4

```
var classifierOptions = new ImageClassificationTrainer.Options()
{
    FeatureColumnName = "Image",
    LableColumnName = "LabelAsKey",
    Arch = ImageClassificationTrainer.Architecture.InceptionV3,
    ReuseTrainSetBottleneckCachedValues = true,    ⚙️ InceptionV3   Architecture
    ReuseValidationSetBottleneckCachedValues = t   ⚙️ MobilenetV2   Architecture
};                                                  ⚙️ ResnetV2101   Architecture
var pipeline = mlContext                            ⚙️ ResnetV250    Architecture
    .MulticlassClassification                       🔧 TryParse            bool
    .Trainers                                       📦 typeof
    .ImageClassification(classifierOptions)         ⬤ ◈ ▦
    .Append(mlContext.Transforms.Conversion.MapKeyToValue("PredictedLabel"));
```

FIGURE 10-4 Supported model architectures in the ML.NET Image Classification API

Aside from properties that set label names, it is relevant to point out the `ReuseTrainSetBottle-neckCachedValues` and `ReuseValidationSetBottleneckCachedValues` properties, which allow you to enable caching of frozen values for performance speed.

> **NOTE** In order to use the Image Classification API, you should also install an additional NuGet package: `Microsoft.ML.Vision`.

The ML Devil's Advocate

Searching for photos, whether for personal fun or business reasons, is challenging because the information being sought is purely visual. Accept it as a fact or not, but there's really little true intelligence in current artificial intelligence. Machine learning, in particular, is the most formidable tool to evolve artificial intelligence towards new peaks, but for the time being, it has more of brute-force than smart analysis of information. As far as images are concerned, the human eye, in cooperation with the human brain, can do infinitely better and much faster.

The Magic of the Human Brain

About a decade ago (around 2013), Google launched a new service enabling logged users to search for their photos stored in the cloud. The service was surprisingly able to retrieve photos based on the content and was, therefore, able to recognize most of the objects present in the photo. It was never advertised as AI, but it was definitely the first sign of modern AI made in some way visible to the masses.

It was proof that computer vision was possible and software could classify images close to human standards. From a pure feature perspective, the service was bringing a number of benefits to the table. First and foremost, thanks to the service, users could stop going with the extremely annoying manual task of tagging photos and could query for photos they never tagged using content-oriented terms that came naturally given the context they were thinking of.

The process through which the human brain recognizes objects is still largely unknown. In a 2019 study, researchers at MIT stated to have found evidence of the crucial involvement of a specific region of the brain—the inferotemporal cortex—in the process of object detection. In particular, in this region, small groups of neurons each seem to recognize specific items, such as faces or objects. While the details of human vision are largely a gray area, in general, the retina feeds visual information to the brain, and the visual cortex transforms the input into coherent perceptions. In other words, it encodes the information in some way that produces the perception of the item seen at the end of a neuronal computation chain. For more details, you might want to check out the following report: https://news.mit.edu/2019/inferotemporal-brain-object-recognition-0313.

In software, image classification works in much the same way. A neural network is used to implement a multi-step computation in which the original input is transformed up to the final answer.

Handcrafted Neural Networks

Image classification is tackled as a supervised problem where the image is assigned to a target class based on its pixel content. The training dataset is made of images (pixel-based files) and the known target class. However, the neural network doesn't process raw pixels because they are a too rigid piece of information. Any image is subject to having many small variations of pixels that should not be accounted for. A slightly smaller dog in a photo taken from a larger distance is still a dog, but pixel-wise, it is a significantly different from another photo of a dog. The same holds for the position of the object, the background, ambient lighting, camera angle, and even the camera's focus. Pure RGB values are patently insufficient for the job.

Textures, shapes, and color histograms offer a more stable representation of the information than raw pixel colors, but the downside is that it just shifts the burden on feature engineering. Which colors are most relevant? Which shapes and how large or small? What about the rotation? How flexible should ideally be the definition of a shape? The boost to image classification came only in recent years with the discovery of a particular type of neural network—convolutional neural networks (CNNs). We'll discuss neural networks and explore their taxonomy in Chapter 11 "Overview of Neural Networks."

In summary, handcrafting neural networks is possible, but it comes much easier if you're Google, and even if you're Google, it turns out to be fairly expensive. And it can still be inaccurate without apt and heavyweight techniques. The biggest cost items of a neural network for image classification are the thousands of hours of training (both CPU and GPU) and similar-looking images' availability. As controversial as it might sound, a computer needs thousands of similar images and hours of training to recognize the same cat that small children spot immediately, regardless of its position or size or the image's background or ambiance.

Retraining

If you're Google (or any other giant company), you can probably take the route of building an in-house neural network of some kind to teach it how to recognize images in a specific domain (for example, certain sport gestures). It's not cheap, but it might be worth the cost.

If you're not a giant company, retraining is the best option, although it's not perfect. Retraining forces you to consciously sit on top of an existing and frozen neural network, and it just lets you change the final step, overriding and customizing the result.

So, you typically take a consolidated and pre-trained image neural network built for general object detection, add your own custom target classes, and train for your own specific types of images. It still takes you hundreds (if not thousands) of custom images to process, but in a few hours of training (and most likely without expensive GPU activity), you can surely get good results.

Summary

Most of the beauty of machine learning is crafting your own model to make it behave the way you want. In a way, this reminds us of the old days of software in which every single procedure had to be handcrafted and was rarely reused. Transfer learning is the same concept of software reuse (and modularity) applied to machine learning.

In this chapter, we tackled the rather fascinating problem of software that recognizes objects present in pictures. It's a tough problem that requires a sophisticated neural network and millions of images and thousands of hours of training. Therefore, a handcrafted solution is simply not affordable for small teams. Large organizations are aware of this, so they have worked out public image neural networks that are pre-trained and accurate enough and have made them customizable. This is the essence of retraining or transfer learning.

In TensorFlow, you can completely replace the penultimate layer, grab the features as the previous layers have computed them, and just change the final step to your needs. In ML.NET, this customization step has been wrapped up in a built-in module (the Image Classification task), and customization is exposed via hyperparameters.

In this chapter, we also looked at model composition, which is another way to transfer learning that consists of running a pre-trained neural network on custom images and then mapping the problem to plain multiclass classification.

That's it for ML tasks. The final two chapters of this book will cover the fascinating theme of neural networks.

CHAPTER 11

Overview of Neural Networks

"Mathematics is a place where you can do things which you can't do in the real world."

—Marcus du Sautoy

In the previous chapters, we went with the idea that for every machine learning task, one of a few possible algorithms that, when properly configured, return a sufficiently accurate response. As intimidating as it might sound, this is a decidedly optimistic perspective. The chances that you will not find algorithms that perform acceptably are higher than many seem to think. This is not to mention that all the algorithms we explored for the various problems work only on numbers and tabular data. What if the input is not numbers but images, videos, or sound?

Beyond a certain level of inherent complexity—in the problem and/or in the data source—you need to go beyond straight algorithms and shallow learning and move toward a deeper form of learning. So, welcome to the dazzling world of neural networks!

Feed-forward Neural Networks

The history of neural networks is surprisingly long and even longer than the history of computers. Embryos of modern computers appeared in the 1950s devised around the Von Neumann machine model. Well, believe it or not, an embryo of a neural network appeared a decade before in the peak of the Second World War.

In 1943, in the United States, Warren McCulloch (neuroscientist) and Walter Pitts (mathematician) devised a mathematical model to describe the processing that takes place when the brain deals with the recognition of highly complex patterns. The model was designed to connect many basic cells in the same topological way that neurons are connected in the physical brain. McCulloch and Pitts also gave an elementary but functional model of an artificial neuron. It was only a mathematical model with no concrete mapping to anything physical such as valves, diodes, and resistors but sufficient to be, years later, the starting point for modern neural networks.

The first family of neural networks derived from the McCulloch and Pitts model is the feed-forward neural network (FFNN). Today, FFNNs represent the most common type of neural network, though it is often not sufficiently powerful to tackle the real-world problems of the 21st century.

Artificial Neurons

A neural network is made of layers of artificial neurons. You can think of an artificial neuron as a function that takes a few values in input and returns a single binary value. (See Figure 11-1.) Originally, input values were also devised to be binary values. Today, they're just real numbers.

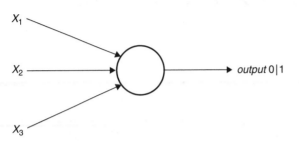

FIGURE 11-1 Overall schema of a perceptron, the first-ever type of artificial neuron

Tightly related to artificial neurons is the concept of an *activation function*.

The Activation Function

The perceptron—the first-ever type of artificial neuron—does two key things:

- It multiplies each value it receives in input for a corresponding coefficient called *weight* and calculates the sum of all products. You can think of this operation as a scalar product of two vectors—input data and weights.

- It returns 1 if the calculated value equals or exceeds a given threshold; otherwise, it returns 0.

Expressed through a formula, it turns out to be the following:

$$Output = \begin{cases} 1 \, if \, \sum_{i=1}^{n} X_i * W_i \geq threshold \\ 0 \, otherwise \end{cases}$$

We can make the function a bit more general by adding an arbitrary term—the *bias*—which is independent of input and weights. When this arbitrary term is added, the formula above changes to the one below. Note that in the formula below, we used a more compact notation for the scalar product of the input vector X and vector of weights W.

$$Output = \begin{cases} 1 \, if \, X \cdot W + b \geq 0 \\ 0 \, if \, X \cdot W + b < 0 \end{cases}$$

Such a function is called an *activation function*. The threshold reminds us of the electrical threshold necessary to activate a synapse (synapse = space where brain cells meet; synapsis = the pairing of two chromosomes during meiosis) in the human brain. The perceptron weighs any received input and makes a decision (that is, it returns 1) only if the actual value is beyond a given level of confidence. The perceptron is a very simple neuron; it is merely a binary and linear classifier, and all it does is draw a hyperplane. In its simplicity, though, the perceptron has a very interesting property: It can be used to simulate a NAND gate.

NAND and Functional Completeness

In electronics, a NAND gate is a logic gate that returns false if all of its inputs are true; otherwise, it returns true. A NAND is the combination of an AND gate and a NOT gate. NAND gates are functionally complete, meaning that all other logic gates (AND, NOT, and OR) can be implemented through a combination of NAND gates. For example, the AND gate can be obtained as a concatenation of two NAND gates. Once you have NAND gates, you can implement any logical expression.

By choosing the proper combination of weights and bias, a perceptron can be used to simulate a NAND gate. Here's an example:

The perceptron in Figure 11-2 has a bias of 3, and −2 is the weight for X_1, X_2 input parameters. Supposing a binary input of 00 (all false), we see that in the former case, the total calculated is 3, which equals the threshold and results in a response of 1. Conversely, assuming an input of 11 (all true), we obtain −, which is not equal to or greater than the threshold, resulting in a response of 0. The same happens for any other variation of 0 and 1 in the input. Hence, the perceptron works as a NAND gate.

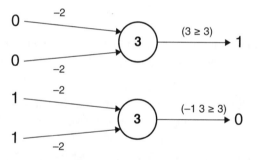

FIGURE 11-2 Using the perceptron to simulate the NAND gate

The NAND equivalence gives perceptrons full expressivity, and by fine-tuning weights and biases, you can calibrate the neuron to make it calculate certain things. In other words, a training process is built on top of perceptrons and can be driven to discover the ideal values of weights and biases that more accurately compute what we want or expect.

Layers of the Network

The power of perceptrons lies in the chance it gives us to approach the flow of any function by simply adding more layers, more inputs, and more connections. The idea is to forward a neuron's output and make it the input of another neuron in a subsequent layer of perceptrons. In this way, the information only travels forward until it reaches the end of the chain.

In essence, that is a feed-forward neural network.

Hidden Layers

The first layer of neurons is the network's input, and the last layer is the output. All intermediate layers—those whose neurons are neither the network's input nor its output as a whole—are known as *hidden layers*. In Figure 11-3, these neurons are rendered as empty circles.

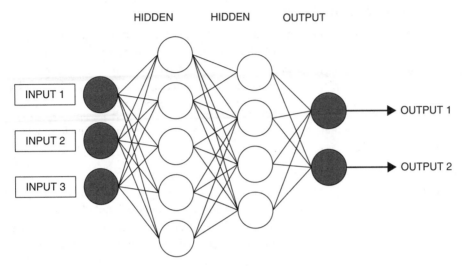

FIGURE 11-3 A sample feed-forward neural network

All neurons belonging to a successive layer receive as input the output calculated by the previous layer's connected neurons. The output of a neuron is obtained through the activation function. Each layer of neurons has its own activation function.

Each layer of a feed-forward neural network adds both complexity and abstraction because you don't work with the raw input data; instead, you are only working with some of its transformations. This is also where the term *deep learning* comes from: the depth of the neural network (or the number of layers in the network) influences and determines the ability to learn. Finally, note that in Figure 11-3, the output layer shows more than just one value. In general, both the input and output of a neural network should be seen as vectors or sequences of vectors.

> **NOTE** Feed-forward neural networks are networks in which the information travels only forward and never backward. In other, more complex types of neural networks, the information can travel back and forth.

Enabling the Network to Learn

So, we now have a neural network that can perform a large set of calculations. The accuracy of those calculations, though, depends on weights and bias. While we can set these values beforehand, it would be great if the network could learn those values by itself. In fact, in real-life scenarios, manually setting weights and bias might be highly impractical given the huge number of connections and weights to deal with.

To set up an effective learning mechanism, though, we need more control over the output. In other words, if we slightly change one of the weights or biases, we also want the output to change slightly and continuously. In this way, through successive refinements, we could manage to obtain just the value we were looking for by simply acting on a specific input without drastically altering all the others and their connections to the output layer.

To enable learning across a neural network, a more sophisticated activation function is needed and consequently (consequently = as a result of; subsequently = following in time not necessarily as a result of) a more sophisticated type of artificial neuron.

The Logistic Neuron

As we've seen, the perceptron employs a *step function* as its activation function. In mathematics, a step function is a piecewise constant function whose entire output is determined by applying constant sub-functions to specific input segments. A step function is neither continuous nor differentiable. To enable learning, instead, we intuitively need more (mathematical) regularity.

Mathematical regularity is the key factor to avoid having a minor change in the input induce a large change in the output. To enable learning, a binary 0/1 choice is no longer enough; we need to attack the entire space of real numbers between 0 and 1.

The Sigmoid Activation Function

Here's then a new type of neuron that replaces the perceptron. The new neuron we consider is called *logistic* (or sigmoid) and has a mathematically continuous activation function.

$$\sigma = Output\left(Z\right) = \frac{1}{1+e^{-Z}}$$

In the formula, Z is given by $X \cdot W + b$ where b is the bias, X is the input vector, W is the vector of weights, and $X \cdot W$ is the scalar product. The function above is a sigmoid, and its curve is plotted below in Figure 11-4.

A sigmoid function is a bounded and differentiable function defined for all real input values. Its output varies between 0 and 1 with continuity even though neither 0 nor 1 are ever reached.

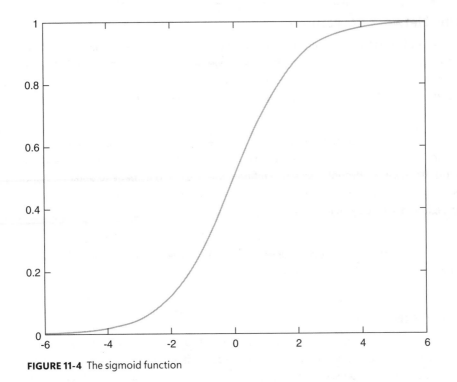

FIGURE 11-4 The sigmoid function

From Step Functions to Sigmoids

Using a sigmoid only modifies the value that each neuron forwards to its connected peers on the next layer, but it doesn't change the number of layers and connections of the feed-forward neural network. The value is no longer a binary value but a continuous value in the 0–1 range. As you see in Figure 11-4, for large values, the sigmoid activation function approaches 1, and for very small values, it stays close to 0. Therefore, at the extremes, the function's behavior is the same as the step function in perceptrons.

We started our discussion of feed-forward neural networks with perceptrons because of their inherent learning value. However, nobody uses perceptrons anymore in real life. The mathematical value of working with continuous values is invaluable and will prove even more useful when dealing with the actual training of a neural network.

Training a Neural Network

For the most part, neural networks are only for supervised learning, and the training is not different from the training of any other machine learning supervised artifacts. The key step of training consists in the identification of the function that represents the best measure of the distance between the predictions made by the network and expected values.

The most common algorithm to train a multi-layer feed-forward network leverages the backward propagation of errors—a technique known as *backpropagation*.

The Backpropagation Algorithm

The backpropagation algorithm was first devised in the late 1960s, but it was never seriously applied to machine learning until the mid-1980s. Today, it's the most commonly used technique.

The algorithm is built around an implementation of the gradient descent. In other words, it is a mathematical tool to find the minimum of a function by exploring values in the direction of the steepest descent. Within the backpropagation algorithm, the calculation of the gradient proceeds backward through the network, from the last to the first layer of neurons. The gradient is first calculated on the final layer's weights, and the error information is pushed backward on the previous layer, where the calculation is repeated on the local weights. The process goes on and on until it reaches the initial layer. In backpropagation, the rule to change the values of the various weights is recursive and proceeds backward from the output layer towards the input layer. (See Figure 11-5.)

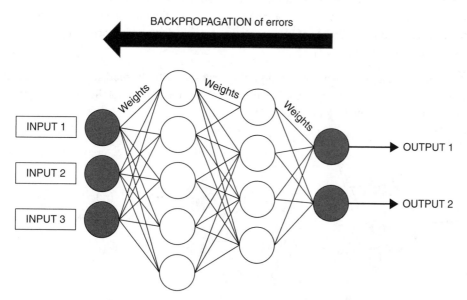

FIGURE 11-5 Error information flows backward from the final layer to the first layer.

Steps of the Algorithm

The backpropagation algorithm is articulated in four key steps nested in three different loops. The outermost loop is on the entire dataset and is referred to as an *epoch*. For each epoch, the training dataset is divided into mini-batches of a given *m* size. The second loop works on every mini-batch of rows. Finally, the innermost loop goes over the data rows in the current mini-batch. Here's some pseudo-code.

```
foreach(var epoch in epochs)
{
    var batches = SplitDatasetInMiniBatches(sizeOfBatches);
    foreach(var batch in batches)
    {
        foreach(var row in batch)
```

```
    {
        // Step 1: Calculate the output for the given row
        // Step 2: Calculate the final vector of errors
        // Step 3: Calculate the error vector for all intermediate layers
        // Step 4: Apply updated weights proceeding backwards
    }
  }
}
```

The first step is the classic feed-forward calculation shown in Figure 11-5. The neural network receives the features of a given data row and returns an output vector (or, in simpler cases, just a scalar value).

The heart of backpropagation is in steps 2 and 3. The error vector is first calculated for the final layer of the network, and then, proceeding backward, it is calculated for all intermediate layers. The reason is that getting errors is easy once the computation has reached the final stage. However, we need to update the weights along the entire set of layers, and we can only do that by proceeding backward from the final layer to the input.

Once all errors at all stages are known, the algorithm proceeds with the gradient descent calculation and finds the weights that minimize the cost function. Even this step is accomplished recursively from the final layer of neurons to the first. (See Figure 11-6.)

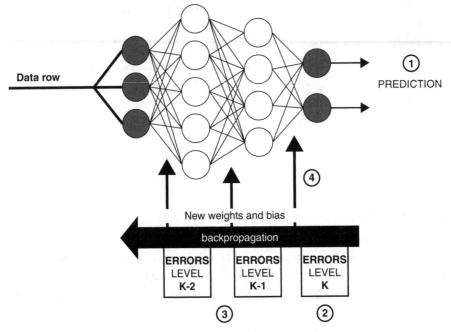

FIGURE 11-6 Schema of the backpropagation algorithm

More Sophisticated Neural Networks

A feed-forward neural network has some limitations, the most relevant of which is that they're essentially stateless and keep no memory of whatever happens. Every prediction is independent of any previous and subsequent predictions. In addition, a feed-forward neural network can't handle images or audio files and is not designed to generate new content.

To overcome these limitations, other types of neural networks have been arranged, such as recurrent neural networks (for stateful networks), convolutional neural networks (for computer vision), and generative adversarial neural networks (for content creation).

Stateful Neural Networks

Unless it is properly architected, a neural network doesn't hold state and works much like an HTTP server. Two consecutive requests are treated as fully independent requests over HTTP, and two consecutive predictions are treated as fully independent predictions by a trained network. The point of (lack of) state applies to both training and production.

The Need for State

Let's consider the following example. To reliably predict a given stock's price, the sole history of the stock used in training may not be sufficient. You might also want to access some of the most recent quotes of the stock. This data is not necessarily incorporated in the trained model unless you retrain and redeploy the model frequently.

As humans, we continually make predictions. When we listen to someone speaking, sometimes we can rightly guess her next few words. When we make decisions, we don't simply evaluate the pros and cons as they appear from the available input data, but we integrate that data with experience and past memories of similar or related facts. We wish a neural network to be able to do the same.

A stateful neural network is referred to as a recurrent network (RNN). The information flows forward from the input layer to the output, but every prediction is made based on the input that results from the combination of the direct input and the state that previous predictions may have determined. Hence, every prediction leaves a track in the new memory layer.

The Memory Context

The memory context is a logical component of the architecture and not necessarily a distinct piece of software. In fact, in some RNN implementations, it is treated just as an additional hidden layer of a feed-forward neural network placed right after the input layer.

At the time t of the ongoing prediction, the component receives a vector of values X from the client application. The input X, combined with the current state H_{t-1} determined at the time $X-1$ of the last prediction, produces an update of the current state to H_t. The component's output is a modified version of the original input transformed in some way based on the state. (We'll see details of this in a moment.)

The output of the component is typically used as input of a regular feed-forward neural network.

Architecture of a Recurrent Network

Figure 11-7 presents the basic component architecture of a recurrent neural network. At least in its simplest form, a recurrent neural network is the concatenation of a memory context and a classic feed-forward neural network.

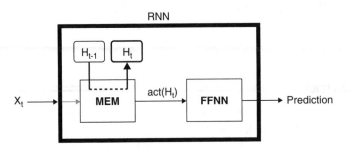

FIGURE 11-7 Component architecture of RNN

The bottom line is that a recurrent neural network is a feed-forward neural network plus an additional component that deals with the state of the network. The schema in the figure can be made as complex as needed, and multiple memory contexts can be concatenated. Moreover, the same FFNN can be split into smaller pieces, and memory contexts can be added in between. The state is a property of the memory context and is sometimes referenced as a *hidden state vector*.

Given an input X_t, the memory context combines it with the pre-existing state H_{t-1} and obtains the snapshot of a new state H_t. The new state, which absorbed the input, is passed to the activation function and becomes the input for the next network architecture component. It's interesting to observe the behavior of an RNN once put on a timeline. (See Figure 11-8.)

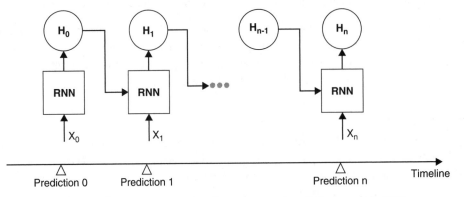

FIGURE 11-8 Impact of state management on the sequence of predictions made by RNN

The cumulative nature of the memory context ensures that every new prediction is done taking into account all the previous predictions.

From RNN to Deep RNN

Figure 11-7 shows the simplest form a recurrent neural network can take. The schema can be extended in various ways as it most suits your needs. For example, you can add one or more hidden layers between the input and the memory context. Or you can configure multiple memory contexts differently (see Figure 11-9). Speech recognition is a real-life scenario in which a more complex RNN architecture is necessary. In fact, in this case, it could make sense for the network to try to predict the next word based on what has been pronounced to date.

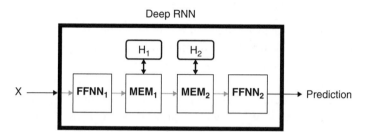

FIGURE 11-9 Possible schema of a "deep" RNN

From an algorithmic point of view, training an RNN is pretty much the same as training a classic feed-forward neural network, and backpropagation is still the key approach. In particular, unrolled over time, as shown in Figure 11-8, the RNN can be assimilated to a chain of feed-forward neural networks that develop the internal state (possibly, multiple hidden states) over the course of the dataset. The variation of the backpropagation algorithm used here is called "backpropagation over time."

Long Short-Term Memory

So far, the RNN architecture discussed presents a unsurmountable drawback in some business contexts: inputs that come sufficiently spaced out may not influence each other as expected. In other words, the hidden state held by the memory context component has a lifetime that is too short. This led to a new branch of research that culminated with the definition of a Long Short-Term Memory (LSTM) neural network.

Overall, an LSTM neural network differs from a plain RNN for a more sophisticated version of the memory context. To prolong the lifetime of the hidden state, the neural network architecture adds a second level of memory referred to as the *cell state*.

Convolutional Neural Networks

FFNNs have been introduced to help with nonlinear regression and classification problems, and flavors of RNNs are commonly used for speech recognition and natural language processing. What about images? A tailormade type of neural network exists to deal with images and pixel-based content—convolutional neural networks (CNN).

Much like a recurrent neural network, a CNN results from the combination of a plain FFNN with multiple, dedicated components. A convolutional neural network incorporates a special layer aimed at reducing large images to a more manageable form without losing relevant information, which might be critical for making a good prediction.

The Convolution Operation

The problem with images is that they are cumbersome objects to deal with. Think, for example, of one of those 4K images taken by a high-end smartphone. It's 16M pixels, and each pixel takes at least 3 bytes for the RGB channel—another 16M points. There should be a way to reduce such a huge amount of data. Mathematics comes to the rescue through the *convolution* operation.

In mathematics, convolution takes two functions and produces a third function that overall indicates how the shape of one is modified by the other. In real-life, convolution finds multiple applications. It's used to figure out the correlation between two signals, to perform pattern matching or, in our case here, to apply filters to incoming data. In this context, a filter is a process that removes some unwanted information from incoming data. For continuous functions, the convolution is calculated as the integral of the product of the two functions after one is rotated by 180 degrees. If the functions involved are not continuous; instead, pieces of their product are simply summed. This is just what happens when images are involved.

Convolution of Images

Let's say we have a matrix that represents an image. We take another (arbitrarily smaller) matrix called the kernel. For images, the convolution consists of moving the kernel matrix over the entire surface of the original image, starting from position 0,0. The kernel will move one cell at a time along the width first and move one cell down once it has reached the right edge. Kernel movement is repeated for each color channel (i.e., RGB). The operation is summarized in Figure 11-10.

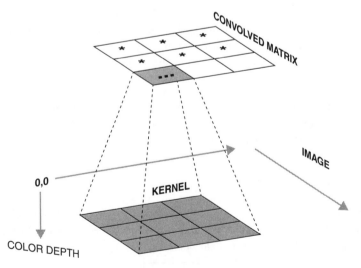

FIGURE 11-10 The convolution operation on one level of depth

At each step, the kernel matrix is multiplied element by element (Hadamard product) to the corresponding section of the original image. Note that the color depth of the kernel has to be the same as the color depth of the original image. The resulting intermediate matrix has the same size of the kernel. All the resulting matrix elements are then summed up, and the value is written to a new matrix—the convolved matrix.

The size of the convolved matrix depends on the both the size of the image and the kernel. The formula is

$$(W_{Image} - W_{Kernel} + 1) \ast (H_{Image} - H_{Kernel} + 1)$$

The dimension of the kernel is a hyperparameter of the CNN, whereas its values are figured out during the training.

Max and Average Pooling

The convolution layer is only the first step that a CNN performs. The second step is pooling. The purpose of pooling is to reduce the convolved matrix's size even more to get rid of all noise and keep only the relevant and dominant features.

Pooling consists of moving another smaller matrix over the surface of the convolved matrix. In this case, we won't call it a kernel matrix because all that matters is the size and not the content. The moving matrix is a sort of window that shows what's underneath applying one of two simple mathematical filters.

One is Max Pooling and returns the maximum value found in the section of the convolved matrix. The other is Average Pooling and returns the arithmetic mean of the values observed. Figure 11-11 shows how to extract a pooling matrix from a 4x4 convolved matrix using a window size of 2x2.

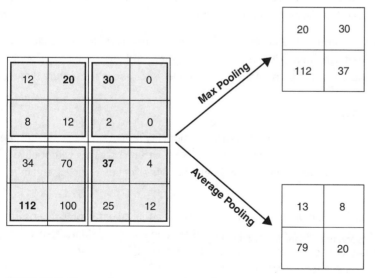

FIGURE 11-11 Max pooling versus verage pooling

Even though convolutional and pooling layers are conceptually distinct, they are often combined in a single comprehensive layer. In a single CNN, there might be multiple convolutional and pooling layers. The more layers, the more powerful the network and, conversely, the more computing power it requires.

Auto-Encoders

An auto-encoder is a system made by two connected neural networks in which the output of the first becomes the input of the second. You can see it as two interacting networks—an encoder and a decoder. An auto-encoder network is depicted in Figure 11-12.

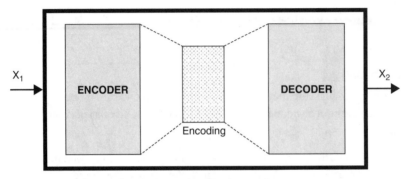

FIGURE 11-12 Schema of an auto-encoder neural network

Schema of an Auto-Encoder

The overall auto-encoder receives an input X_1 and passes it to the first layer (the encoder). The encoder encodes the input creating a sort of more compact representation known as *encoding*. Typically, the encoding is a single dimension data compared to n-dimensional data being the input. The encoding is then passed to the second layer (the decoder), which tries to re-create the original input as X_2. If X_1 and X_2.

It is important to notice that Figure 11-12 illustrates the schema of the network as we train it. Once the network is trained and deployed to production, it gets an input X_1 and outputs its compact representation (the encoding). Therefore, the point of the auto-encoder is to reduce the feature dimensions.

Applications of Auto-Encoders

The primary business application of auto-encoders is a dimensionality reduction—a classic unsupervised problem—where we aim to condense larger data into fewer features, possibly without loss of important information. Other applications are anomaly detection, information retrieval, and image processing.

Training an auto-encoder for anomaly detection requires only canonical data points to ensure optimal performance on standard elements and poor on unseen and anomalous data. Hence the auto-encoder for anomaly detection will return a Boolean answer based on the distance between the original input value and the value reconstructed from the encoding.

Information retrieval, especially when large objects are involved (such as images), is simplified by checking the encoding rather than the whole object. This leads to the third application—image processing and, in particular, image compression. Other scenarios are image denoising and increased resolution. Ultimately, image compression is a form of dimensionality reduction, and interesting experiments with auto-encoders have been run to compress images that are competitive with the JPEG standard.

Summary

Neural networks are not a recent discovery in computer science, but they have received a boost in the past decade for business and computing reasons. New types of neural networks flourished, expanding the capabilities of the first canonical type of network created—the feed-forward neural network. In a feed-forward neural network, information flows in only one direction from the input nodes to the output nodes traversing any layer of intermediate nodes that may be defined.

In this chapter, we first reviewed the structure of a feed-forward neural network, the types of neurons you can have, and how the training of a neural network takes place through the backpropagation technique. Next, we provided an overview of more sophisticated types of neural networks, such as recurrent and convolutional networks.

In the next chapter, we'll add some practical considerations and examples of solving problems using neural networks

CHAPTER 12

A Neural Network to Recognize Passports

"In math, you're either right or you're wrong."

—*Katherine Johnson*

Most of the hype around AI refers to making some common operations simpler and faster. It's about automating chores and reducing the number of manual steps required to accomplish a task. One of the plusses of AI is just in simplifying and streamlining workflows obtaining the same results with less effort and more error-prone actions from human operators.

In this final chapter, we just aim at illustrating one of these scenarios: a canonical array of form fields automatically filled by some smarter-than-usual software. The specific scenario we'll address in the chapter is a registration form that requires users to upload a passport photo. Usually, the backend service needs a plain photo of the passport. Also, it requires some text information to be extracted from the photo and stored as independent information, such as the first and last name, birth date, country of residence, and, of course, release date, expiry date, and number.

Often, users are presented with a file upload input field and additional input fields to insert first, last name, and even number and dates of the passport. Instead, why not simply upload the photo and let some other software do the rest of the job? Isn't this just what happens in hotels and airport check-in desks? However, in such environments, it's a dedicated Optical Character Recognition (OCR) reader that does the job of recognizing the information and passing it via cable to connected PC software.

Machine learning extends the core capabilities of OCR and makes the use of a dedicated reader unnecessary.

Using Azure Cognitive Services

There are two main ways to build a pure software solution for extracting personal information from a passport and use it to, say, create a prefilled user profile record. One way is to take advantage of the Azure Cognitive Services API, passing an image via URL or stream and receiving a JSON object with the content recognized in all detected text zones. The other way is to craft a handmade neural network to do the same. It's the umpteenth implementation of the old buy-or-build dilemma.

Let's start by seeing what it takes to go the Azure Cognitive Services route.

Anatomy and Solution of the Problem

Given a passport photo, we want to figure out the crucial personal information stored in it. In particular, we want to be able to receive the entire content of the passport's Machine-Readable Zone (MRZ) in a structured, property-based way. Ideally, we want to place a single call, pass the input, and get the response in the expected format.

> **NOTE** In a passport (and a variety of other documents), an MRZ consists of two (in some cases, three) lines of vital personal information encoded into a standardized format that is made to measure for a quick read and automated machine-led verification. In passports, the MRZ is placed at the bottom of the first page. Historically, the MRZ was introduced in the 1980s to speed up operations at borders and airports.

The Image Input

From a computer perspective, an image is not simply a photo. A computer image has a width and height, a density of colors, and, of particular relevance, might be vertical or horizontal and rotated by any angle. It can also be a single-page or two-page photo of a paper passport.

If you manage to build your own black-box software for passport analysis, then the various sizes and orientations of the input image are aspects you have to find a way to neutralize. This is mostly conventional software work—sort of a morphologic manipulation of image data. Its output is an image with fixed settings as far as size, orientation, and colors are concerned.

The ability to process input images of any size and orientation is crucial for the success of the solution. In the real world, users would upload passport images taken in myriad ways, and the software must be able to normalize the content somehow.

Text Detection

Any passport is made of two distinct types of content—plain text and MRZ. Here, the term "plain text" refers to whatever personal information appears on the passport pages, including details such as residence, eye color, and height. In addition to plain text fields, passports feature the machine-readable zone, which stores a subset of the information about the holder's identity.

A passport analysis software must be able to spot all zones in the images where some text appears. The output is a list of bounding boxes within the image that are estimated to contain text.

Text Recognition

Finally, the text in each detected bounding box must be turned into literals. This is just the type of job that an Optical Character Recognition (OCR) is designed to perform. The recognition process will turn prints of text into literal strings that another piece of software can further process.

An interesting plus of OCR systems, when embedded into broader services such as Azure Cognitive Services, is giving some interpretation over the raw text. The OCR turns font drawings into literals, but some sequences of literals (for example, dates) are special. A smart cognitive service at work on a known type of document can turn, say, 061074 into a `DateTime` object or a human-friendly representation of the date.

Working with the ID Form Recognizer

The Azure Form Recognizer cloud service analyzes information from government-issued ID documents such as passports. The service uses a prebuilt ID model as the learning foundation for each supported document type to look for bounding text boxes. The service combines OCR capabilities with ID knowledge coming from dozens of countries and U.S. states. Furthermore, the API extracts key information from IDs, such as first and last name, number, and birth and expiry dates, and returns this data in a JSON-structured format. The MRZ is sent as one of the fields in the JSON feed.

Let's see what it takes to work with the Azure service.

Preliminary Work

The first step is to register your own dedicated machine learning Azure service from the portal. Conceptually, it is not really different from creating an app service for hosting a web application. (See Figure 12-1.)

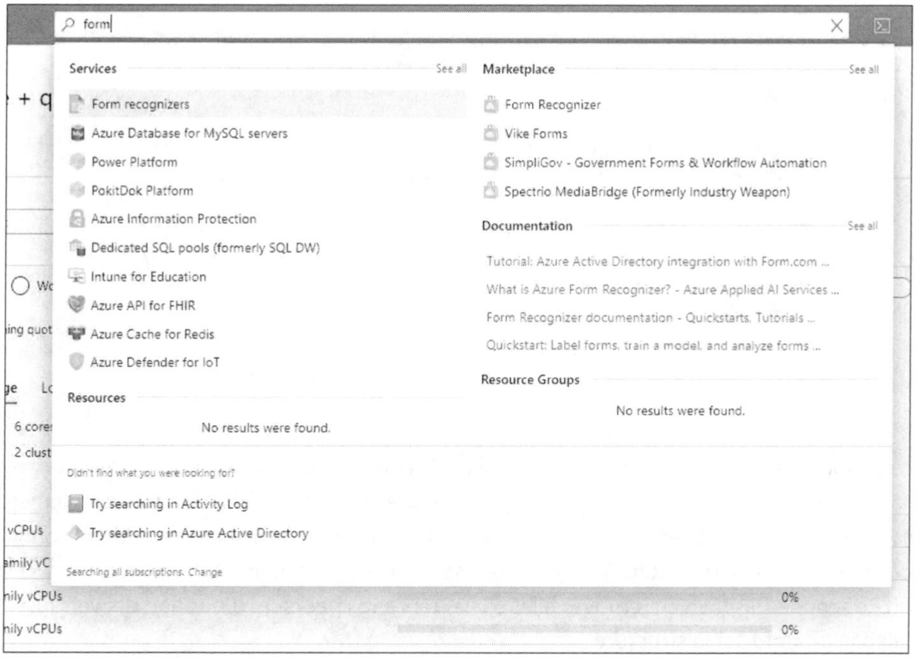

FIGURE 12-1 Creating a new Form Recognizer service

After successfully completing the procedure, you get the actual endpoint used for further calls and the personal API key.

To build a client application that consumes the service, you also need to install the Azure. AI.FormRecognizer NuGet package in the Visual Studio solution.

All that remains is the plain coding.

A Sample Client Application

The following code shows a form recognizer service created in Visual Studio:

```
class Program
{
    // Any "xxxx" is specific to your account
    const string Endpoint = "https://xxxxxxxx.cognitiveservices.azure.com/";
    const string ApiKey = "xxxxxxxxxxxxxxxxxxxxxxxx";

    static async Task Main(string[] args)
    {
        if (args == null)
        {
            Console.WriteLine("No file specified");
            return;
        }

        var passportFile = args[0];

        Console.WriteLine("Uploading and parsing...");
        var response = await ParsePassportFile(passportFile);
        Console.WriteLine("\n");

        // Parse MRZ to some intelligible data structure
        var mrz = new PassportResponse(response.Data.Replace(" "," ""));
        Console.WriteLine(mrz);
        Console.WriteLine($"CONFIDENCE: {response.Confidence}");

        Console.WriteLine("\n\nPress any key!");
        Console.ReadLine();
    }

    // More code here ...
}
```

The code above receives the file name from the command line and passes it up to the internal helper named ParsePassportFile. The helper method returns a tuple in which the first element (Data) contains the raw MRZ sequence, and the latter (Confidence) expresses the level of confidence the neural network has in the result. Finally, the raw sequence is parsed into an instance of the custom PassportResponse class, which removes filler characters and checksum digits and delivers just actual data packed in a comfortable structure.

The passport file can be a PDF or image file and will be uploaded to the cloud service to be analyzed. Here's the code:

```
static async Task<(string Data, float Confidence)> ParsePassportFile(string file)
{
    // Upload the passport file
    await using var stream = new FileStream(file, FileMode.Open);
    var client = new FormRecognizerClient(new Uri(Endpoint), new AzureKeyCredential(ApiKey));
    var operation = await client.StartRecognizeIdentityDocumentsAsync(stream);

    // Get a document as a response
    var response = await operation.WaitForCompletionAsync();
    RecognizedFormCollection documents = response.Value;
    if (identityDocuments.Count == 0)
        return (null, 0);
    RecognizedForm document = documents.Single();

    // Extract MRZ info
    if (!document.Fields.TryGetValue("MachineReadableZone," out FormField mrz))
        return (null, 0);

    if (mrz.Value.ValueType == FieldValueType.Dictionary)
        return (mrz.ValueData.Text, mrz.Confidence);

    return (null, 0);
}
```

The service returns a list of documents, the first of which is of interest to us. The document provides a list of fields from which we select MachineReadableZone. The ParsePassportFile method returns the raw text of the MRZ field. The full list of document fields beyond the MachineReadableZone is documented here: *https://docs.microsoft.com/en-us/azure/cognitive-services/form-recognizer/concept-identification-cards*.

After obtaining the raw MRZ sequence, the remaining steps consist of parsing the sequence and extracting the actual pieces of information stored there, such as name, surname, gender, expiry date, and number. A helper PassportResponse class and an internal MrzParser class will do the job. The full source code of these classes is included in the book samples, but the core of the code is shown here:

```
// Parsing step
var mrz = new PassportResponse(response.Data.Replace(" ," ""));

// Render out facts
Console.WriteLine(mrz);
Console.WriteLine($"CONFIDENCE: {response.Confidence}");
```

An interesting point to emphasize is that that blank spaces must be removed from the raw MRZ sequence. The MRZ is laid out in two rows in passports, but the form recognizer returns it as a single string with a blank sequence to denote the break on a new line. Instead, our handcrafted MRZ parser assumes a canonical MRZ sequence is passed, which is exactly 88 characters long. Instead, the sequence returned by the form recognizer is 89 because of the extra space. Figure 12-2 shows the sample application at work on a specimen passport template.

FIGURE 12-2 A sample application that encapsulates the Azure ID Form Recognizer cloud service

> **NOTE** The Form Recognizer service comes with a free plan that allows up to 500 pages per month at a rate of a maximum of 20 calls per minute. Likely, you don't need training for standard passports, but the free plan allows for a maximum of 1 call per minute. Also, note that container support has been added to Form Recognizers to allow you run this AI engine right in your environment.

Crafting Your Own Neural Network

To be honest, if your business problem is extracting clean passport data from a PDF or image file all you want to do is using the ID Form Recognizer, whether as a cloud service or embedded in your environment via a licensed Docker container. Are there edge situations in which you want to look somewhere else and consider crafting your own neural network?

We'll return to the aforementioned buy-or-build dilemma of neural networks in the "ML Devil's Advocate" section later in this chapter, but for now, suffice it to say that we see three main reasons for considering a custom solution:

- For some reason, you can't use any existing cloud service or on-premises third-party container
- You can't afford the costs of the service and the latency it might introduce
- You have ad hoc documents to deal with and find the response you're getting to be inaccurate.

In general, we're talking about very specific and rare conditions that are more likely to happen with custom forms and receipts than with government-issued ID documents. Anyway, here are a few considerations and some practical experience on crafting a dedicated neural network for extracting the MRZ sequence from a passport photo.

Topology of the Neural Network

A neural network is a software artifact that gets some well-defined numeric input and returns some well-defined numeric output. More often than not, the well-defined numeric input is not natively available in the right format but results from some preliminary software manipulation or is the output of some other neural network. Likewise, the well-defined numeric output can become the input of another neural network or be subject to further software manipulation that turns it into data usable for the purposes of the application.

The Neural Pipeline

In the real world, a neural network is almost always the heart of a learning pipeline with canonical (non-machine learning) pieces of software sprinkled all around. The whole pipeline has a well-defined business-specific input (such as an image file) and a business-acceptable response, whether in a string (sequence) or an array of numbers. In our case, the input is the passport file; the output is the MRZ raw sequence.

Processing the Input Image

Let's say it up front: The Azure ID Form Recognizer makes it look trivially easy and straightforward, but it is not likely so. The Azure service blissfully accepts passport files in a variety of formats, including PDF and JPG. Doing the same in a custom pipeline poses a number of challenges:

- Having or writing libraries to extract pixel or meta information for each of the file types you intend to support

- Writing methods to normalize the position of the image

- Writing methods to neutralize colors and fonts

- Writing methods to perform morphological operations on the image (for example, erosion, dilation)

Reading and writing files in a given format is not the most challenging problem. However, things get much more complicated when it comes to understanding and neutralizing the possible rotation of the image, reducing color spaces, and understanding the essence of shapes rendered with fonts beyond the glyphs.

We often use OpenCV, an open-source library released under the BSD 3-clause license and free for commercial applications. The library is available for multiple programming languages here: *https://opencv.org*.

The OpenCV Library

The OpenCV library provides an amazing number of services that range from reading and displaying images and videos to image processing functions such as changing color spaces, geometric transformations, finding edges, smoothing, and thresholding.

The library is also good at doing morphological transformations like erosion and dilation on binary, black-whited images. Erosion eats away the boundaries of any foreground object, making its thickness decrease. Dilation does the exact opposite and enlarges the size of the foreground object. Erosion and dilation are sometimes performed one after the other.

Video analysis, plotting, 3D visualization, image stitching, and blending complete the image processing module. Additional modules deal more with machine learning-oriented functionalities such as object and barcode detection, face analysis, and text recognition.

Extracting the MRZ Region

For our purposes, an MRZ is of type 3 (see *https://en.wikipedia.org/wiki/Machine-readable_passport*) and develops on two lines of text, each of which is 44 characters long. At first, one may think that some deep (or just shallow) learning is unavoidable to detect the MRZ region in a passport photo. The reality is a bit different, and with the help of a great computer vision framework, such as OpenCV, the task can be accomplished with the sole use of image processing techniques, including morphological erosion, blurring, and contours detection.

Let's review the necessary steps for image processing that spot the location of the MRZ region in the file.

1. Resize the image to a fixed dimension.

2. Apply a 3x3 pixel Gaussian blurring to reduce high-frequency noise.

3. Apply a black-hat filter to find dark regions (MRZ text) on a light background (passport paper).

The black-hat filter is a common edge-detection filter that most image processing programs provide. The combined effect on some original image of Gaussian blurring and black-hat is analogous to Figure 12-3.

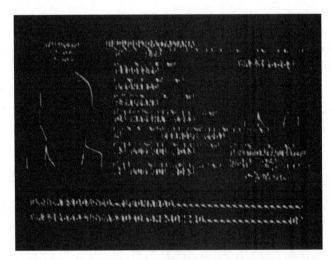

FIGURE 12-3 Morphological black-hat operator applied to a sample passport image

Next up, we compute the Scharr gradient along the x-axis of the black-hat image. The purpose is to get rid of all the regions that do not represent text.

1. Apply the gradient to mark those regions that are not simply dark on a light background but also contain changes in the vertical gradient.

2. Scale the image back into the range 0–255 (black/white) using min/max scaling.

3. Apply a closing operator (erosion followed by dilation) using a rectangular kernel.

The ultimate purpose of the Closing operation is to close the gaps between characters in the MRZ region. Figure 12-4 shows a realistic example of the current state of the original image.

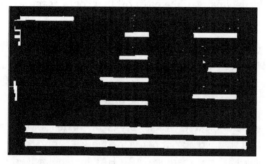
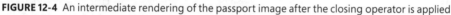

FIGURE 12-4 An intermediate rendering of the passport image after the closing operator is applied

At this stage, the image spots all areas with some text. Instead, we want a single region for the whole MRZ and get rid of all the rest.

4. Apply another closing operator with a square kernel.

Figure 12-5 shows the new stage of the original passport photo.

FIGURE 12-5 The MRZ region is now a single area of the image, and all other text has been darkened as irrelevant

The final step of the process is finding the area's contours, defining the coordinates of the bounding box, and extracting the actual pixels from the original image.

> **NOTE** One crucial point we have so far left behind is: what if the original image is rotated at some angle? The approach followed largely shields us from this (rather common) occurrence. In fact, what we actually do is find the minimum area rectangle that fits the MRZ and crop it. The cropped image, though, is now perfectly horizontal.

Recognizing the MRZ Content

All the work done so far has nothing to do with pure machine learning. However, manual machine learning becomes necessary for the concrete step of figuring out the text in the selected region of the original image. In other words, we now hold a smaller image of the passport that contains the sole MRZ area. On that, we now need to do text recognition.

The OpenCV library does have a module for text recognition that is slated to parse an image and turn recognized shapes of literals into a string. However, it's a rather generic OCR library and not fully appropriate for a delicate task such as extracting personal data from a passport. Not just OpenCV but also most consolidated, yet general-purpose, OCR libraries have the same drawback.

Then to reliably parse out the text, we need some dedicated OCR library tailor-made for MRZ captures of a passport document. For this, we just want to build up our neural network. Beyond reading MRZ content, a custom neural network is also useful for, say, reading CAPTCHAs. In general, if you need to be substantially sure about what you parse—and you parse small texts—a custom neural network is a reasonable way to go.

To build a neural network, TensorFlow is an excellent choice, especially if coded using the topmost layer of Keras. Figure 12-6 presents the list of layers in the Keras-based neural network. Each block in the middle column represents a Keras layer of the specified type (such as Conv 2D, Dense, and the like).

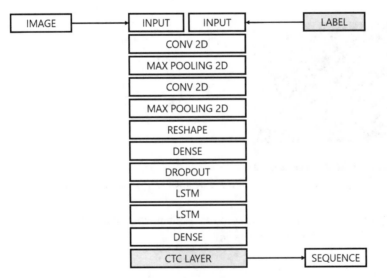

FIGURE 12-6 Schema of an OCR neural network

The neural network is quite articulated and composed of several distinct layers involved in processing the input image to produce a sequence of characters. The image is rendered as an array of values in a single black-white color channel (no RGB). We also need a second piece of input for training purposes, which is the expected MRZ sequence (the label). Under normal conditions, this would not be necessary, but in this case, we have to use a custom loss function (see later), and this label serves to optimize the performance of the loss function. Both the label and loss function layer will be removed in production.

Right after the input layer, there are a couple of 2D convolution layers, each of which runs a convolution kernel on its input data. Both layers use a 3x3 kernel and a ReLU activation function. (The ReLU function is a piecewise linear function that will output the same input if positive and zero if negative.) The output dimensionality of the first Conv2D layer is 64, whereas the second produces 32 values. Each Conv2D is followed by a MaxPooling2D layer, which downsamples the input along the height and width by taking the maximum value over an input window of 2x2. Both MaxPooling2D layers are configured in the same way.

At this point, the image is four times smaller, so the Reshape and Dense layers will reduce the input size accordingly before getting into the recurrent (LSTM) part of the neural network. The Dropout is only used during training to prevent overfitting. The recurrent LSTM layers provide the crucial part of the network. The first has 128 output values, which become the input for the second LSTM, which outputs 64 values. Both layers use the default hyperbolic tangent activation function and return the full state sequence. A softmax activation on the final layer produces the output. The softmax function turns a vector of N values into a vector of N values that sum to 1.

As mentioned, for training purposes, we need to add a custom error layer—the CTC layer. A Connectionist Temporal Classification (CTC) loss function is ideal to use whenever a good alignment between sequences is required and key for the quality of the response. A canonical example is aligning each character to its location in an image file. No predefined CTC layer exists in Keras, and it must be written manually as a Python class. (See the source code included on this book's web site for details.)

Training Pains

While designing a functional neural network for specific text recognition tasks is not a mission-impossible task, training such a network for passport images poses additional and nontrivial issues. Where do you get data to train a passport neural network? No such dataset exists, and none should actually exist for security and privacy reasons!

Using an MRZ Generator

An MRZ sequence is not simply the combination of first, last name, birth date, document number, and the like. It contains filler characters and, more importantly, a few checksum digits in specific locations. Arranging an MRZ generator is a two-step operation.

First, you create a C# class that can randomly generate a valid MRZ sequence, and then you use some publicly available tool (or write your own) to turn those strings into JPG or PNG images. In this way, you can create a dataset of the desired size and make it even larger in the case of retraining. (One tool for Python solutions is TextRecognitionDataGenerator, which is available at *https://github.com/ Belval/TextRecognitionDataGenerator.*)

Using TensorFlow Generators

Another aspect to consider is how to feed hundreds of thousands of images to the TensorFlow training pipeline that Keras relies on. Unless you have unlimited RAM and computing power, it is far more preferable to use a cursor-based approach and feed items of the dataset only on-demand.

In TensorFlow, you pass the dataset through a generator, which produces any due item on demand. This dramatically reduces the amount of memory needed to train the network. However, the TensorFlow data generator is only a shell (conceptually similar to ML.NET DataView objects), and it must be connected to some real generator that does the actual job.

We have two options here: One is to accumulate all the sample MRZ images into a folder and use a built-in folder-based generator or pass the list of MRZ strings as the dataset and connect it to a custom generator capable of turning text into images.

The ML Devil's Advocate

So far in this chapter, we have presented two ways to solve the same problem: using a dedicated cloud service or crafting a bespoke neural network. In doing so, we recalled the old software dilemma of build-or-buy. Paraphrasing it for machine learning, it becomes close to another commodity-or-vertical dilemma.

Commodity Versus Vertical Solutions

Applied AI solutions become more and more standardized and general enough to be adaptable to multiple scenarios just via hyperparameters. More and more shards of vertical problems, immersed in specific business contexts, are taken out of their native environment and commoditized. When this is the case, then there's no real reason to insist on creating custom solutions.

Let us tell you a story about software commodities.

A year before we actually embarked on writing this chapter, passport detection was not as efficient and shrink-wrapped as it is today. At that time, the only option was to use a general-purpose OCR, which returned bounding boxes and text recognized in it. It was good enough but not as good as it should be for a crucial task such as parsing a passport file.

Today, the situation is fairly different, and the ID Form Recognizer does a much better job. A year ago, crafting a dedicated neural network seemed reasonable. Today, it is likely overkill.

In our opinion, the trend of commoditizing aspects of real problems with cloud services will continue indefinitely. In light of this, most applied AI solutions will end up being just some orchestration software around one or more cloud services.

Does this mean that just everything is destined to be commoditized?

In nearly any industry segment, there are problems that only apparently lend themselves to being commoditized. For example, think of predictive maintenance, price prediction, anomaly, or fraud detection. You can find challenges on Kaggle for most of them, but in reality, it is radically different. You need a dedicated solution for each scenario. The more you reuse, the more you risk losing in terms of accuracy. For example, in wind turbine predictive maintenance, it is ideal to have a model for each turbine in a wind farm with a dataset that logs time series every five seconds or so.

Commercial solutions exist, but more often than not, what works for customer X doesn't work the same for customer Y. So, if you're a company with enough budget, you can seriously plan to craft the ideal solution for your scenario, given your context, business model, and specific settings.

When Are Custom Solutions Inevitable?

In a nutshell, custom neural networks remain necessary to solve problems you can't solve otherwise or that haven't yet been commoditized in some way. Existing services can give you the direct or partial solution that can be adapted to final with some surrounding standard code. In any other case, a custom solution is an option to consider seriously.

In earlier chapters, we solved anomaly detection problems with a simple chunk of ML.NET code. The point is that not everything that falls under the umbrella of "anomaly detection" is really solvable effectively with a shallow learning algorithm. And not everything you can envision as a business instance of "anomaly detection" can be effectively solved with a direct, plain algorithm or even a single multi-layer neural network.

The bottom line is that, in the end, AI is just software written using more powerful tools than the primitives of programming languages, class libraries, and software frameworks.

Summary

In this chapter, we attempted to illustrate two different approaches to solve a common problem in many web forms: figuring out the vital information stored in a passport from an image file. Too often, we are still required to upload a passport photo on many web desks and then manually enter the same information (name, dates, and numbers) that are already recognizable via software from the image itself.

We first used a new Azure service—the ID Form Recognizer cloud service—to upload a file and receive the sequence of characters in the machine-readable zone of the document. The operation comprehends two steps—extraction of the MRZ region from the original image and an OCR pass to turn pixels into a string.

Next, we attempted to do the same using a custom neural network. Aside from the effort (and skills) necessary for creating a brand-new neural network, training is the key differentiator. You don't need any training if you call a service. However, if you want to do it yourself, you need a high-quality dataset and sufficient computing time.

The world of AI is split into two main families of solutions: commodities and vertical solutions. If you have a good enough commodity, by all means, use it. Be aware, though, that platforms and cloud services exist that may not be specific to the business workflows of the specific company you work for. If you can't solve the problem in any consolidated and commoditized way, then it's time to try a custom neural network.

AI, in the end, is just software.

Model Explainability

"Anyone who attempts to generate random numbers by deterministic means is, of course, living in a state of sin.."

—*John Von Neumann*

We could put it down abruptly like this: machine learning today is not really as intelligent as media (and even common sense) lead us to think. Worse yet, from a pure perspective of applied intelligence, an expert system—a primordial form of software intelligence than deep learning and neural networks—are more intelligent. So, what is intelligence, and what is intelligence in software?

Although with slightly different wording, nearly all worldwide dictionaries provide a definition of *intelligence* that goes with the following statement:

The ability to acquire knowledge and turn that into expertise.

However, in the folds of the definition, there's another layer of meaning that is worth surfacing and that we can summarize in the three further points:

- Form judgment and opinions out of the acquired knowledge

- Act based on that

- React to unknown events

In a nutshell, human intelligence combines cognitive capabilities, including perception, memory, language, and reasoning, and uses an unparalleled learning schema to extract, transform and store information.

Software Intelligence

In software, intelligence is close to sensing the surrounding environment and reacting to detected changes. An expert system does that by deducing the appropriate behavior from a finite and hard-coded (though high) number of cases and scenarios. Instead, machine learning–based software—what media love to call artificial intelligence—is software that can learn from what it processes. In other words, the number of cases and scenarios from which answers are deduced is not hard-coded by a human team of developers but is determined programmatically via training. Training, in turn, is driven by the data you provide. It goes without saying that if data is biased (willingly or not), then answers are biased (willingly or not).

A trained model that goes into production is a total black box that not even developers know what they are going to return in front of a certain input. All we know is that the model during training showed an acceptable degree of error compared to provided expected results. Nobody knows—for sure—if all that was however correct, honest, or biased, and in which direction. Nobody knows—for sure—why neural networks make the decisions they actually make.

All this is scary if you think of the critical business systems these algorithms can interact with (or be a constituent part of), such as security surveillance, insurance/financial decision systems, and medical diagnostics.

Today's huge emphasis on ethics in AI starts with the lack of a broadly accepted explainability model that could help make sense of and accept the output of deep-learning models.

The Super Theory of Artificial Intelligence

Neural networks—the most sophisticated way to do machine learning—have been in the works for several decades, approximately since the 1960s. It is curious to note that the will to build intelligent machines came up even before building comprehensive software applications for common tasks. We could even say that software engineering in itself is a byproduct of the quest for intelligent machines!

For many years, though, the focus on AI has been primarily academic and theoretical. The most prominent result of this first stage of research is surely the back-propagation training method of neural networks. There have been two major winter seasons in AI (namely, a substantial stopping of funding and research) before the 2000s. After that, much more computing power, better learning algorithms, as well as the availability of large volumes of data radically changed the landscape and produced significant advances. Around 2012, deep learning started becoming the dominant approach to getting accurate and even superhuman results. Hence, the number of domains in which deep learning was employed proliferated—from healthcare to finance, energy to general industry, and to retail.

However, the key factor is that such an improved accuracy in prediction brought a significantly increased complexity in the underlying model as a side effect. The increased power mostly comes from two sources: more sophisticated network topologies and ridiculously vast amounts of data provided in training. In other words, the boost in the prediction power comes more from brute force than from effective improvements in the learning techniques. The bottom line is that we know very little about the inner workings of neural networks, and we get results but do not fully understand why those results have been produced. And we don't actually know how to interpret them. Should we blindly trust or refuse all results? At what costs?

The cheap answer to this yet unsolvable problem is ethics in AI (or Responsible AI). But ethics only scratches the surface of things.

Instead, a more thoughtful answer is that we currently lack a comprehensive and well-defined mathematical model that explains the actual dynamics of deep neural networks. This is just what we pompously called the "super theory of artificial intelligence" in the title of this section. Prominent scientists also said, with trepidation, that we risk incurring in a third winter of AI if this fails to move the bar from a brute-force approach to a more mathematical approach. The pontifical statement that AI will take over humans and change the way we live and work is seriously at risk because of the lack of this super theory.

Machine Learning Black Boxes

In machine learning, a model is a computational graph, much more complex in structure, but it is conceptually analogous to a plain polynomial. A black-box model is a model that an algorithm creates directly from data. The black-box nature lies in the fact that even those who design the network can't really explain how variables are combined to produce numbers interpreted as predictions or classifications.

Developers do define the list of the input variables, but black-box models are usually such intricated functions of the input that no human can realistically understand how input variables are jointly related to each other. Internally, the state of a neural network at work is comparable to a chaotic system. And, as in chaotic systems, a minimal change anywhere—in input as well as in one of the thousands of interconnections—could end up in radically different outputs.

Interpretability and Explainability

Two concepts are invoked when it comes to making sense of machine learning black box models: interpretability and explainability. While these two terms are often used interchangeably, a subtle yet neat difference exists between them. It is crucial to note that there is currently no rigorous mathematical definition or measurable metric for both terms. Some broadly accepted definitions stand, however. A model is interpretable if the connections between input and output are obvious, understandable, and reproducible.

Lack of interpretability is not an issue in low-risk scenarios where machine learning is applied. For example, a model that recommends that you stay in a hotel that you would not stay in is not a big issue unless you're a large company like Booking.com, and you don't want your recommendations to disappoint customers. Likewise, getting a naïve price prediction for a taxi ride might not be a disaster unless you're Uber and want to give an edge to competitors. At the same time, predicting the evolution of the market price of energy is a different story. You want accuracy and to know what makes the suggested price a reasonable value and whether a model is better than another. Interpretability must be high in high-risk scenarios such as healthcare or insurance/finance. The model gives a prediction, but a human subscribes to that prediction and uses it to make an actual decision. Would you trust a machine? What if you do? And what if you don't? An AI system with high interpretability would also allow users to try the system as sort of what-if game.

Explainability, instead, relates to the internal mechanics of a machine learning system. Internally to a neural network, the back-propagation step—the core learning algorithm—updates the weights on neurons based on its error function. The setting of these values is largely uncontrolled by developers and hardly reproducible. Yet, assigning these values is key to obtaining an output from a given input. As shown in Figure A-1, everything in a neural network but the input and the output values are hidden dynamics (and largely unknown details). Ultimately, lack of explainability means that nobody can easily predict the effect of changing a single weight on one of the hidden connections.

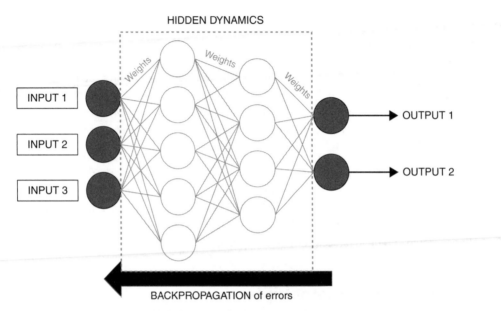

FIGURE A-1 Input and output in the learning of a neural network

The hidden layers (the black box) allow a model to make associations among the given data points, and based on that, predict better results. Note that here "better" refers to minimizing an error function. Explainability measures the level of understanding engineers have about the internal flow of data that takes place while the network is training.

What's the relationship between interpretability and explainability?

An interpretable model is not necessarily a model whose internals engineers know in detail. Yet, it is a model whose cause-and-effect relationship between input and output is relatively easy to spot. On the other hand, an explainable model is a model in which the role played by input values in the calculation of the output is intelligible, but it's not necessarily the cause-and-effect relationship between input and output. In summary, machine learning interpretability does not axiomatically entail machine learning explainability and vice versa. However, interpretability tends to be considered a broader term than explainability.

Explainability Techniques

There are actually a few different ways to make sense of the decisions a model makes. Some of them are already implemented in ML.NET, and others will likely appear in the future. However, the overall idea is finding ways to understand which features are the most salient for a given model to predict.

Basically, you have two options when it comes to building a model. You can go for an interpretable model, namely a model whose decisional steps can be explained to a human to reproduce the results. Alternatively, you can go for a black-box model and make a post-mortem analysis on how explainable it is. The canonical example of interpretable models is a decision tree. In general, shallow learning algorithms are more interpretable than neural networks and are much less accurate and effective in some cases.

This leads us straight to enumerate a few common methods for model explainability:

- Decision-tree visualization

- Training pipeline visualization

- Feature contribution calculation

- Permutation feature importance

A decision tree is a supervised shallow algorithm that uses a binary tree graph to assign each data sample a target value. Decision-tree learning is the process of finding the optimal rules for splitting the data sample according to the metric in use. Visualizing the final tree is relatively automatic, and many tools exist to plot the tree either graphically or via a text console. For example, in Python scikit-learn, there's the `plot_tree` method, which when used in a Jupyter notebook, gives you an instant view of the final tree.

Another Python package useful for both decision-tree and training pipeline visualization is Graphviz. Using it, you can take the training pipeline of an ML.NET solution and render it in a Python Jupyter notebook via NimbusML, which is a Microsoft Python framework that makes ML.NET models available in a Python environment. To mix .NET and Python, you can also count on .NET Interactive Notebooks and the .NET DataFrame API.

Feature contribution calculation is a method that computes model-specific contribution scores for each feature of the input vector. The idea is to process a dataset with a trained model and predict each data item. It can be useful to inspect which features significantly influenced the prediction to understand and explain these predictions. In ML.NET, you find a built-in transformer for this method in the `ExplainabilityCatalog` object. The transformer returns positive scores if the feature increases the accuracy of the prediction or a negative value if the feature negatively impacts the prediction. A near-zero value indicates that the feature is not relevant for the prediction.

While feature contribution measures the actual contribution that a feature gives to the prediction, feature importance refers to measuring how useful a given feature is at predicting a target variable. The foundation of permutation feature importance (PFI) is that valuable information only useful for prediction comes from certain features, and you want to know which. So, if you randomly shuffle the feature values and the quality of your predictions decreases, then that means you removed a crucial feature. Conversely, if the decrease in quality is small, then the information in the original dropped features wasn't very relevant for the predictions, and you can even remove them definitely simplifying the model. In ML.NET, regression, classification, and ranking catalogs present a `PermutationFeatureImportance` method for the purpose.

Conclusion

As members of a global society, we are under the effect of two opposite forces. One is the hype of progress driven by artificial intelligence, making everything easier and smoother for everyone. The other is the force of singularity, which warns us about the risks of giving machines more and more decisional power, allowing them to decide for us and take control of our lives and jobs.

Lack of explainability is a fact, and no mathematical theory exists that either defines or overcomes it. So, most sophisticated models—such as those used in vital scenarios—are at risk of blind trust, and nobody really likes that. So, ethics are a bold theme when it comes to AI.

While explainability can be achieved mostly as a post-training explanation, ethics in AI is primarily the stimulus to search for explainable and interpretable models as much and often as possible. As for the direct impact of AI on people's lives and our positions, AI is slated to replace tasks much more than actual jobs in most cases.

Index

A

J-K

L

M

Q-R

S